International Risk Management

International Risk Management

1st Edition • 1st Printing

The Institutes
720 Providence Road, Suite 100
Malvern, Pennsylvania 19355-3433

1st Edition • 1st Printing • August 2016

ISBN 978-0-89463-899-2

Foreword

The Institutes are the trusted leader in delivering proven knowledge solutions that drive powerful business results for the risk management and property-casualty insurance industry. For more than 100 years, The Institutes have been meeting the industry's changing professional development needs with customer-driven products and services.

In conjunction with industry experts and members of the academic community, our Knowledge Resources Department develops our course and program content, including Institutes study materials. Practical and technical knowledge gained from Institutes courses enhances qualifications, improves performance, and contributes to professional growth—all of which drive results.

The Institutes' proven knowledge helps individuals and organizations achieve powerful results with a variety of flexible, customer-focused options:

Recognized Credentials—The Institutes offer an unmatched range of widely recognized and industry-respected specialty credentials. The Institutes' Chartered Property Casualty Underwriter (CPCU®) professional designation is designed to provide a broad understanding of the property-casualty insurance industry. Depending on professional needs, CPCU students may select either a commercial insurance focus or a personal risk management and insurance focus and may choose from a variety of electives.

In addition, The Institutes offer certificate or designation programs in a variety of disciplines, including these:

- Claims
- Commercial underwriting
- Fidelity and surety bonding
- General insurance
- Insurance accounting and finance
- Insurance information technology
- Insurance production and agency management
- Insurance regulation and compliance

- Management
- Marine insurance
- Personal insurance
- Premium auditing
- Quality insurance services
- Reinsurance
- Risk management
- Surplus lines

Ethics—Ethical behavior is crucial to preserving not only the trust on which insurance transactions are based, but also the public's trust in our industry as a whole. All Institutes designations now have an ethics requirement, which is delivered online and free of charge. The ethics requirement content is designed specifically for insurance practitioners and uses insurance-based case studies to outline an ethical framework. More information is available in the Programs section of our website, TheInstitutes.org.

Flexible Online Learning—The Institutes have an unmatched variety of technical insurance content covering topics from accounting to underwriting, which we now deliver through hundreds of online courses. These cost-effective self-study courses are a convenient way to fill gaps in technical knowledge in a matter of hours without ever leaving the office.

Continuing Education—A majority of The Institutes' courses are filed for CE credit in most states. We also deliver quality, affordable, online CE courses quickly and conveniently through CEU. Visit CEU.com to learn more. CEU is powered by The Institutes.

College Credits—Most Institutes courses carry college credit recommendations from the American Council on Education. A variety of courses also qualify for credits toward certain associate, bachelor's, and master's degrees at several prestigious colleges and universities. More information is available in the Student Services section of our website, TheInstitutes.org.

Custom Applications—The Institutes collaborate with corporate customers to use our trusted course content and flexible delivery options in developing customized solutions that help them achieve their unique organizational goals.

Insightful Analysis—Our Insurance Research Council (IRC) division conducts public policy research on important contemporary issues in property-casualty insurance and risk management. Visit www.insurance-research.org to learn more or purchase its most recent studies.

The Institutes look forward to serving the risk management and property-casualty insurance industry for another 100 years. We welcome comments from our students and course leaders; your feedback helps us continue to improve the quality of our study materials.

Peter L. Miller, CPCU
President and CEO
The Institutes

Contents

Assignment 1
Enterprise Risk Management
Framework and Process   1.1

Risk Classifications   1.3

Modeling an Enterprise Risk
Management Framework and
Process   1.9

Designing and Implementing an
Enterprise Risk Management
Framework and Process   1.15

ISO 31000 Risk Management—
Principles and Guidelines   1.21

COSO Enterprise Risk
Management—Integrated
Framework   1.25

Applying the Enterprise Risk
Management Framework and
Process   1.30

Summary   1.41

Assignment 2
Business Continuity Management   2.1

Introduction to Business Continuity
Management   2.3

Business Continuity Planning   2.6

Strategic Redeployment Planning   2.10

Supply Chain Risk Management   2.13

Crisis Communication   2.17

Mitigating Supply Chain Risk   2.20

Summary   2.29

Assignment 3
Legal and Regulatory Risk   3.1

Basis for Legal and Regulatory Risk   3.3

Legal and Regulatory Risk
Consequences   3.8

Modifying Legal and
Regulatory Risk   3.10

Legal Systems   3.16

International Law   3.22

Commercial Liability Loss
Exposures   3.24

Assessing and Treating Legal and
Regulatory Risk   3.30

Summary   3.35

Assignment 4
International Insurance   4.1

Insurers' Global Expansion   4.3

Methods of Engaging in
International Business   4.9

Overview of International
Insurance   4.17

Regulatory Compliance   4.24

Reverse Flow Business   4.30

International Insurance Solutions   4.35

Selecting International Insurance
Solutions   4.43

Structuring an International
Insurance Program   4.54

Captives and Multinational
Insurance Programs   4.59

Summary   4.66

Assignment 5
Climate Change Risk, Cyber Risk
and Terrorism Risk   5.1

Climate Change Risk   5.3

Cyber Risk Loss Exposures   5.8

**Controlling and Financing Cyber
Risk Loss Exposures**   5.15

Cyber Risk Insurance Policies   5.21

The Terrorism Risk Insurance Act 5.29

**The Terrorism Risk Insurance
Program Reauthorization Act of
2015 (TRIPRA 2015)**   5.33

**Terrorism Endorsements for
Commercial Property and Liability
Forms**   5.36

Summary   5.43

Index   1

Direct Your Learning ▶▶

1

Enterprise Risk Management Framework and Process

Outline

Risk Classifications

Modeling an Enterprise Risk Management Framework and Process

Designing and Implementing an Enterprise Risk Management Framework and Process

ISO 31000 Risk Management—Principles and Guidelines

COSO Enterprise Risk Management—Integrated Framework

Applying the Enterprise Risk Management Framework and Process

Summary

Educational Objectives

After learning the content of this assignment, you should be able to:

▷ Explain how the following classifications of risk apply and how they help in risk management:

- Pure and speculative risk

- Subjective and objective risk

- Diversifiable and nondiversifiable risk

- Quadrants of risk (hazard, operational, financial, and strategic)

▷ Describe the purpose and component parts of an enterprise risk management framework.

▷ Explain how to design and implement an enterprise risk management framework and process.

▷ Explain how ISO 31000 provides a framework and a process for an organization to manage its risks.

▷ Explain how the Committee of Sponsoring Organizations' Enterprise Risk Management—Integrated Framework provides a standard by which an organization can manage its risks.

▷ Apply the enterprise risk management framework and process to an organization's hazard risk.

Enterprise Risk Management Framework and Process

RISK CLASSIFICATIONS

Classifying the various types of risk can help an organization understand and manage its risks. The categories should align with an organization's objectives and risk management goals.

Classification can help with assessing risks, because many risks in the same classification have similar attributes. It also can help with managing risk, because many risks in the same classification can be managed with similar techniques. Finally, classification helps with the administrative function of risk management by helping to ensure that risks in the same classification are less likely to be overlooked.

These classifications of risk are some of the most commonly used:

- Pure and speculative risk
- Subjective and objective risk
- Diversifiable and nondiversifiable risk
- Quadrants of risk (hazard, operational, financial, and strategic)

These classifications are not mutually exclusive and can be applied to any given risk.

Pure and Speculative Risk

A **pure risk** is a chance of loss or no loss, but no chance of gain. For example, the owner of a commercial building faces the risk associated with a possible fire loss. The building will either burn or not burn. If the building burns, the owner suffers a financial loss. If the building does not burn, the owner's financial condition is unchanged. Neither of the possible outcomes would produce a gain. Because there is no opportunity for financial gain, pure risks are always undesirable. See the exhibit "Classifications of Risk."

In comparison, **speculative risk** involves a chance of gain. As a result, it can be desirable, as evidenced by the fact that every business venture involves speculative risks. For example, an investor who purchases an apartment building to rent to tenants expects to profit from this investment, so it is a desirable speculative risk. However, the venture could be unprofitable if rental price controls limit the amount of rent that can be charged.

> **Pure risk**
> A chance of loss or no loss, but no chance of gain.

> **Speculative risk**
> A chance of loss, no loss, or gain.

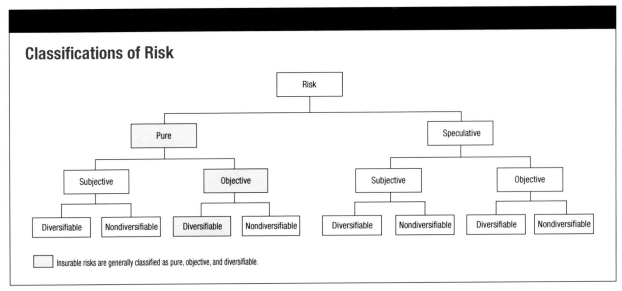

Classifications of Risk

Risk
- Pure
  - Subjective
    - Diversifiable
    - Nondiversifiable
  - Objective
    - Diversifiable
    - Nondiversifiable
- Speculative
  - Subjective
    - Diversifiable
    - Nondiversifiable
  - Objective
    - Diversifiable
    - Nondiversifiable

Insurable risks are generally classified as pure, objective, and diversifiable.

[DA02396]

Credit risk

The risk that customers or other creditors will fail to make promised payments as they come due.

Certain businesses involve speculative risks, such as these:

- Price risk—Uncertainty over the size of cash flows resulting from possible changes in the cost of raw materials and other inputs (such as lumber, gas, or electricity), as well as cost-related changes in the market for completed products and other outputs.

- **Credit risk**—Although a credit risk is particularly significant for banks and other financial institutions, it can be relevant to any organization with accounts receivable.

Financial investments, such as the purchase of stock shares, involve a distinct set of speculative risks. See the exhibit "Speculative Risks in Investments."

Insurance deals primarily with risks of loss, not risks of gain; that is, with pure risks rather than speculative risks. However, the distinction between these two classifications of risk is not always precise—many risks have both pure and speculative aspects.

Distinguishing between pure and speculative risks is important because those risks must often be managed differently. For example, although a commercial building owner faces a pure risk from causes of loss such as fire, he or she also faces the speculative risk that the market value of the building will increase or decrease during any one year. Similarly, although an investor who purchases an apartment building to rent to tenants faces speculative risk because rental income may produce a profit or loss, the investor also faces a pure risk from causes of loss such as fire.

To properly manage these investments, the commercial building owner and the apartment owner must consider both the speculative and the pure risks. For example, they may choose to manage the pure risk by buying insurance or taking other measures to address property loss exposures. The speculative

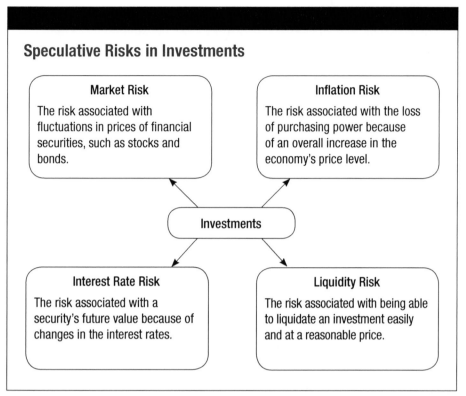

Speculative Risks in Investments

Market Risk

The risk associated with fluctuations in prices of financial securities, such as stocks and bonds.

Inflation Risk

The risk associated with the loss of purchasing power because of an overall increase in the economy's price level.

Investments

Interest Rate Risk

The risk associated with a security's future value because of changes in the interest rates.

Liquidity Risk

The risk associated with being able to liquidate an investment easily and at a reasonable price.

[DA02398]

risk might be managed by obtaining a favorable mortgage and maintaining the property to enhance its resale value.

Subjective and Objective Risk

When individuals and organizations must make a decision that involves risk, they usually base it on the individual's or organization's assessment of the risk. The assessment can be based on opinions, which are subjective, or facts, which are objective.

Because it is based on opinion rather than fact, **subjective risk** may be quite different from the actual underlying risk that is present. In fact, subjective risk can exist even where **objective risk** does not. The closer an individual's or organization's subjective interpretation of risk is to the objective risk, the more effective its risk management plan will likely be.

The reasons that subjective and objective risk can differ substantially include these:

• Familiarity and control—For example, although many people consider air travel (over which they have no control) to carry a high degree of risk,

Subjective risk

The perceived amount of risk based on an individual's or organization's opinion.

Objective risk

The measurable variation in uncertain outcomes based on facts and data.

they are much more likely to suffer a serious injury when driving their cars, where the perception of control is much greater.

- Consequences over likelihood—People often have two views of low-likelihood, high-consequence events. The first misconception is the "It can't happen to me" view, which assigns a probability of zero to low-likelihood events such as natural disasters, murder, fires, accidents, and so on. The second misconception is overstating the probability of a low-likelihood event, which is common for people who have personally been exposed to the event previously. If the effect of a particular event can be severe, such as the potentially destructive effects of a hurricane or earthquake, the perception of the likelihood of deaths resulting from such an event is heightened. This perception may be enhanced by the increased media coverage given to high-severity events.

- Risk awareness—Organizations differ in terms of their level of risk awareness and, therefore, perceive risks differently. An organization that is not aware of its risks would perceive the likelihood of something happening as very low.

Both risk management and insurance depend on the ability to objectively identify and analyze risks. However, subjectivity is also necessary because facts are often not available to objectively assess risk.

Diversifiable and Nondiversifiable Risk

Diversifiable risk is not highly correlated and can be managed through diversification, or spread, of risk. An example of a diversifiable risk is a fire, which is likely to affect only one or a small number of businesses. For instance, an insurer can diversify the risks associated with fire insurance by insuring many buildings in several different locations. Similarly, business investors often diversify their holdings, as opposed to investing in only one business, hoping those that succeed will more than offset those that fail.

Diversifiable risk

A risk that affects only some individuals, businesses, or small groups.

Examples of **nondiversifiable risks** include inflation, unemployment, and natural disasters such as hurricanes. Nondiversifiable risks are correlated—that is, their gains or losses tend to occur simultaneously rather than randomly. For example, under certain monetary conditions, interest rates increase for all firms at the same time. If an insurer were to insure firms against interest rate increases, it would not be able to diversify its portfolio of interest rate risks by underwriting a large number of insureds, because all of them would suffer losses at the same time.

Nondiversifiable risk

A risk that affects a large segment of society at the same time.

Systemic risks are generally nondiversifiable. For example, if excess leverage by financial institutions causes systemic risk resulting in an event that disrupts the financial system, this risk will have an effect on the entire economy and, therefore, on all organizations. Because of the global interconnections in finance and industry, many risks that were once viewed as nonsystemic (affecting only one organization) are now viewed as systemic. For instance, many economists view the failure of Lehman Brothers in early 2008 as a trig-

Systemic risk

The potential for a major disruption in the function of an entire market or financial system.

ger event: highlighting the systemic risk in the banking sector that resulted in the financial crisis.

Quadrants of Risk: Hazard, Operational, Financial, and Strategic

Although no consensus exists about how an organization should categorize its risks, one approach involves dividing them into risk quadrants:

- Hazard risks arise from property, liability, or personnel loss exposures and are generally the subject of insurance.

- Operational risks fall outside the hazard risk category and arise from people or a failure in processes, systems, or controls, including those involving information technology.

- Financial risks arise from the effect of market forces on financial assets or liabilities and include **market risk**, credit risk, **liquidity risk**, and price risk.

- Strategic risks arise from trends in the economy and society, including changes in the economic, political, and competitive environments, as well as from demographic shifts.

Hazard and operational risks are classified as pure risks, and financial and strategic risks are classified as speculative risks.

The focus of the risk quadrants is different from the risk classifications previously discussed. Whereas the classifications of risk focus on some aspect of the risk itself, the four quadrants of risk focus on the risk source and who traditionally manages it. For example, the chief financial officer traditionally manages financial risk, and the risk manager traditionally manages hazard risk. Just as a particular risk can fall into more than one classification, a risk can also fall into multiple risk quadrants. For example, embezzlement of funds by an employee can be considered both a hazard risk, because it is an insurable pure risk, and an operational risk, because it involves a failure of controls. See the exhibit "Risk Quadrants."

Organizations define types of risk differently. Some organizations consider legal risks as operational risk, and some may characterize certain hazard risks as operational risk. Financial institutions generally use the categories of market, credit, and operational risk (defined as all other risk, including hazard risk). Each organization should select categories that align with its objectives and processes.

Market risk

Uncertainty about an investment's future value because of potential changes in the market for that type of investment.

Liquidity risk

The risk that an asset cannot be sold on short notice without incurring a loss.

Risk Quadrants

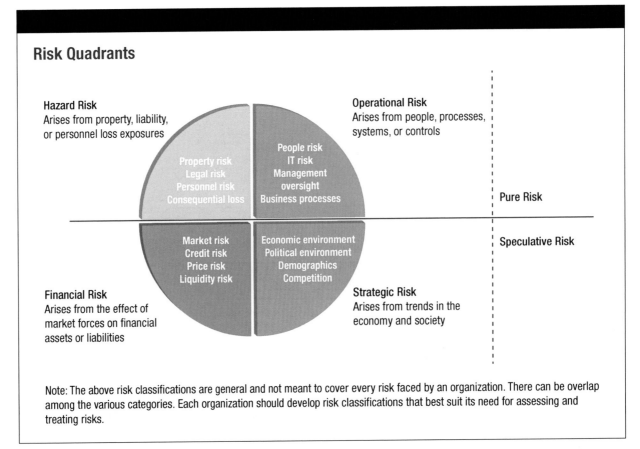

Hazard Risk
Arises from property, liability, or personnel loss exposures

Property risk
Legal risk
Personnel risk
Consequential loss

Operational Risk
Arises from people, processes, systems, or controls

People risk
IT risk
Management oversight
Business processes

Pure Risk

Market risk
Credit risk
Price risk
Liquidity risk

Economic environment
Political environment
Demographics
Competition

Speculative Risk

Financial Risk
Arises from the effect of market forces on financial assets or liabilities

Strategic Risk
Arises from trends in the economy and society

Note: The above risk classifications are general and not meant to cover every risk faced by an organization. There can be overlap among the various categories. Each organization should develop risk classifications that best suit its need for assessing and treating risks.

[DA08677]

Apply Your Knowledge

The New Company manufactures electronic consumer products. The company's manufacturing plant is highly automated and located in the United States. However, it purchases components from three companies in Asia. The majority of its sales are in the U.S., but European sales represent a growing percentage.

Describe the types of risk New Company would have in each of the four risk quadrants.

Feedback: In the hazard risk quadrant, New Company would have property damage risks to its plant and equipment resulting from fire, storms, or other events. It would also have risk of injury to its employees and liability risks associated with its products.

In the operational risk quadrant, New Company would have risks from employee turnover or the inability to find skilled employees. It would also have business process risk related to how it manages its supply chain and information technology risk related to its automated manufacturing process.

In the financial risk quadrant, New Company would have exchange rate risk related to its European sales. It would also have price risk for raw materials and supplies.

Strategic risks include competition, economic factors that could affect consumer demand, and the political risk arising from countries in which the company's component suppliers are located.

MODELING AN ENTERPRISE RISK MANAGEMENT FRAMEWORK AND PROCESS

All recognized risk management standards contain frameworks for organizations to use as they design their risk management programs. Some also specify a risk management process, while others do not. Just as a building is constructed on a frame, a risk management program should be built on a framework.

A risk management framework designed according to best practices will include several major components. These components apply on an enterprise basis across all of the organization's risks. Adapting these components to an organization's objectives and operations will provide a good start toward developing a successful risk management program.

Purpose of a Risk Management Framework

The fundamental purpose of a **risk management framework** is to integrate risk management throughout the organization. The framework is intended to support a risk management process. A risk management framework from an international risk management standard, such as the ISO 31000 framework or the COSO ERM framework, can be applied to any type of organization and can be customized to the needs of a particular one. The principle that underlies a risk management framework is that risk management should add value to the organization. It should not only reduce negative risk but also contribute to profit, reputation, and health and safety.

Risk management framework

A foundation for applying the risk management process throughout the organization.

Enterprise Risk Management Framework and Process Model

The enterprise risk management framework and process model illustrates the components of a framework and the steps of a process. This model encapsulates key concepts from various international risk management standards and is just one of many forms an ERM framework and process can take. Each organization should adopt an ERM framework and process that best meets its needs.

These are the four components of the framework model:

- Lead and establish accountability
- Align and integrate
- Allocate resources
- Communicate and report

These are the five steps of the process model:

- Scan environment
- Identify risks
- Analyze risks
- Treat risks
- Monitor and assure

An organization's framework and process should be reviewed periodically to make sure they continue to meet the organization's needs. See the exhibit "Enterprise Risk Management Framework and Process Model."

The model also illustrates that the risk management process occurs within and is supported by the risk management framework. The risk management process occurs at various levels and applies to various functions throughout the organization. Typically, the framework will be established by an organization's senior management and chief risk officer, while the process may be established by just the chief risk officer or another risk management professional.

Components of a Risk Management Framework

The four components of the risk management framework model demonstrate the organization's commitment to risk management and help drive the integration of risk management throughout the organization. The framework components also support the risk management process. They are not meant to be carried out in any particular order, and an organization should adapt the components to suit its specific circumstances.

Lead and Establish Accountability

The first component of a risk management framework involves an organization's senior management, usually the chief executive officer (CEO), leading and establishing accountability for risk management. Leadership includes development of the organization's risk management philosophy and mission. It also includes commitment to risk management at the highest levels of an organization. The tone for major projects and initiatives is set at the top of the organization, and a tone of sincere commitment to and support for risk management is essential for the process to be successful. Senior management's commitment also involves holding everyone in the organization

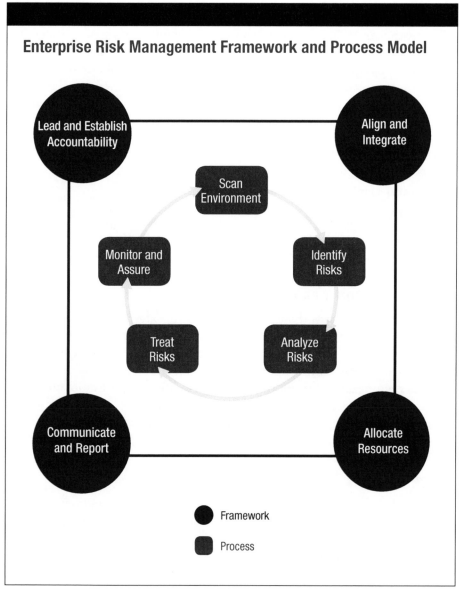

Enterprise Risk Management Framework and Process Model

[DA08717_1]

accountable for risk management. These techniques can be used to establish accountability:

- Identify **risk owners** and their roles in the organization
- Establish **key performance indicators (KPI)**
- Establish **key risk indicators (KRI)** and use them to evaluate performance
- Develop **risk criteria** to evaluate the significance of risks

Risk owner

An individual accountable for the identification, assessment, treatment, and monitoring of risks in a specific environment.

Key performance indicator (KPI)

Financial or nonfinancial measurement that defines how successfully an organization is progressing toward its long-term goals.

Key risk indicator (KRI)

A tool used by an organization to measure the uncertainty of meeting a strategic business objective.

Risk criteria

Information used as a basis for measuring the significance of a risk.

Align and Integrate

The second component of the framework is alignment of risk management with an organization's objectives and integration of the risk management process. Risk management objectives should be aligned with objectives at both the strategic and operational levels of the organization. After this alignment has been developed, the risk management process must be integrated with organizational processes, including these:

- Strategic planning
- Performance management
- Process management
- Internal control
- Compliance
- Governance

Allocate Resources

The third component of the framework is the allocation of resources. A clear indication of senior management's commitment to risk management is the willingness to allocate the resources necessary to effectively implement a risk management process throughout the organization. Typical resource needs include training and adaptation of systems. Additionally, the chief financial officer (CFO) must determine an appropriate risk-based capital allocation according to regulatory requirements and the risk characteristics of the organization's business units or products.

Communicate and Report

The fourth component of the framework is communication and reporting. Senior management must effectively communicate the purpose and importance of the risk management process to the entire organization. Communication across organizational functions is also necessary for the design and implementation of an effective risk management process. After the process is integrated, proficient communication of results must take place to provide the basis for ongoing monitoring and improvement.

The risk management framework should include procedures to report information about risks and the results of risk management to appropriate stakeholders. Senior management should receive executive summary reports at regular intervals. More detailed reports should be prepared and reviewed by managers regarding risks in their areas of responsibility. For the risk management process to be optimally effective, information about emerging risks should be included in risk reports.

Risk Management Policy

To obtain buy-in from managers and employees throughout the organization, a clear statement of the risk management policy should be present. The policy should support the risk management framework and be communicated throughout the organization and to appropriate external stakeholders. See the exhibit "Example of Risk Management Policy Statement."

The risk management policy statement shown in the exhibit touches on several aspects of components in the risk management framework model. It mentions establishing senior management commitment and support, applying processes, maintaining effective communication, and training.

Example of Risk Management Policy Statement

Policy Statement on Risk Management

Mission Statement

Canterbury City Council's Risk Management Policy is to adopt best practice in the identification, evaluation and cost-effective control of risks, to ensure that they are either eliminated or reduced to an acceptable level.

Risk is a factor of everyday life and can never be eliminated completely. All employees must understand the nature of risk and accept responsibility for risks associated with their area of authority. The necessary support, assistance and commitment of senior management will be provided.

Our Risk Management objectives are to:

1. Integrate Risk Management into the culture of the organisation.

2. Manage risk in accordance with best practice.

3. Consider legal compliance as an absolute minimum.

4. Anticipate and respond quickly to social, environmental and legislative change.

5. Prevent injury and damage and reduce the cost of risk.

6. Raise awareness of the need for risk management.

These objectives will be achieved by:

1. Establishing a Corporate Governance/Risk Management organisational structure to act in an advisory and guiding capacity and which is accessible to all employees.

2. Include Corporate Governance/Risk Management as one of the implications to be considered in every committee report.

3. Adopt processes, which demonstrate that Corporate Governance/Risk Management principles are being applied across the whole organisation.

4. Provide training in risk awareness and Corporate Governance.

5. Maintain documented procedures for the control of risk and provision of suitable information, training and supervision.

6. Maintain an appropriate system for recording incidents and carrying out post event checks to ascertain causes and identify preventive measures against re-occurrence.

7. Devise and maintain contingency plans in key risk areas to secure business continuity where there is a potential for an event having a major impact upon the council's ability to function.

8. Maintain effective communication and involvement of all staff and members.

9. Monitor arrangements on an ongoing basis.

Canterbury City Council Online, "Policy Statement on Risk Management," www.canterbury.gov.uk/main. cfm?objectid=938 (accessed April 10, 2012). [DA08834]

DESIGNING AND IMPLEMENTING AN ENTERPRISE RISK MANAGEMENT FRAMEWORK AND PROCESS

Risk management professionals should use a recognized international standard as a model for the framework and process that will integrate risk management practices throughout their organizations. A recognized standard is more likely both to meet any regulatory risk management guidelines and to provide effective methods for organizations.

Before designing a risk management framework and process, risk management professionals should understand the major international risk management standards and consider which one best reflects the needs of the organization. After a standard is selected, risk management professionals should use the standard as broad guidance as they design and develop an appropriate framework and process for their organizations.

As a risk management professional, how would you design and implement a risk management framework and process for your organization, based on a recognized international standard?

Risk management professionals can adapt a risk management framework and process to their organizations' needs. Best practices in risk management involve continuously reviewing the framework and process as results are obtained and analyzed. Any major change within the organization should also prompt a reevaluation of the framework and process. These are the stages in designing and implementing a risk management framework and process:

- Gap analysis
- Evaluation of internal and external environments
- Integration into existing processes
- Commitment of resources
- Communication and reporting
- Monitoring and improvement

Gap Analysis

A risk management professional should first compare an organization's existing risk management framework and process against that of an internationally recognized standard, such as ISO 31000 or COSO ERM. Each component of the selected risk management framework and process should be matched with a similar aspect of the current risk management program and the responsible organizational function.

Any component or subcomponent of the framework and process that does not have a match in the organization's current risk management program represents a gap. Identifying these gaps allows the organization to better use resources. Additionally, matched components can form key supports of the framework and process because they are already integrated within the organization's procedures and culture.

Evaluation of Internal and External Environments

After performing a gap analysis, risk management professionals should evaluate the internal and external environments in which the organization operates.

Internal Environment

Evaluating the internal environment begins by understanding the organization's overall objectives and risk appetite—the total exposed amount that an organization wishes to undertake on the basis of risk-return trade-offs for one or more desired and expected outcomes.[1] Then the evaluation proceeds to the organization's key strategies. For example, applying a risk management framework to an organization that is pursuing an organic growth strategy will be different from applying one to a company with a mergers-and-acquisitions strategy.

Risk management professionals, usually with a team representing key organizational functions, should next evaluate the organizational structure and the major categories of risk within each area. Results of the gap analysis can be used to identify areas in which application of the risk management framework and process needs to be modified. For example, the gap analysis may indicate that risk management is not explicitly included in an organization's procurement process. Procurement could then become a focus in the design of the risk management framework and process.

After mapping the organizational structure and its key risk categories, the risk management team should evaluate the resources necessary to implement and maintain the risk management framework and process. These resources may include equipment, systems, and people. For example, integrating risk management into procurement may involve training employees and acquiring computer software.

The internal context evaluation should also provide an overview of the formal and informal communication channels within the organization. This should include perspectives on the corporate culture. Is the overall culture risk taking or risk averse? What are the general attitudes and viewpoints of subgroups on risk management? Surveys and discussion groups can be used to gather this information.

External Environment

The external environment of an organization includes these factors:

- Economic
- Political
- Legal and regulatory
- Technology
- Natural
- Competitive landscape

Risk management professionals should evaluate the external environment for all of the organization's operations. The key risk categories for each factor should be included in this evaluation. For example, risks associated with the natural environment will have different effects on energy providers, insurers, farming organizations, and electronic manufacturers.

Integration Into Existing Processes

There are two major keys to successful integration of the risk management framework and process. The first is to align risk management objectives and policy with the organization's overall objectives and risk appetite. The second is to use existing processes.

The gap analysis will identify existing risk management policies and procedures. Using existing processes as components of the risk management framework and process serves two purposes. First, any long-existing process is likely embedded into the organization's culture; therefore, the organization will not experience the usual resistance to change from introducing new procedures. Second, resources will not have to be allocated to designing and implementing pieces of the framework and process that already exist.

Traditionally, most organizations have risk management procedures to address human resources practices, employee safety, product safety, credit risk, financial processes, and regulatory requirements. Although a risk management framework and process can be designed with existing components, risk management professionals should consider how well the current procedures meet the organization's needs and how these processes should be adapted to comply with a recognized standard. Additionally, this consideration should address how well the current procedures meet the organization's needs.

As the framework is being designed, those involved in its planning and implementation should consider where new paradigms might better achieve objectives. For example, in many organizations, different functions purchase supplies and services. In a manufacturing organization, a central purchasing division may procure the components and materials used in production. However, a risk management department may purchase property and casualty insurance, a human resources department may purchase health and disability insurance, and an information technology department may purchase computers and related services. The organization may want to consider adding cross-functional risk management to coordinate these various processes.

A critical component of the integration is assigning responsibility and accountability for risk management within each of the organization's functions. Ideally, everyone in the organization would embrace the risk management vision, but specific persons would be designated as responsible for risk management. Typically, managers of divisions and business units are responsible for managing the risks in their areas of operations: for example, the chief financial officer (CFO) has regulatory responsibility for most financial risk, and managers reporting to the CFO have responsibility for their functions.

Commitment of Resources

Plans for the risk management framework and process should include the additional resources required and a commitment from senior management to provide those resources. These are categories of necessary resources:

- Technology, including equipment and systems
- Administrative persons
- Specialists, either internal or external
- Analysts
- Training

The nature and extent of these resources vary widely in different organizations. The size of the organization, how many locations it has, the geographical dispersion of its business units, the nature of its operations, and the extent of existing risk management all determine what resources are necessary.

For many organizations, implementing a risk management framework and process takes several years. A large quantity of information needs to be assembled and evaluated to design an effective framework and process, determine the necessary resources, and integrate the framework and process throughout the organization. A lengthy time frame allows organizations to allocate the necessary funds in stages.

Communication and Reporting

Communication is a key aspect of the risk management framework and process. A framework should establish the types and channels of communication within the organization. This is a complex process, and key stakeholders within the organization should be involved during the planning of risk management communication. These stakeholders should also be included in designing metrics for both evaluating risk management and reporting results.

Communication

Communicating the risk management policy is a key step in integrating the risk management framework and process throughout the organization. The way the policy is communicated sets the tone. For example, a chief executive officer who visits a manufacturing organization's factories to deliver the policy and discuss it with employees sends a powerful message that the policy is important to the organization's objectives.

Many other types of communication besides policy dissemination must occur before, during, and following implementation of the risk management framework and process. Successful integration of the framework and process will depend on the quality of these communications.

During design of the framework and process, detailed and thoughtful communication should occur among all key areas of the organization. A task force comprised of representatives of these areas who can commit significant amounts of time to the risk management framework and process can be an effective resource. Often, organizations will use an external risk management consultant to facilitate the process of developing the communication plan.

The implementation phase requires communication of both the policy and procedures that will be integrated throughout the organization. Training may be required, especially for those responsible and accountable for results.

Communication after the framework and policy are in place should focus not only on metrics and analysis of results, but also on how well the organizational culture is adapting to the policies and procedures. Any areas of resistance to the integration of the framework and process should be identified and addressed through both formal and informal communication, training, surveys, and other methods.

Reporting

Those who are responsible and accountable for risk management results in an organization must receive timely and relevant information regarding key metrics for their areas of responsibility. Many organizations use a scorecard approach and distribute results quarterly. If an organization reports financial results quarterly, tying risk metrics to the quarterly financial results can be a valuable way of determining and reporting on the effect of risk management on the organization's overall objectives. For example, improvements in customers' credit quality could be tied to its effect on the organization's balance sheet.

In addition to internal reports, most organizations must produce reports to external stakeholders to meet regulatory or other requirements. These mandated reports should be included in the design of the risk management framework with defined reporting responsibilities.

Monitoring and Improvement

An effective risk management program should lead to improvements in results. As objectives are met, new objectives are set to encourage continual improvement. The risk management framework and process should provide mechanisms to encourage continuous improvement, such as regular review of objectives, team discussion of results, and benchmarking to other organizations in the same industry.

P-D-C-A Cycle

The P-D-C-A Cycle, also known as the Shewhart cycle and the Deming cycle, is an expansion of an approach to process improvement. The steps include Plan, Do, Check, and Act.

The plan-do-check-act cycle (**P-D-C-A Cycle**) can be used in many different settings as an improvement model. The "act" step of the cycle simultaneously restarts it, with evaluation of the implemented improvement reinitiating the "plan" phase.

Additionally, risk management professionals and other key stakeholders should participate in educational programs and professional associations, read professional journals, and stay current on broad business trends. The risk management framework and process should be able to adapt and respond to changing circumstances. For example, if a new regulation will change capital or reporting requirements, risk and financial managers should be aware of the potential change and how it will affect the organization. Plans should be made to address it within the risk management framework.

Apply Your Knowledge

After studying the methods to design and implement a risk management framework and process based on an internationally recognized standard, explain a risk management professional's first step in designing and implementing a risk management framework and process for an organization.

Feedback: The risk management professional should first conduct a gap analysis of the organization. This step involves determining the existing risk management program, including procedures in different areas of the organization. The structure of the entire organization should be charted, indicating which functions have explicit risk management processes. Additionally, key risk categories for each area should be mapped. Next, those functions that do not have explicit risk management procedures, as well as key risks that are not currently addressed, should be identified. The risk management framework and process can be designed using the risk management components that are already in place.

ISO 31000 RISK MANAGEMENT—PRINCIPLES AND GUIDELINES

An organization should reference a recognized standard when developing a risk management program. The International Organization for Standardization (ISO) provides an international standard, ISO 31000, that any organization can adapt to manage its operational, financial, strategic, and hazard risks.

For example, an electronics manufacturer with factories and suppliers in Asia and the United States would like to develop a risk management program for its supply-chain risks. As a recognized international standard, ISO 31000 could provide the framework and process for the organization's risk management program.

Background

ISO is a nongovernmental group. Its membership consists of the national standards institutes of 163 countries, some of which are government entities, while others are in the private sector. In 2009, ISO published ISO 31000:2009, Risk Management—Principles and Guidelines, an international risk management standard.

ISO 31000:2009, or ISO 31000, was developed largely from the Australian and New Zealand Risk Management Standard, AS/NZS 4360:1995.[2] ISO 31000 contains principles, a framework, and a process to manage risk; it can be tailored to meet the objectives of any organization. See the exhibit "ISO 31000 Standard: Risk Management Principles, Framework, and Process."

Scope

The ISO 31000 standard can be applied to all operations and most activities of the organization and to any type of risk, including hazard, operational, financial, and strategic risks. It also applies regardless of whether the risk has positive and/or negative consequences.

Although the standard is universally applicable, it is not intended to produce uniformity. On the contrary, its emphasis is on tailoring its process and framework to each organization.

Principles

ISO 31000 lists eleven principles of risk management. In general, these principles relate to uses, qualities, and application of effective risk management. Uses include protecting the organization's value, informing decision making, and dealing with uncertainty. The qualities of effective risk management include structure, timeliness, transparency, inclusiveness, dynamism, and

ISO 31000 Standard: Risk Management Principles, Framework, and Process

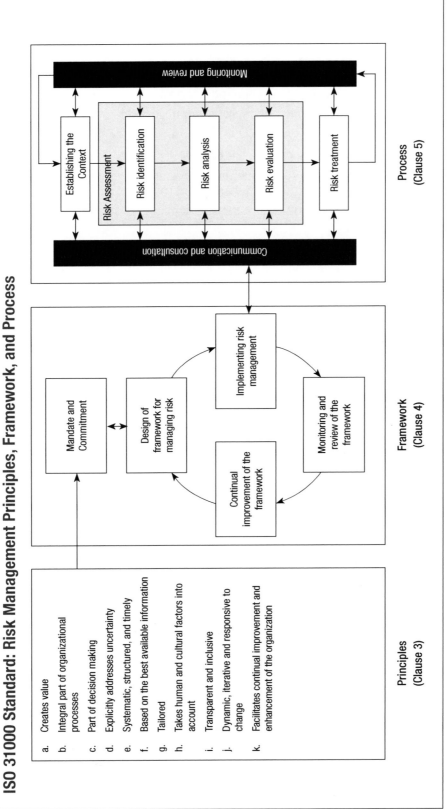

Principles
(Clause 3)

a. Creates value
b. Integral part of organizational processes
c. Part of decision making
d. Explicitly addresses uncertainty
e. Systematic, structured, and timely
f. Based on the best available information
g. Tailored
h. Takes human and cultural factors into account
i. Transparent and inclusive
j. Dynamic, iterative and responsive to change
k. Facilitates continual improvement and enhancement of the organization

Framework
(Clause 4)

Mandate and Commitment

Design of framework for managing risk

Implementing risk management

Monitoring and review of the framework

Continual improvement of the framework

Process
(Clause 5)

Monitoring and review

Communication and consultation

Establishing the Context

Risk Assessment

Risk identification

Risk analysis

Risk evaluation

Risk treatment

responsiveness to change. Effectively applied, risk management is integrated into all of an organization's processes, is based on the best available information (and an understanding of the limitations of such information), and considers human and cultural factors.[3]

Framework

ISO 31000 includes a generic risk management framework that organizations can use to integrate the risk management process into their management and operational systems. The framework can be adapted to an organization's specific operations and objectives. A strong mandate and commitment from managers must be in place to implement a successful, company-specific risk management framework.

Designing a tailored framework begins with an evaluation of an organization's risk contexts, including all major factors both inside and outside the organization that affect its objectives and operations. For example, in January 2012, Apple's supply chain was disrupted by a fire at the factory of one of its major suppliers in China that caused injury and death to several skilled workers and required the plant, and the supply chain, to be shut down for a period of time.[4] An ISO 31000 framework would have assisted in identifying and addressing the related risks.

Based on a thorough understanding of its contexts, an organization can establish its risk management policy. This policy should address how the organization will identify risks and how it will measure, review, and communicate its risk management efforts. The framework also must incorporate accountability procedures for meeting risk management goals and must integrate risk management throughout the entire organization.

Appropriate resources should be available for designing and implementing the risk management framework. These resources should include staff with the necessary skills and any necessary equipment, such as that used for training or data management. Finally, the framework must establish internal communication and reporting methods and external communication with relevant stakeholders.[5]

Process

The ISO 31000 risk management process consists of several activities besides establishing the internal and external contexts of the organization and communicating: specifically, assessing risks, treating risks, and monitoring and reviewing the changes resulting from application of the process. Because the process is applied to different risks and functions of the organization, the specific context for each risk management process should be defined, in addition to the overall organizational context.

For example, an electronics manufacturer will have financial, marketing, manufacturing, distribution, and information technology functions. The manufacturing operations may have multiple plants in different countries with different suppliers. Therefore, particular risk management processes, such as the one for managing supply-chain risks, will need to be established in detail within the context of each country in which the organization does business, as well as within the overall context of the organization.

As part of establishing the internal and external contexts, an organization should define risk criteria. Risk criteria are based on measures used to evaluate the significance of the organization's various risks in relation to the organization's values and objectives as well as the legal and regulatory requirements to which it is subject. In establishing risk criteria, an organization considers factors such as possible consequences resulting from each risk, their likelihood of occurring, how they will be measured, and the organization's tolerance to the risk. An organization could use multiple measures for a single risk, such as its effect on both net income and reputation.

Risk Assessment

The ISO 31000 definition of risk assessment includes risk identification, risk analysis, and risk evaluation.

An organization should develop a comprehensive list of risks that can have either a positive or negative effect on objectives. From a traditional risk management viewpoint, this assessment has focused on hazard risks, which can result only in negative consequences. However, the risk management process has evolved for most standards, regulators, and organizations to include risks that have the possibility of negative or positive consequences. For example, an organization that chooses a plant location or supplier in a catastrophe-prone region, where labor costs are lower than in other areas and where currency exchange rates are favorable, is accepting risk with an expected positive outcome resulting from lower costs as well as risk with an expected negative outcome associated with supply-chain interruptions.

It is important to identify as many risks as possible, prioritizing key risks in terms of their effect on the organization's objectives. It is also essential that both line management and executive management are involved in identifying risks, as unidentified, or missed, risks will not be analyzed or addressed in the risk management process and, therefore, pose a greater threat of damage.

After risks are identified, the next step is analysis—quantitative, qualitative, or a combination of the two. This analysis includes determining the level of risk and its potential effects on the organization. Both the tangible and intangible effects of consequences should be considered.

The third step in risk assessment is evaluating the organization's risks. This step involves applying the selected risk criteria to the levels of risk determined during the analysis. The subsequent evaluation will allow decisions to be made regarding risk treatment.

Risk Treatment

Risk treatment is the ongoing process of deciding on an option for modifying risk and whether the residual level of risk is acceptable, selecting a new risk treatment if the current one is not effective, and then repeating this assessment.

In treating risks, an organization may choose to avoid, retain, or transfer all or part of a risk. Risks may also be treated by eliminating their sources, altering the likelihood that an event will result from a risk, or changing the consequences of events resulting from risk. For risks that present the possibility of positive outcomes, an organization may choose to assume a risk or even increase it. Selection of the risk treatment should include determining those within and outside the organization who are accountable, as well as performance measures that will be used in ongoing assessments of the risk treatment.

Risk treatment options can be applied individually or in combination following a deliberate sequence. For example, an organization may find it economical to alter the likelihood of an event and its consequences before transferring the risk.

Many organizations experienced severe supply-chain disruptions when they could not receive parts manufactured in Japan after the devastating earthquake and tsunami in 2011. As a result, an electronics manufacturer might now choose suppliers that are not located in earthquake-prone regions to eliminate the source of this risk.

Risk Monitoring and Review

Monitoring and reviewing both internal and external changes and how these changes affect risks and their treatment should be a planned part of the risk management process. Monitoring should also include recording the assessments and reporting them internally and externally, as needed; determining the frequency, distribution, and method of reporting is an integral part of developing the risk management process.

COSO ENTERPRISE RISK MANAGEMENT— INTEGRATED FRAMEWORK

The Committee of Sponsoring Organizations (COSO) is a voluntary organization in the private sector. COSO includes the Institute of Internal Auditors (IIA), the American Accounting Association (AAA), the American Institute of Certified Public Accountants (AICPA), Financial Executives International (FEI), and the Association of Accountants and Financial Professionals in Business (IMA).

In 2004, COSO issued a risk management standard. There are many similarities between COSO 2004 and other risk management standards, such as ISO 31000. A major difference, however, between COSO 2004 and other standards is that the COSO framework's components do not address root cause analysis. Although the framework can be applied to all the risks of an organization, the origin of the COSO standards is in financial risk.

Additionally, COSO defines the term "risk" somewhat differently than does ISO 31000. COSO defines risk as the possibility that an event will occur and adversely affect an organization's objectives, whereas ISO 31000 defines risk as "the effect of uncertainty on objectives." However, COSO does reflect in its framework for risk management that an event can have a positive as well as a negative effect.

An organization decides on the risk management standard(s) to use for all or part of the organization's risks. A bank, for example, might select COSO 2004 as its risk management standard because of this standard's historical focus on financial controls and its robust emphasis on control activities in the COSO Enterprise Risk Management—Integrated Framework and risk management process.

Additionally, internal auditors, primarily in the United States, frequently use COSO 2004 as a standard when evaluating an organization's risk management. Internal auditors do not select or implement an organization's risk management standard. However, auditors have an important role in monitoring, reviewing, and evaluating the risk management process. Auditors can advise an organization on how well controls are working in different areas of operations and recommend improvements.

Background

COSO was organized in 1985 to sponsor the National Commission on Fraudulent Financial Reporting. This was an independent private-sector initiative to study the factors that lead to fraudulent financial reporting. The initiative developed recommendations for public companies and their independent auditors, the U.S. Securities and Exchange Commission and other regulators, and educational institutions.[6]

In 1992, COSO published a framework for the evaluation of internal control systems titled "Internal Control—Integrated Framework." This was updated in 2004 to be the Enterprise Risk Management—Integrated Framework, expanding beyond internal controls to include strategic objectives. A major reason for the development of this framework was to meet the requirements of the U.S.'s Sarbanes-Oxley Act.

Framework

The COSO Enterprise Risk Management—Integrated Framework is designed to help an organization achieve its objectives in four categories:

- Strategic—high-level goals, aligned with and supporting its mission
- Operations—effective and efficient use of its resources
- Reporting—reliability of reporting
- Compliance—compliance with applicable laws and regulations

There are eight interrelated components of the COSO framework that should be integrated within an organization's risk management process:

- Internal environment—Determine risk management philosophy and risk appetite, integrity and ethical values, and the operating environment. A board of directors is an important part of the internal environment with influence on the other aspects of the environment. In this component of the risk management process, senior management aligns the people, processes, and infrastructure to make it possible for the organization to stay within its risk appetite.
- Objective setting—Align risk management objectives with the organization's mission and risk appetite. Objectives must be determined before management can identify the events that might affect their achievement.
- Event identification—Identify internal and external events that affect achievement of objectives, and distinguish between negative risk and opportunity risk. External events include economic, political, social, and technological elements. Internal factors include management decisions, people, infrastructure, processes, and technology.
- Risk assessment—Analyze risks, considering likelihood and impact. Likelihood is the possibility that a given event will occur. Impact is the effect of an event if it does occur. Risk assessment is first applied to **inherent risk**. After the development of risk responses, **residual risk** is determined.
- Risk response—Select how to respond to the risks identified, for example, by avoidance, reduction, or transfer.
- Control activities—Establish policies and procedures to carry out effective risk responses. Control activities are the policies and procedures to determine that risk responses are performed correctly.
- Information and communication—Use effective communication that flows down, across, and up the organization. An organization should use both historical and current data to have an effective risk management program.
- Monitoring—Make modifications through ongoing monitoring of the risk management process. An organization may use both internal and independent evaluations to monitor its risk management.

Inherent risk

Risk to an entity apart from any action to alter either the likelihood or impact of the risk.

Residual risk

Risk remaining after actions to alter the risk's likelihood or impact.

COSO states that "risk management is not strictly a serial process, where one component affects only the next. It is a multidirectional…process in which almost any component can and does influence another."[7] The process should be applied across all four levels of an organization: entity, division, business unit, and subsidiary. See the exhibit "COSO Risk Management: Relationship of Objectives and Components."

COSO Risk Management: Relationship of Objectives and Components

There is a direct relationship between objectives, which an organization strives to achieve, and risk management components, which are necessary to achieve them.

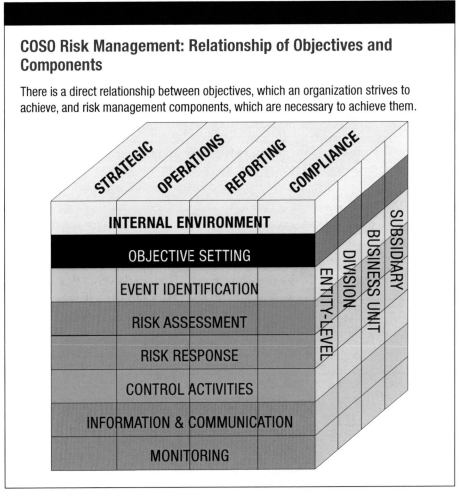

In the example of a bank, the organization would identify its strategic objectives to include return on capital, profit, and growth. The bank's operational objectives would support its strategic objectives in areas such as loan activity, customer growth, acquisitions, and expansion. The reporting and compliance objectives would focus on meeting regulatory requirements. The bank's managers would then apply the eight components of the COSO risk management framework across all of the organization's levels to align the bank's operations with its risk appetite and strategic objectives.

Control Activities

Section 404 of the Sarbanes-Oxley Act states that public companies are required to publish information in their annual reports regarding the scope and adequacy of their internal control structure and procedures for financial reporting. Additionally, the companies are required to assess the effectiveness of these internal controls and procedures. The registered accounting firm that provides an audit of the financial statement is required to attest to and report on the assessment of the effectiveness of the internal control structure and procedures for financial reporting.

Because COSO 2004 historically focused on financial controls and developed its risk management framework in the context of internal audits related to compliance with Sarbanes-Oxley, control activities are a key feature of this standard in comparison with other risk management standards.

Control activities are policies and procedures applied to each of the four categories of objectives—strategic, operations, reporting, and compliance. Overlap may exist in how controls relate to objectives and areas of operation. The most important function of a control is its role in achieving its objective. For example, a control activity may have the objective of ensuring that all bank loans conform to the bank's guidelines. The organization may apply this control activity across regional divisions and branch offices.

Control activities typically have two parts. The first part is the policy that states what should be done, and the second part is the procedure to accomplish the policy. For example, a policy states that all bank loans should conform to guidelines. The procedure is to enter all loan information into the bank's computer system and produce daily reports for branch managers, weekly reports for regional managers, and monthly reports for the risk manager.

The risk management process should be monitored to determine the effectiveness of control activities in meeting objectives. There are two types of monitoring. The first type is ongoing regular monitoring by an organization's management. For example, the percentage of nonconforming loans is compared to the guidelines on a daily basis. The second type is periodic evaluation, often by internal auditors. Internal auditors can identify areas where control activities are deficient and make recommendations to improve them.

Apply Your Knowledge

An internal auditor discovers that 17 percent of a bank's loans do not conform to the bank's guidelines. The control objective is that all loans conform to guidelines. The procedure includes entering information regarding each loan into the computer and producing reports for managers. Which one of the following is the auditor likely to recommend?

a. Review the objective
b. Review the procedure
c. Review both the objective and the procedure

Feedback: c. The auditor is likely to recommend a review of both the objective and the procedure. Has the bank changed its risk appetite? If so, the objective and loan guidelines may need to be revised. The bank's managers may want to do further review of the nonconforming loans and evaluate the effect on the bank's performance objectives. Additionally, the procedures regarding the quality of the information entered into the computer and how the reports are prepared and analyzed should be reviewed.

APPLYING THE ENTERPRISE RISK MANAGEMENT FRAMEWORK AND PROCESS

Applying the enterprise risk management framework and process to the facts of a case can help risk management professionals understand how their organizations' risks can be managed. Although this process can be applied to all of an organization's risks, this case focuses on hazard risk.

Case Facts

Power, Inc., is a regional energy provider located in the northeastern United States. Power owns and operates natural gas plants in seven states. Its operations include installing and maintaining gas pipelines and customer hookups. Power has a fleet of service trucks used to connect and disconnect customer gas service and a fleet of maintenance vehicles used to perform repairs to main gas pipes. Additionally, Power has an office building where fifty employees perform accounting, administrative, legal, and human resources functions.

Power had an increasing frequency of vehicle accidents over the past three years, although the severity of those accidents remained essentially the same. Service technicians, however, have experienced less frequent but more severe injuries during the same time period. Two minor injuries involving Power's clerical employees occurred at the company's office building. Nationally, one tropical storm during the previous three years caused major damage to a key pipeline and resulted in injury to employees who repaired damage during the storm.

During the three-year period, three ruptures to pipelines necessitated evacuating the immediate area because of a release of gas. No injuries resulted. There has been an increase in the number of property damage claims from customers alleging damage to appliances and homes resulting from Power's installations and maintenance. One lawsuit filed involved the deaths of a family from a gas explosion, and several lawsuits were filed related to nonfatal injuries in similar incidents.

Power's senior management includes a chief executive officer (CEO), a chief financial officer (CFO), and a chief operating officer (COO). A vice president is in charge of each of its plants and each corporate division (legal, human resources, and procurement). Line managers are responsible for direct management of areas of operation and for employees at each of the plants, such as energy generation and service.

This case provides an opportunity for you to apply the enterprise risk management framework and process to Power's hazard risks.

Overview of Steps

These are the four components of the enterprise risk management framework:

- Lead and establish accountability
- Align and integrate
- Allocate resources
- Communicate and report

These are the steps in the enterprise risk management process:

- Scan environment
- Identify risks
- Analyze risks
- Treat risks
- Monitor and assure

Applying the Risk Management Framework

When an organization adapts an enterprise risk management approach, it must develop a framework. The main purpose of the framework is to integrate risk management throughout the organization; however, it also supports the risk management process.

Lead and Establish Accountability

Senior management must provide the leadership to develop and integrate enterprise risk management. The commitment of the organization's leaders is necessary, and they must also establish accountability for results among the organization's risk owners.

Knowledge to Action

What performance standards can Power's senior management use to establish accountability from line managers for hazard risk? Select all that apply.

a.   Key performance indicators (KPIs)

b.   Severity of employee injuries

c.   Key risk indicators (KRIs)

d.   Storm response time

Feedback: a. and c. Power's senior management should design KPIs and KRIs that align with Power's risk management and strategic objectives. The organization's managers have little direct control over the severity of employee injuries (b.). Although storm response time (d.) could be included as a KPI, an evaluation would need to be performed of the storm's severity and other factors that are beyond the managers' control.

Align and Integrate

The risk management framework must align the organization's risk management approach with its strategic objectives and integrate risk management throughout the organization.

Knowledge to Action

Explain which levels in Power's organizational structure need to be involved in the integration of an enterprise risk management process.

Feedback: All levels of Power's organizational structure need to be involved in the integration of the risk management process. Each level must take ownership of risk and be accountable for results. Senior management is responsible for the risk management policy and commitment. Plant and division managers are responsible for results in their areas of operation. Line managers are responsible for their functions. Additionally, employees must be risk owners and accountable for results.

Allocate Resources

Senior management demonstrates its commitment to risk management by allocating resources, such as training, systems, equipment, and consultants.

Knowledge to Action

What type(s) of resources would best assist Power's risk management process? Select all that apply.

a.   Technician training in installation and maintenance procedures

b.   Driver training

c.   New computer system

d.   Lightning rods

Feedback: a. and b. Property damage claims have increased in frequency as a result of installations and maintenance. Vehicle accident frequency has also experienced an increase. Training service technicians in safe driving techniques and proper installation and maintenance procedures would be an appropriate allocation of resources to assist the risk management process. Power has identified its hazard risks and found no need for a new computer system at this time (c.). Lightning rods (d.) could not be effectively deployed along all of Power's pipelines.

Communicate and Report

Communication and reporting is an essential component of the risk management framework.

Knowledge to Action

Who would be the best person(s) in the organization to communicate Power's commitment to risk management?

a.   CEO

b.   Vice president of human resources

c.   Plant managers

d.   Line managers

Feedback: a. Communication from the top is important to emphasize an organization's commitment to risk management. However, communication at all levels is also important as the risk management process is integrated.

Applying the Risk Management Process

Once the risk management framework is in place, the risk management process can be designed and integrated throughout the organization.

Scan Environment

The first step in the process involves scanning the internal and external environments and defining the criteria that will be used in the assessment of risk.

Knowledge to Action

Which factors would you include in the external environment for Power's hazard risk management?

Feedback: Factors in the external environment for Power's hazard risk management include the regulatory, legal, and natural environments. Regulations affect many aspects of Power's hazard risk management process—for example, there are federal regulations regarding employee safety and state regulations regarding utilities, vehicles, and employee injuries. The legal environment affects the likelihood and potential outcome of litigation, and the natural environment affects risks such as storms or wildfires.

Identify Risks

The next step in the risk management process is risk identification.

Knowledge to Action

Identify Power's key hazard risks. Categorize these risks according to whether they arise from external causes (such as weather) or internal causes (such as employee operations).

Feedback: These are Power's key hazard risks arising from external causes:

- Weather-related damage to property or injury to employees
- Explosion of gas pipelines related to fire or other external causes
- Damage to pipelines that causes release of gas

These are Power's key hazard risks arising from internal causes:

- Vehicle accidents with vehicle or other property damage
- Vehicle accidents with personal injury
- Various risks of employee injury while working on gas pipes or installing equipment
- Risk of injury to clerical employees
- Damage to customers' property from interruption to gas supply, gas leakage, or explosion
- Injury to customers from interruption to gas supply, gas leakage, or explosion

Analyze Risks

Risk analysis focuses on the causes of risks, their likelihood, and their consequences.

Knowledge to Action

Place each of Power's risks into one of these categories:

- High potential impact/high likelihood
- High potential impact/low likelihood
- Low potential impact/high likelihood
- Low potential impact/low likelihood

Feedback: These are the risks in the high potential impact/high likelihood category:

- Vehicle accidents with personal injury
- Various risks of employee injury while working on gas pipes or installing equipment

These are the risks in the high potential impact/low likelihood category:

- Weather-related damage to property or injury to employees
- Explosion of gas pipelines related to fire or other external causes
- Damage to pipelines that causes release of gas
- Injury to customers from interruption to gas supply, gas leakage, or explosion

These are the risks in the low potential impact/high likelihood category:

- Vehicle accidents with property damage
- Damage to customers' property from interruption to gas supply, gas leakage, or explosion

This is the risk in the low potential impact/low likelihood category: risk of injury to clerical employees.

Treat Risks

The first step in treating risk is to decide which risks qualify for risk treatment and to prioritize them.

Knowledge to Action

Select and prioritize Power's risks for risk treatment.

Feedback: These are the risks Power faces that are suited for risk treatment:

- Explosion of gas pipelines
- Weather-related damage to property or injury to employees
- Damage to pipelines that causes release of gas
- Injury to customers from interruption to gas supply, gas leakage, or explosion
- Vehicle accidents with personal injury
- Employee injuries

Risks with high potential impacts and low likelihood are most suitable for risk treatment. Risks with high potential impact and high likelihood are also suitable for risk treatment options. Also, various regulations, determined during the first step of scanning the environment, necessitate risk treatment for vehicle and employee injuries.

Risks with low potential impact and high likelihood should be addressed through operational procedures. Finally, risks with low impact and low likelihood are the lowest priority for risk treatment.

After risks have been evaluated and prioritized, treatment options can be selected. These risk treatment options can be used in various combinations:

- Avoiding the risk
- Changing the likelihood/impact
- Financing the risk
- Retaining the risk

Knowledge to Action

Which risk treatment approach(es) would you recommend for risk of damage to pipelines from weather or other external causes? Select all that apply.

a. Avoiding the risk
b. Changing the likelihood/impact
c. Financing the risk
d. Retaining the risk

Feedback: c. and d. It is impossible for Power to avoid the risk from external events to pipelines (a.). Although an engineering evaluation may determine methods to change the potential impact (b.), such as more-resistant piping material, the best combination of risk treatment for Power is to retain a portion of the risk and to finance the remainder through insurance.

Which risk treatment approach(es) would you recommend for risks to employees from severe weather? Select all that apply.

a. Avoiding the risk
b. Changing the likelihood/impact
c. Financing the risk
d. Retaining the risk

Feedback: b., c., and d. Power cannot completely avoid the risk to its employees from severe weather. Damage to gas pipelines must often be dealt with immediately to avoid additional hazards. Power can change the likelihood of employee injury by carefully selecting employees for its crisis response teams, training them, and providing protective equipment. Power should also use a combination of retention and financing to treat this risk.

Which risk treatment approach(es) would you recommend for the risk of injury to customers? Select all that apply.

a. Avoiding the risk
b. Changing the likelihood/impact
c. Financing the risk
d. Retaining the risk

Feedback: b., c., and d. Power cannot avoid the risk associated with its gas pipes and service without losing its customers. It can, however, change the likelihood of injury to its customers by training and supervising its employees, and it should also use a combination of retention and financing to treat this risk.

Which risk treatment approach(es) would you recommend for Power's risk of vehicle accidents with injuries? Select all that apply.

a. Avoiding the risk
b. Changing the likelihood/impact
c. Financing the risk
d. Retaining the risk

Feedback: b., c., and d. The severity of Power's vehicle accidents has remained level, while the frequency has increased. This risk cannot be avoided because vehicles must be used to perform essential business functions. Power can change the likelihood of vehicle accidents by hiring drivers with safe driving histories and training the drivers it employs. A combination of financing and retaining this risk is also recommended. In addition to meeting state requirements for auto liability insurance, Power would benefit from limiting the potential impact of this risk within its ability to do so, such as through electronic monitoring of its drivers.

Which risk treatment approach(es) would you recommend for Power's risk of injury to its service technicians? Select all that apply.

a. Avoiding the risk

b. Changing the likelihood/impact

c. Financing the risk

d. Retaining the risk

Feedback: b., c., and d. Although the frequency of Power's employee injuries has been decreasing, an ongoing focus on safety and injury prevention will probably lower both likelihood and impact. A review of Power's return-to-work and claims programs can also help improve the impact of employee injuries. Workers compensation insurance is required in almost every state, and Power should use a combination of retention and financing for this risk.

Although the risk of damage to customers' property has low potential consequences because of the lower cost compared with the risk of injury, this risk—in combination with increasing frequency of vehicle accidents—indicates a need for better risk management of service technicians' work performance. Hiring, training, and supervising service technicians should be important risk management priorities for Power.

Monitor and Assure

To be effective over time, a risk management process should be monitored to provide assurance that risks are being managed appropriately.

Knowledge to Action

Which activity or activities of the risk manager can assist with monitoring and assurance of hazard risk management? Select all that apply.

a. Reporting results, such as accident statistics

b. Meeting with managers to review results

c. Writing warnings to employees who have accidents

d. Conducting employee training

Feedback: a. and b. The risk manager's activities should include reporting results and meeting with managers to review results. Performance management (c.) and training of employees (d.) should be conducted by employees' managers or by trainers with subject-matter expertise, such as in safe driving techniques.

Review Questions

1. Describe how classifying risk helps an organization's risk management process.

2. Compare pure risk with speculative risk.

3. Explain why it is important to distinguish between speculative risks and pure risks when making risk management decisions.

4. Explain the reasons why subjective and objective risk may differ.

5. Contrast diversifiable with nondiversifiable risk.

6. Describe the quadrants of risk.

7. Describe the fundamental purpose of a risk management framework.

8. Compare an organization's internal and external environments.

9. List the four components of the framework model.

10. Identify the techniques an organization can use to establish accountability for risk management.

11. Describe the reporting aspect of the enterprise-wide risk management process.

12. Explain the importance of a risk management policy statement.

13. Explain the purpose and process of a gap analysis in designing and implementing a risk management framework.

14. Compare evaluations of an organization's internal and external environments for the risk management framework.

15. Describe the two key elements to successful implementation of a risk management framework and process into existing organizational processes.

16. List the categories of necessary resources to implement a risk management framework and process.

17. Explain the importance of communicating an organization's risk management policy.

18. Explain the purpose of the plan-do-check-act (P-D-C-A) cycle in risk management.

19. Explain whether the ISO 31000 risk management standard is designed to produce uniformity.

20. Describe in general what a risk management policy should address.

21. Identify the three processes included in the ISO 31000 definition of risk assessment.

22. Describe risk treatment in the ISO 31000 risk management standard.

23. Describe the monitoring phase of the ISO 31000 risk management standard.

24. Describe how the Committee of Sponsoring Organizations (COSO) defines risk.

25. Identify the four categories in which the COSO Enterprise Risk Management—Integrated Framework is intended to help an organization achieve its objectives.

26. Explain how the COSO risk management framework should be applied across an organization.

27. Explain why control activities are a key feature of the COSO Enterprise Risk Management—Integrated Framework.

28. Describe control activities in the COSO Enterprise Risk Management—Integrated Framework.

29. Explain the two types of monitoring of control activities in the COSO Enterprise Risk Management—Integrated Framework.

Application Questions

1. Classify each of these risks as pure or speculative, subjective or objective, and diversifiable or nondiversifiable:

    a. Damage to an office building resulting from a hurricane

    b. Reduction in value of retirement savings

    c. Products liability claim against a manufacturer

2. Write a statement of commitment to risk management that your organization could use in its risk management policy. (Answers may vary.)

3. Beth's organization has decided to use an enterprise risk management framework. As Beth works on the design of this framework, what should she do to optimize resources?

4. A risk manager is developing a control activity for a bank's mortgage underwriting. The bank's objective is that all mortgages conform to guidelines. Explain the control activity the risk manager might develop and how compliance would be determined.

5. Sol-Ar is a growing organization that installs solar panels. It is based in a southwestern city in the United States, and its assembly plant employs sixty people. It has six trucks that are used for installation and service, with fifteen technicians and twenty-five assistant technicians employed in the installation and service division.

    As Sol-Ar has grown over its five years of existence, its losses have also grown. Employee injuries have increased more than sales. The most frequent and severe injuries are back strains at the plant, but Sol-Ar had one serious injury to a technician who fell from a roof during the installation of a panel. Vehicle accidents have increased in frequency but not severity. One serious liability claim occurred related to a solar panel that fell during installation, injuring a bystander, and several minor liability claims occurred related to property damage from leakage around the panel installation.

    Sol-Ar recently decided to hire a risk manager to assist the chief financial officer (CFO) with risk management. Janet has just started in that role.

a. Identify Sol-Ar's key hazard risks arising from internal causes, and categorize them according to high or low potential impact and high or low potential likelihood.

b. For each of the identified risks, determine whether Janet should recommend risk treatment and, if so, which treatment.

SUMMARY

Classifying the various types of risk can help organizations manage risk. Some of the most commonly used classifications are pure and speculative risk, subjective and objective risk, and diversifiable and nondiversifiable risk. An organization's risks can also be categorized into quadrants as hazard risk, operational risk, financial risk, and strategic risk.

The primary purposes of a risk management framework are to integrate risk management throughout an organization and to support the risk management process. These are the four components of the risk management framework:

- Lead and establish accountability
- Align and integrate
- Allocate resources
- Communicate and report

An established risk management policy statement should clearly communicate the policy to everyone in an organization.

A gap analysis of an organization's current risk management program compared with an internationally recognized standard is the first step in designing and implementing a risk management framework and process. After completing the gap analysis and a study of the organization's internal and external environments, an organization can design a framework and process and integrate them throughout all areas.

ISO 31000 provides an internationally recognized standard that any organization can use to manage all of its risks. This standard includes guiding principles and provides a generic framework that organizations can tailor to support their own risk management processes.

Similar to other risk management standards, the COSO Enterprise Risk Management—Integrated Framework assists organizations in meeting their objectives. COSO was originally developed to provide a framework for financial controls. Although its standard was expanded in 2004 to provide strategic risk management, it continues to emphasize control activities.

You should be able to apply the enterprise risk management framework and process to an organization's risks. The components of the framework will allow you to integrate and support the risk management process in the organization. The process begins with scanning the environment, including the relevant laws and regulations. The next steps in the process enable you to identify and analyze risks. After risks have been identified and analyzed, the most appropriate risk treatment options can be selected. Monitoring the process assures an organization's managers that optimal risk management is in place. Although this case focused on hazard risk, you should be able to apply this process to all of an organization's risks.

ASSIGNMENT NOTES

1. Risk and Insurance Management Society, "Exploring Risk Appetite and Risk Tolerance," RIMS Executive Report, 2012, www.rims.org/resources/ERM/Documents/RIMS_Exploring_Risk_Appetite_Risk_Tolerance_0412.pdf (accessed June 1, 2012).

2. AS/NZS-ISO 31000:2009: Risk Management—Principles and Guidelines, Standards Australia/Standards New Zealand, SAI Global, http://sherq.org/31000.pdf (accessed July 13, 2012).

3. "Risk Management—Principles and Guidelines," pp. 7-8.

4. Charles Duhigg and David Barboza, "In China, Human Costs Are Built Into an iPad," The New York Times, January 25, 2012, www.nytimes.com/2012/01/26/business/ieconomy-apples-ipad-and-the-human-costs-for-workers-in-china.html?_r=1&ref=todayspaper (accessed July 13, 2012).

5. "Risk Management—Principles and Guidelines," pp. 8-12.

6. Committee of Sponsoring Organizations of the Treadway Commission, "About Us," www.coso.org/aboutus.htm (accessed February 7, 2012).

7. Committee of Sponsoring Organizations of the Treadway Commission, "Enterprise Risk Management—Integrated Framework: Executive Summary," September 2004, pp. 3-4, www.coso.org/documents/coso_erm_executivesummary.pdf (accessed February 8, 2012).

Business Continuity Management

Educational Objectives

After learning the content of this assignment, you should be able to:

▶ Describe the evolution of business continuity management and its alignment with risk management.

▶ Explain how risk mitigation is achieved through business continuity planning.

▶ Describe the scope and stages of strategic risk redeployment planning.

▶ Explain how supply chain risk management is used to assess and mitigate risks that could disrupt an organization's flow of goods and services.

▶ Explain how risk mitigation is achieved through efficient communication in times of crisis.

▶ Given a scenario involving a supply chain, recommend the risk-appropriate mitigation tools.

Outline

Introduction to Business Continuity Management

Business Continuity Planning

Strategic Redeployment Planning

Supply Chain Risk Management

Crisis Communication

Mitigating Supply Chain Risk

Summary

Business Continuity Management | 2

INTRODUCTION TO BUSINESS CONTINUITY MANAGEMENT

When an organization suffers any level of disruption—from a relatively minor occurrence, such as a market downturn, or a major catastrophic event—its leaders must act to restore normal operations.

An organization can use business continuity management (BCM) to address potential threats to its operations, such as natural disasters, major physical damage to a building, or the loss of a critical supplier. BCM involves examining such threats and establishing an operational plan with contingencies that allow the organization's key operations and critical functions to continue if a disruption occurs. Many organizations call BCM "business resiliency" because continuity planning for risk helps organizations withstand disruptive events and, ultimately, survive.

BCM seeks to minimize the loss of resources essential to an organization's recovery from a disruption in operations. This is accomplished by focusing an organization's efforts on effective pre- and post-loss actions.

Evolution of BCM

The terms "emergency preparedness," "disaster recovery," and "business continuity" are often used interchangeably. Although the concepts are closely related, they differ in scope and focus, having evolved over the past century as organizations' goals changed from merely surviving a catastrophe to responding to one with resilience.[1]

The roots of BCM are in emergency preparedness and response planning. Such planning developed early in the last century and centered on providing emergency supplies and trained personnel to ensure the safety of both people and an organization's physical assets during and after catastrophes such as hurricanes and fires. Although limited to disasters, emergency preparedness planning helped establish the need for comprehensive planning.

Disaster recovery planning arose from organizations' increasing use of and dependence on technology in the latter part of the last century. Organizations became vulnerable to loss of systems responsible for data management and storage, inventory management, communication, and other critical systems. In response, information technology (IT) departments developed plans for protecting data and equipment and for recovering data. In many organizations, disaster recovery is still considered an IT function. However, as technology became pervasive in nearly all business operational functions, the concept of disaster recovery planning expanded to include planning for the protection and recovery of operational systems in the event of a disaster.

In the broader sense, disaster recovery plans seek to ensure that an effective response occurs amid the confusion and emotional distraction of a disaster. Disaster recovery plans typically focus on actions that can be taken before and immediately after a disaster to ensure the safety of personnel and the viability of future operations.

The concept of BCM developed gradually, as organizations realized that, to plan adequately for recovery after a disaster, they had to look beyond their organizations to other systems on which they depended, including supply and distribution chains. From the emergency preparedness focus on protecting people, buildings, and equipment after a disaster, through the disaster recovery focus on protecting data and technological systems from disaster, BCM expanded to encompass the need to ensure continuing business operations and recovery—not just in the event of a disaster, but in the event of any serious disruption in operations.

Events such as the September 11, 2001, terrorist attacks on the World Trade Center; Hurricane Katrina in the southeastern United States in 2005; and the earthquake, tsunami, and resulting nuclear crisis in Japan in 2011 have reinforced the importance of BCM. Organizations far from those disaster sites felt the effects of when suppliers' and customers' facilities, business data, and financial records were destroyed and supply and distributions channels were disrupted, often at multiple points along the chain. These experiences have expanded the practice and application of BCM, prompted more organizations to adopt or expand their BCM programs, and spurred the development of businesses created solely to provide BCM services for other entities.

Aligning Business Continuity Management With Risk Management

Some organizations include BCM within the purview of their risk management function. Others separate the roles of business continuity managers and risk managers; they might or might not coordinate their efforts, or they might even compete.

Risk management and BCM are similar in that they both involve planning, organizing, leading, and controlling an organization's resources and activities to achieve a particular result. However, BCM deals primarily with consequences of disruption; its focus on minimizing the results of disruptions to operations means it typically deals with operational risk. In contrast, risk management focuses more broadly on ongoing risk assessment and risk treatment and deals not only with operational risk, but also with hazard risk (property, liability, and personnel loss exposures), financial risk (resulting from the effect of market forces on financial assets or liabilities), and strategic risk (resulting from economic and societal trends).

Organizations that treat BCM and risk management as complementary rather than competing functions can benefit from an integrated approach. For example, risk management's identification of hazard risks and related data can be useful to BCM in determining exposures that could result in operational disruptions, and an effective risk management program can reduce some types of disruptive exposures. To coordinate efforts, organizations should clearly define the roles, responsibilities, and reporting structures of both functions.

Business Continuity Certifications and Standards

The United States Department of Homeland Security (DHS), created after the September 11, 2001, terrorists attacks on New York City and Washington, D.C., has pressed for voluntary adoption of emergency-preparedness standards by private-sector businesses. DHS has adopted three internationally recognized standards that promote private-sector preparedness, including disaster management, emergency management, and business continuity management:

Standards to help organizations

- ASIS SPC.1-2009, "Organizational Resilience: Security, Preparedness, and Continuity Management Systems"—Developed by ASIS International, an organization that disseminates information about security, this standard emphasizes organizational resilience in emergencies. It provides guidelines for the implementation of policies, objectives, and programs that reinforce organizational resilience through business continuity management.
- British Standard 25999-2:2007, "Business Continuity Management"— Identified as the best practice standard for business continuity, this standard defines requirements for a management systems approach to business continuity.
- National Fire Protection Association 1600:2010, "Standard on Disaster/ Emergency Management and Business Continuity Programs"—This standard focuses on disaster and emergency management and business continuity, including prevention, mitigation, preparedness, response, and recovery from disasters. It aligns with the related disciplines and practices of risk management, security, and loss prevention.

The standards seek to encourage more U.S. organizations to prepare for emergencies. They provide organizations with guidelines for assessing their preparedness for hazards and for developing plans to protect their employees and to ensure recovery and continuity following disasters or other emergencies. DHS's adoption of three different standards allows organizations to choose the standard that most appropriately applies to their particular industry.

Although compliance with the standards is voluntary, an organization that chooses to apply them must commit organizational resources to the endeavor.

If an organization chooses to participate, it develops a preparedness plan under one of the three standards and submits it to a DHS accrediting organization. Certification confirms that the organization's plan complies with the standard chosen. Once an organization is certified, periodic audits are conducted to confirm that its plan continues to comply with the chosen standard.

BUSINESS CONTINUITY PLANNING

An organization can develop a detailed plan of action to mitigate risk and maintain operations regardless of external and internal events that could otherwise prove disastrous.

Over half of all businesses subjected to a catastrophic event fail immediately. Of those businesses that survive a catastrophe, half fail within two years. While government agencies may not fail immediately, a catastrophe could result in the reassessment of their effectiveness and mission, a change of leadership, or reorganization, leading to further disruption.

The development of a business continuity plan (BCP) is an important component of business continuity management (BCM). A BCP allows an organization to analyze all possible eventualities to determine the critical functions that must continue during a disruption so that the organization survives, recovers, and resumes growth. The development and implementation of a BCP entails seven steps:

1. Understanding the business
2. Conducting a business impact analysis (BIA)
3. Performing a risk assessment
4. Developing the continuity plan
5. Implementing the continuity plan
6. Building a BCM/BCP culture
7. Maintaining and updating the plan

While BCP and BCM contain the word "business," both terms refer to securing continuity of operations. Thus, applying the concept to other than for-profit entities can be accomplished by considering the "business of the agency" or the "business of the charity," for example. Thus, "business" considers the mission, vision, and strategy of the enterprise in addition to its survival.

Understanding the Business

To complete a business continuity plan, an organization must first understand all aspects of its business. This includes determining key objectives and how and when they will be met, as well as the internal and external parties involved in achieving them.

Once the organization determines its key objectives (for example, a key objective may be "continuing to manufacture and sell widgets"), it must examine how it uses its facilities, materials supply chain, human resources, communications, information systems, processes, distribution channels, and customers to achieve them. This allows the organization to identify the key processes that will constitute the basis for its BIA.

Conducting a Business Impact Analysis

An organization conducts a BIA to identify and assess the risks that may affect it. A BIA assesses what events may occur, when they may occur, and how they could affect achievement of key objectives. The BIA also measures the financial and nonfinancial effect of risks and explores organizational vulnerabilities, critical elements in developing strategies to protect organizational resources.

The analysis also distinguishes between critical and noncritical processes. This allows the organization to use the BIA to determine its recovery time objective, which is the time period within which a critical process must be recovered in order for the organization to resume operations after a disruption of operations.

Various international standards, such as ISO 31000:2009, take different approaches or use different terminology for the BIA. In some standards, the BIA and the risk assessment are combined. In other standards, the BIA goes beyond a more traditional risk assessment, which often focuses only on hazard risks and fails to assess the full impact of risk on all aspects of the operation.

Performing a Risk Assessment

An organization performs a risk assessment to identify and evaluate potential exposures and the probability that certain events will occur. It also indicates how susceptible the organization may be to particular disruptions. This helps the organization prioritize its BCM strategy and risk controls and assists management in making decisions regarding organizational risk appetite. A thorough risk assessment will reveal exposures and can assist in establishing methods for future risk mitigation efforts. Finally, the risk assessment helps the organization determine an action plan.

Assessments can be conducted at various levels. Convergys Corporation, for example, conducts three levels of assessment:[2]

- Enterprise assessment—a global assessment of risks that could affect the enterprise's overall business goals
- Site assessment—an assessment by risk owners at risk centers of risks associated with particular sites or locations or even specific geographies
- Program or project assessments—an assessment of a project's capabilities, resources, and limitations in relationship to a viable recovery strategy

Developing the Continuity Plan

After it has conducted the BIA and performed a risk assessment to establish recovery time objectives, an organization can begin to develop strategies to maintain critical functions during disruptions. Organizations may use one strategy or a combination of strategies to ensure resiliency:

- Active backup model—The organization establishes a second site that includes all of the necessary production equipment housed at the primary site. Staff may be relocated to the second site if operations are disrupted at the primary site.

- Split operations model—In this model, an organization maintains two or more active sites that are geographically dispersed. Capacity at each site is sufficient to handle total output in the event of a disruption at either site.

- Alternative site model—An organization that uses this strategy maintains a production site and an active backup site that functions as the primary site as needed.

- Contingency model—This strategy involves the organization's developing an alternate way to maintain production, perhaps using manual processes.

All of these strategies involve three levels of planning:[3]

- BCM organizational strategy
- BCM process level strategy
- BCM resource recovery strategy

These planning levels require the organization to examine its basic processes, determine potential points of failure, and create alternate operational methods.

Strategic choices for addressing a disruption of operations include these options:

- An insurance policy—This allows the organization to recover some of its financial losses if it suffers an insurable loss.

- Transfer processing—This entails the organization's entering reciprocal arrangements with another company or division to perform a necessary function in the event of a disruption of operations.

- Termination—With this strategy, an organization ceases production of the affected product or service.

- Loss mitigation—This entails implementation of risk controls and plans to reduce, minimize, or divert any loss.

- Do nothing—If an organization does nothing in the event of a disruption of operations, it absorbs the potential loss. This represents an increase of its risk appetite.

— Top down [handwritten]

Implementing the Continuity Plan

Senior management must impress upon the organization that the BCP is integral to its survival and success. The business continuity coordinator (BCC) assists and directs each department in formulating a departmental plan. This ensures that the organization's component parts work effectively for the entire organization.

Each department's plan must include these elements:[4]

- Statement of acceptable level of functioning
- Recovery time objectives, resources needed, and potential failure points
- Tasks and activities required
- Procedures or processes
- Supporting documentation and information
- Structure to support the plan
- Description of division teams—purpose, team members, mission
- Explanation of interdependencies among the various division teams

The BCC presents the drafted BCP to senior management for approval. Once the BCP is approved, the BCC and senior management begin to influence the organization's culture to accept, practice, and maintain the BCP.

Building a BCM/BCP Culture

Senior management provides the vision statement and support for the BCP. It must also set expectations and objectives for middle management concerning maintenance of departmental plans. See the exhibit "Business Continuity Management (BCM) Encompasses All Divisions."

Business Continuity Management (BCM) Encompasses All Divisions

Risk Management	Facilities Management	Human Capital Management	Technology Management
Intellectual Property Management	Reputation Management	Market Share Management	Supply and Distribution Management

[DA03892]

Staff must be educated on the importance of maintaining the BCP. One way management can achieve this is to hold semiannual exercises in which staff members react to a hypothetical disaster scenario by using the plan to maintain operations. If successful, these exercises may find "holes" in the BCP that

— common sense [handwritten]

need to be addressed. Exercises also provide opportunities to amend the BCP as new processes are introduced and used.

External suppliers and customers should know that the organization has a BCP and be encouraged to provide their own contingency plans. When key suppliers and customers are prepared for a disruption of operations, their relationship with the organization is improved.

Maintaining and Updating the Plan

Organizational environments, processes, and products change rapidly in today's business environment, and so too should the BCP. A BCP is effective only if it is kept fresh and updated. The BCP should be reviewed in detail and amended as internal or external conditions warrant. Analyzing the written BCP is essential and should be done semiannually or when a significant change has occurred in product line, processes, or management. An organization must also determine how best to store its BCP. Companies often maintain electronic copies of the BCP on a secure server accessible from several locations, while written copies are also maintained by key members of the organization.

Business continuity planning may not be effective in all cases. When an organization's survival is threatened, strategic redeployment planning is required.

STRATEGIC REDEPLOYMENT PLANNING

Following a business disruption caused by chaotic events, an organization can use strategic redeployment to determine how to resume its business operations and ensure its survival and recovery.

Small disruptions within an organization can develop into major disruptions that jeopardize its survival. During major disruptions, business continuity plans may be insufficient for fully restoring the organization and ensuring its survival. Once a disruption has occurred, management must determine whether existing organizational strategies are still valid and, if not, make necessary strategic adjustments to ensure the organization's survival. When an analysis of the situation reveals that the disruption is due to a chaotic situation, the organization must reorganize its resources. In such cases, strategic redeployment becomes necessary for the organization to determine how to realign itself in order to survive, regain its position in the marketplace, and protect its reputation.

Strategic Redeployment Planning Stages

A strategic redeployment plan (SRP) is a comprehensive plan for resiliency after a severe disruption. It is designed to bring the organization back from a state of chaos in four stages:

- Emergency stage
- Alternate marketing stage
- Contingency production stage
- Communication stage

The communication stage in strategic redeployment planning has a distinct meaning and context. However, effective, accurate, and timely communication to both internal and external stakeholders is required at all of the stages of strategic redeployment, not just the communication stage.

Emergency Stage

The emergency stage, sometimes referred to as disaster recovery, starts at the moment of disruption and constitutes the organization's immediate response. This stage is designed to accomplish three objectives:

- Protect people—For example, by contacting emergency authorities, evacuating the area, and warning neighbors
- Protect physical assets—For example, by guarding the site and organizing salvage operations
- Protect reputation—For example, by communicating with all economic stakeholders and maintaining control of all media releases

The emergency stage may include closing and cleaning the facility, recalling products, and meeting with employees and news media to communicate the status of the emergency response.

Alternate Marketing Stage

The second stage of strategic redeployment requires the organization to evaluate the impact of the disruption on the organization's reputation and market share. The organization must determine whether it needs a new marketing strategy. It must also consider consumer loyalty—will customers remain loyal during the crisis, or will they seek substitute products or services? Will suppliers and subcontractors work with the organization during this interval? Will competitors use the organization's disruption as an opportunity to increase their market share or capture the affected organization's current suppliers? In the alternate marketing stage, no course of action to save the core business or resources should be ruled out, including pulling out of a market or a business. The organization's leadership should set up a center of operations or data room where reliable data and business intelligence information are available for testing various scenarios.

Some organizations may use a color-coded approach at this stage, using "red," "yellow," or "green" to denote the level of disruption. Green indicates that the current strategy should be maintained.

A new marketing strategy developed during this stage may determine, at a minimum, whether the organization will maintain production of its traditional products and services. For instance, the organization may decide that a limited output of products or services should be continued for supplying certain customer segments. Yellow coding may be used to designate such intermediate situations.

If the organization decides to discontinue low-priority products or services, it must analyze the ultimate effect of discontinuance on the organization and on any synergies associated with those products or services. The organization must also evaluate the loss of revenue from current and potential customers of these products or services.

In instances in which the current strategy cannot be maintained and a new marketing strategy is needed, red coding can indicate the need for a radical alteration to the business model or even its complete replacement. In this case, the organization must consider substitutions for the current products or services; what synergies may be created; what resources are needed; and, ultimately, how to restore desired goals and outcomes.

Contingency Production Stage

The analysis completed in the alternate marketing stage leads to the contingency production stage. At this stage, any downtime for the organization must be minimized. The organization must decide what products or services it will provide depending on the facilities available and whether its technology and machinery are adequate. It must also consider its supply chain with respect to the quality and cost of resources needed and determine whether the product packaging must be adapted for a new product. Other considerations during this stage include the availability of transportation and of routes to distribute products and services.

Communication Stage

The sole objective of the communication stage is to preserve or enhance stakeholders' trust and confidence in the organization. This stage begins when a disruption has occurred and is initially referred to as crisis communication. When the organization's production and reputation have been restored, the crisis communication becomes post-crisis communication. To meet the objectives of crisis and post-crisis communication, the organization must identify and address the concerns and expectations of all internal and external stakeholders, including these four basic concerns:

- Safety and security of all stakeholders
- Transparency in all of management's decisions
- Clarity and consistency in communications
- Perceived lack of trust in management and the organization

The key to effective communication in a time of disruption is a good relationship with the news media, established before any crisis. The organization must maintain a permanent link with the media so that when a crisis occurs, it can leverage the goodwill created in normal times. To achieve clarity and consistency, information released to the media must echo the information provided to employees. The organization must keep open channels of communication with local authorities and industry associations. Employees need up-to-date information as soon as it is practical. Keeping employees, customers, suppliers, and other stakeholders well informed during a crisis will not only prevent defection to competitors, but also strengthen loyalty and rebuild trust in the organization.

Conditions for Success

Strategic redeployment requires attention to the increasing concerns of internal and external stakeholders. If an organization fails to protect its reputation before a disruption, it may not survive the disruption. The manner in which the organization interacts with internal and external stakeholders determines its credibility in the marketplace. Successful redeployment is an organization-wide effort.

Depending on the nature of the crisis, an SRP may not always involve major changes for an organization. In some dire circumstances, however, the plan may be drastic and may involve major changes that take an organization in a new direction.

SUPPLY CHAIN RISK MANAGEMENT

Market globalization and outsourcing for economic efficiency have substantially increased interdependencies between events and the production of goods and services in different regions and industries.

Supply chains may be viewed as branches of a tree connected to one another through a common trunk. A disruption in the availability of one good or service may have far-reaching effects on an organization, including, in the short term, inability to deliver on contractual promises and, in the long term, destruction of shareholder value.

Supply chain risk management entails assessing and mitigating all the threats that might interrupt the normal flow of goods and services from and to an organization's stakeholders. When applied to the production of goods, supply chain risk management encompasses managing the volatility related to producing, transporting, and storing goods, as well as managing the distribution channels from the initial raw materials to the final consumer product. Disruptions in an organization's production affect its immediate financial condition and may damage its brand reputation irreparably.

When applied to services, supply chain risk management encompasses managing the volatility associated with delivering the service to its end users, taking into consideration all the components of the value chain. Organizations must identify the risks and opportunities within supply chains and balance efficiency and best practices against vulnerability to disruptions. Supply chain risk management visibility has increased with the introduction of ISO 28000: *Supply Chain Security Management Requirements*.

Threats and Opportunities Inherent in Supply Chains

An organization must assess supply chain risk by examining both internal and external exposures and vulnerabilities. Internal exposures and vulnerabilities include these:

- Production location—Facilities may be vulnerable to natural disaster, manmade disaster, or terrorism.
- Production bottlenecks—Production may depend on a key machine or material; a malfunction or breakdown in the machine would slow or halt production.
- Information technology—The data center may be vulnerable, information backup may be unavailable, or staff may fail to follow restoration protocols.
- Infrastructure—Damage to infrastructure can impede or halt production altogether.
- Strikes or other employment issues—Production may cease, inventory cannot be moved, and orders are not filled.
- Machinery breakdown—Production may stall, or a critical backup in production may occur, while new parts (or new machines) are ordered and installed.

External exposures and vulnerabilities include these:

- Third-party suppliers—Disruption in production from the supplier could undermine an organization's ability to generate its product and to satisfy customer demand.
- Sole-source suppliers—Disruption in supply when only one supplier of goods is available will reduce or potentially shut down an organization's ability to produce and satisfy customer demand.

- Single source supplier—Disruptions in supply can also occur when an organization chooses to rely on only one supplier, even when multiple suppliers are available.

- Change in demand level—Incremental or substantial changes in demand because of changes in customer taste or to competition can cause over- or under production. If demand is not accurately forecasted, market reputation could be damaged.

- Financial risks—Increases in the cost of materials or transportation charges will cause costs to rise. Organizations may not be able to pass on increased costs because of consumer preferences, prior contracts, and competition. Exchange rate fluctuations may cause increases in materials costs and may also reduce the attractiveness of the product in overseas markets.

- Geopolitical environment—Imports and exports may be affected by government regulation or taxation. Unstable governments increase the chance of nationalization of an organization's overseas assets.

- Natural or manmade catastrophes—Storms, earthquakes, volcanic eruptions, and other natural disasters can damage an organization's facilities or interfere with its transportation routes. Pandemics may interrupt an organization's activities if too few employees are available to work. Terrorist activity can disrupt normal supply and distribution channels for extended periods.

- Merger of a key supplier with a competitor—Changes in ownership of key suppliers can affect the price of materials and the availability of supplies.

Organizations can also assess supply chains to uncover potential opportunities that may include these:

- Inventory and storage costs can be reduced by using the supply chain for just-in-time deliveries and work processes.

- Improvements in technology can be leveraged to improve process efficiencies.

- Supplier relationships can be improved to build positive relationships that strengthen communication and minimize potential supply chain disruptions.

Balance Between Efficiency and Vulnerability to Disruptions

Once an organization assesses potential risks of disruption in its supply chain, it must determine how it will defend its production processes, distribution channels, and market reputation. It also should examine various options to maintain production efficiency, as well as test and consider its ability to accurately forecast demand for materials, labor, and sales. Flexibility in supply sources as well as product design can help balance efficiency against potential disruptions.

The business impact analysis of a supply chain disruption must take into account all the components of a potential loss, such as loss of net revenues, increased costs, and any mitigation costs. If the organization determines that a potential disruption would have little or no impact on the flow of revenues, it may choose not to consider such a disruption in its business continuity plan. To ensure continuity, the organization must thoroughly analyze the short-, medium-, and long-term consequences of any threat or disruption. Such consequences could include potential downgrades by a financial rating agency and/or legal requirements in foreign countries to ensure continuity for industries deemed vital in that jurisdiction.

Supply Chain Best Practices

The organization must periodically assess its supply chain and establish best practices for various disruption scenarios. This assessment requires a multidisciplinary team of managers to prioritize potential risks and determine disruption timing and recovery time. As it analyzes each type of disruption, the team should consider various responses. The response to each situation should depend on the likelihood and impact (the level and duration) of the potential disruption.

Based on this review, the team will establish best practices and then take action as needed. Such action includes the regular use of dry-running and updating the business continuity plan on a regular basis as conditions change. See the exhibit "Supply Chain Best Practices and Mitigation Techniques."

Supply Chain Best Practices and Mitigation Techniques

Internal Disruption	Best Practices/Mitigation
Production location	Diversify locations
Production bottlenecks	Redesign product or production process to reduce or eliminate bottlenecks
IT and infrastructure failures	Maintain appropriate backup protocols, redundant systems, and maintenance
Strikes or employment issues	Maintain and educate staff on proper human resource management
Machinery breakdown	Maintain spare parts or establish changeover processes
External Disruption	**Best Practices/Mitigation**
Third-party/single suppliers	Diversify suppliers, contract carefully, maintain ongoing dialogue with suppliers
Sole-source supplier	Consult with the supplier to mitigate some of the risks (expand to several production sites) and/or design technological innovations
Change in demand	Monitor and forecast changes in competition and environment
Financial risks	Legal contracts to provide protection for some risk, insurance contracts for others, and monitoring the environment to identify emerging financial trends that could affect costs
Geopolitical environment	Understand and monitor the political environments in which the organization operates
Natural or manmade catastrophes	Maintain and update the business continuity plan
Merger of a key supplier	Diversify suppliers, contract carefully, and maintain ongoing dialogue with suppliers

[DA03893]

CRISIS COMMUNICATION

An organization's ability to communicate plans and activities to stakeholders during a crisis is critical to overcoming the situation and contributes to the success of any redeployment strategy.

Consider this scenario: Smoke is billowing out of the fourth, fifth, and sixth floors of a building. Firefighters, police, and emergency medical technicians dart into the building and back to their rapid-response vehicles. Employees rush out of the building. Some are covered in soot, coughing, or screaming for co-workers, while several are brought out on stretchers. The news media are on the scene, reporting live and questioning distraught employees. Executives' cell phones start ringing as calls come in from members of the board of directors, key clients and suppliers, and the press.

This situation has clearly triggered reactions from many stakeholders, as well as from the media. This is the instant that the organization must begin to manage the crisis and protect its reputation. Crisis management, properly handled, can help mitigate organizational risk on several levels. Communication is a key element in managing a crisis.

Mitigating Risk Through Crisis Communication

Risk management is a complex system based on a web of relationships among internal and external stakeholders. Good risk management practices should be embedded within the organization and include all financial partners, suppliers, customers, and other stakeholders. This is particularly true in times of crisis.

When an organization implements its crisis management plan, its prime objective is to survive the crisis event. Survival depends on the organization's speedy return to normal operations—brought about by proper continuity, contingency, or disaster recovery planning—and the successful implementation of its strategic redeployment plan. Although crisis management includes several vital components, the quality of an organization's crisis communication is essential to its resiliency.

Stakeholder Communications

Crisis communication begins before any threats have materialized; it involves establishing a baseline of trust with all stakeholders. Every stakeholder must believe that management will competently handle and resolve any crisis. When a crisis occurs, the organization's message must be candid, address the prominent issues, and engage all stakeholders in order to be effective in restoring and maintaining stakeholders' trust. As part of its crisis communication plan, the organization should maintain an open dialogue with the media (press, television, and radio).

Additionally, effective communication that conveys to various stakeholders that the organization has considered all risks helps engender trust. A theme emphasizing corporate involvement in safety and security should underlie such messages. Communications must also demonstrate that senior management is committed to maintaining an environment of transparency in its decision making. All crisis communications must be consistent and tailored to specific audiences. To maintain stakeholders' trust in the organization and its management, the messages must embody corporate integrity and authenticity.

Communication with different stakeholder groups continues after the immediate crisis. The organization will operate differently and face both threats and opportunities differently after a crisis. It is important for the organization to examine and carefully select various communication tools for use with internal and external stakeholders in order to analyze the specific concerns of the stakeholders, provide the solution, and speak the stakeholders' language.

Internal Stakeholders

Internal stakeholders' individual needs must be acknowledged. Employees must be informed continuously, especially regarding how the crisis will affect their jobs and working conditions. New safety concerns may emerge and will need to be addressed. This can be done through meetings, displays of visual aids in the workplace, hands-on training, and the organization's intranet site.

Unit and operational managers must be made aware of ongoing risks. Their assistance in training and maintaining attentiveness to potential risks is crucial to the plan's success. Because risk management is a key responsibility of line managers, managers must be held accountable for specific aspects of the crisis management plan.

Stockholders must be informed of all steps taken to manage, mitigate, and even prevent future crises. Communicating organizational health in the annual report and during quarterly meetings is imperative. Senior management must report major trends and pending claims as well as demonstrate corporate resilience. The board of directors must also be informed regularly about strategic exposures, governance issues, and long-term resilience.

External Stakeholders

In addition to communicating with internal stakeholders, the organization must keep external stakeholders informed. Suppliers must be notified of procedures for scheduled deliveries during the period of disruption and of how the organization will make required payments. Maintaining goodwill with suppliers during a crisis will help them work with the post-crisis organization, which is a critical component of the organization's resilience.

Customers should be assured of the organization's continuity and safety. A sound communication plan can help build trust and maintain consumer loyalty during the period of recovery.

Public officials and local authorities must be informed of the organization's efforts to ensure public safety and health and to demonstrate its commitment to the community. Statutory compliance must be monitored and reported. Other external stakeholders include local associations and special interest groups, which should be informed of the organization's recuperation efforts immediately after a crisis and as part of an ongoing effort to maintain strong relationships with these groups.

The media can be leveraged to transmit information to many internal and external stakeholders. Press releases and interviews on health, safety, and financial progress can help restore and retain marketplace confidence.

Every communication from the organization must be truthful. Risk managers must speak clearly and honestly about current conditions, known risks, and potential risks. The organization must manage and monitor its communication with every stakeholder.

Benefits of Crisis Communication

Regular communication before and throughout a crisis will improve relationships between the organization and its internal and external stakeholders. Good communication will create an open and truthful environment that encourages future investments in the organization and continues to provide it with favorable access to capital. As a long-term result of effective communication, the organization will be able to attract and retain the most talented employees because it has preserved its reputation post crisis. Externally, this reputation will help the organization to continue to build relationships with new and existing suppliers and customers.

Protection of the organization's reputation through good crisis communication reduces barriers to the development of new markets. A successful and well-communicated crisis management plan will promote trust in the organization's products and services. As a result, the organization may be able to gain a competitive advantage based on its reputation and its stringent attention to managing past, current, and potential risks. Additionally, a well-communicated and well-executed crisis management plan may help to minimize litigation arising from the crisis event.

MITIGATING SUPPLY CHAIN RISK

The twenty-first-century consumer can choose goods and services provided by vendors throughout the global market. A breakdown in one link of the supply chain can have disastrous results for an organization. Every organization must prepare for a disruption in order to keep its goods and services flowing to its consumers.

When an organization analyzes its supply chain to determine and recommend risk mitigation tools, it is important to understand these concepts:

- Cascading disruption—seemingly unrelated events that can cause major disruptions
- Supply chain management—the development of sound relationships and diversity among suppliers
- Business resiliency planning—the development of plans that prepare the organization to respond to disruptions

To determine appropriate mitigation tools, an organization should analyze the companies with which it has a business relationship to identify potential dependencies. The organization must then determine how to mitigate the immediate damage that would result from each exposure and select methods to reduce future risk.

The purpose of this analysis is to determine apparent exposures and the impact of losses related to those exposures and to consider possible alternatives to mitigate losses.

Case Facts

Bakeries, Inc., manufactures organic whole-grain sesame bread and crackers. The company purchases its ingredients—whole-grain flour, sugar, eggs, canola oil, and sesame seeds—from organic farms and processors. Bakeries' whole-grain flour is processed by Mille Company, which Bakeries uses exclusively. The products are sold to high-end retail stores specializing in organic foods.

Bakeries is the sole supplier of sesame bread and crackers to Health Foods, a regional high-end wholesome food specialty shop. Health Foods operates on a 3 percent margin, and Bakeries, Inc., products constitute 35 percent of the shop's retail sales.

Originally privately owned, Mille Company has 300 employees. The company culture was built on the premise of providing organic alternatives to the public. Management actively solicited employee feedback on its products and processes and encouraged employee involvement. Three months ago, however, Mille Company was sold to a large food manufacturer. Rather than continue with the existing culture and corporate environment, new management began making production changes to increase the organization's bottom line. Several of the organic farms supplying wheat to Mille Company were unable to increase their production quickly enough to meet the levels demanded by the new corporate owners. Contracts were not renewed, and the new Mille organization began mixing nonorganic grain with organic grain to lower costs and increase supplies. A disgruntled employee reported Mille Company to the Food and Drug Administration (FDA).

The FDA investigated Mille Company, and the results of the investigation were made public. As a result of this investigation, Mille was required to cease branding its flour as "organic." Enraged consumer groups sued Mille Company for product fraud and fraudulent advertising.

Bakeries, Inc., was unable to locate an immediate alternate source of whole-grain flour, and its production subsequently decreased by 60 percent. Canceling its contract with Mille Company required three months' notice, and cancellation within the contract period would result in a penalty. Bakeries, Inc., also missed its production goals by 40 percent and was unable to fulfill its contract with Health Foods.

Health Foods lost profits and customers and sued Bakeries, Inc., for breach of contract and false advertising. Bakeries, in turn, sued Mille Company, citing the same causes of action, along with an additional one: products liability.

Case Analysis Tools

Analyzing exposures and determining appropriate risk mitigation tools for the three organizations involved in this scenario requires analysis of this information:

- Supply chain elements
- Relationships between elements
- Existing contractual arrangements
- Available mitigation tools

Overview of Analysis

Analyzing an organization and its supply chains to develop risk mitigation tools involves a series of steps. Following these steps will assist all three organizations in effectively uncovering potential solutions:

- Identify the exposures and types of risk for each company independently
- Determine co-dependencies between each company
- Analyze the exposures and determine how each company can avoid or mitigate losses to these exposures

Exposure Identification

The first step in developing supply chain risk mitigation tools is to identify exposures. An organization begins this process by examining the upstream and downstream flow of materials to identify the entities involved. A business continuity plan can be a valuable resource in this process. The exclusive relationship Bakeries, Inc., has with Mille Company to purchase all the organic flour it needs creates the potential for Bakeries' overdependence on a single supplier. Bakeries' contract with Mille Company specifies that Mille must deliver organically grown and processed flour. It also requires Bakeries to give Mille Company three months' notice if it wants to change the tonnage of flour purchased or, if it fails to give such notice, pay a monetary penalty to Mille Company. When negotiating this contract, which is favorable to Mille Company, Bakeries, Inc., failed to insist on inclusion of a renegotiation clause if ownership of Mille Company changed. Further, Bakeries, Inc., had no contingency plan in place to address problems that could occur with production at Mille Company. Bakeries, Inc., also neglected to monitor the organizational changes at Mille Company.

Bakeries supplies its products to only one company—Health Foods. Bakeries' failure to deliver contracted products to Health Foods jeopardizes not only Bakeries' future sales but also its survival. Because Health Foods can purchase similar products from other manufacturers, there is a good possibility that Bakeries will not recover its previous market share.

Defending the company in litigation will be costly, further straining Bakeries' shrinking profits. Failure to deliver its product and the resulting negative publicity can cause a major disruption for Bakeries, Inc. With production and sales decreased by 60 percent, Bakeries may not survive. See the exhibit "Bakeries, Inc.: Manufacturer of Whole-Grain Organic Products."

Bakeries, Inc.: Manufacturer of Whole-Grain Organic Products

Exposure	Type of Risk
One key supplier	Financial
Unbalanced customer base	Financial
Litigation—Mille Company and Healthy Foods	Financial/Reputation
Reputation	Financial/Reputation
Survival	Financial/Reputation

[DA03894]

Mille Company, purchased by a large corporation, is undergoing internal cultural changes. Seeking to increase profits and production, the new management at Mille Company is improperly handling the need for an increased grain supply. It has no quality assurance program in place and may have purchased nonorganically grown wheat in order to produce the quantities required. Employees, who are already unhappy due to changes in the organization, noticed that the wheat purchased for processing had not been organically grown and made this fact public.

FDA involvement will be costly to the organization because every shipment of wheat purchased must now be scrutinized. Flour production has decreased, and Mille Company is unable to adhere to its production and delivery schedules. Mille Company is receiving negative media coverage, and several consumer groups are launching independent investigations.

Wheat farms supplying Mille Company are coming under investigation regarding their farming methods. Many customers are canceling their orders to avoid being tainted by the negative publicity. Consumer trust is at an all-time low.

Breach of contract litigation is also expensive. The new corporate parent is forced to defend Mille Company but may ultimately decide to close the facility. See the exhibit "Mille Company: Processes Whole-Grain Organic Flour and Sells It to Bakeries, Inc.."

Health Foods has contracted with Bakeries, Inc., as a supplier of sesame bread and crackers, which account for 35 percent of Health Foods' profits. Health Foods does not have another supplier for these products immediately

Mille Company: Processes Whole-Grain Organic Flour and Sells It to Bakeries, Inc.

Exposure	Type of Risk
New management and culture—employee risk	Social/Political/Legal
Broad number of questionable suppliers	Financial
FDA investigation	Legal/Reputation/Ethical
Small market	Financial
Reputation	Financial/Reputation/Social
Litigation	Financial/Reputation
Survival	Financial/Reputation

[DA03895]

available. Customers wishing to purchase these products are finding alternative sources, notably a large grocery chain. Sales of other products have also dropped due to decreased customer visits to Health Foods. Selling products reputed to be inorganic is tarnishing the company's reputation. Health Foods' management believes its only option is to sue Bakeries, Inc., for breach of contract and faulty advertising. See the exhibit "Healthy Foods: Retail Chain Selling Organic Baked Foods Supplied by Bakeries, Inc.."

Healthy Foods: Retail Chain Selling Organic Baked Foods Supplied by Bakeries, Inc.

Exposure	Type of Risk
One key supplier	Financial
Customer loyalty	Reputation/Financial
Reputation	Financial/Reputation
Litigation	Financial/Reputation

[DA03896]

Determination of Co-Dependencies

Once the individual exposures have been identified, the co-dependencies between the organizations must be determined.

Specific organic farmers are contractually bound to deliver organically grown wheat to Mille Company. Mille Company contracts for a certain tonnage and reserves the right to purchase additional wheat. The farmers agree to grow the wheat using only organic methods, and any violation of this agreement voids the contract.

Mille Company processes the wheat using no additives or preservatives. The company supplies flour to Bakeries, Inc., based on a delivery schedule outlined in the contract. Mille Company is the exclusive supplier to Bakeries, Inc., which must give Mille three months' notice if the contracted amount is to be changed. Bakeries, Inc., is tied to Mille Company by contract and by reputation.

Using the flour it receives from Mille Company, Bakeries produces the whole-grain organic sesame bread and crackers sold at Health Foods' store. Based on the amount of product sold to Health Foods, it is Bakeries' principal customer. Failure to supply product on time to Health Foods constitutes a breach of contract that can drive Bakeries out of business. See the exhibit "Organizational Co-Dependencies."

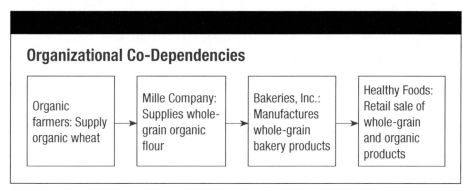

Organizational Co-Dependencies

Organic farmers: Supply organic wheat → Mille Company: Supplies whole-grain organic flour → Bakeries, Inc.: Manufactures whole-grain bakery products → Healthy Foods: Retail sale of whole-grain and organic products

[DA03901]

Analysis of Exposures

With the information resulting from identification of exposures and co-dependencies, the exposures are then analyzed to determine how each company can avoid or mitigate losses. Mitigation plans are based on the analysis of the exposures and co-dependencies between the supply chain elements. Mitigation plans, which establish strategies in advance of a disruption, are an important part of any business continuity plan.

Bakeries, Inc., is in crisis due to its broken supply chain. It needs to quickly find a substitute supplier of organic flour in order to resume baking operations. Concerns that other products it has sold may also have nonorganic components should be addressed with all stakeholders. Communication with customers is critical to the company's survival. Bakeries may need to increase production of other products to keep its operations going and to offset losses arising from its sesame bread and crackers line.

Mitigation plans for Bakeries, Inc., include these:

- Find a new source of organic flour
- Communicate to its business partners the steps it is taking to ensure that the products sold are truly organic
- Communicate those same steps to customers
- Use buffer inventory
- Use hold-harmless agreements to its advantage
- Review existing business continuity plan

Mille Company must communicate with its business partners and the public. If the FDA's allegations are untrue, Mille Company must salvage—and may even rebuild—its reputation as quickly as possible. Cooperation with the FDA investigation will expedite the end of the crisis.

Mille Company may choose to increase its advertising when the FDA issues its report. Depending on the veracity of the allegation, Mille Company may need to redesign its business plan. The company is in crisis because of a failure to meld organizational cultures. Internal communication must be handled as carefully as external communication.

Mitigation plans for Mille Company include these:

- Cooperate with FDA investigation
- Repair employee relations by improving communications
- Communicate with customers
- Redefine its business plan

Health Foods lost valuable inventory items and needs to find an alternate supplier to lure customers back. Its reputation may be damaged, and it must find ways to communicate with the public to regain consumer trust.

Mitigation plans for Health Foods include these:

- Obtain new bakery product suppliers
- Increase advertising
- Regain customer trust

The root cause of this disruption was the change of ownership of one company, Mille Company. The company's new management did not handle the change of culture well, incurring employee anger and ultimately a costly investigation and scandal.

Bakeries, Inc., did not foresee that a change in its supplier's ownership and culture could affect its business. The disruption in its supply caused a loss in revenue, increased costs due to litigation, and a damaged reputation. Bakeries, Inc., failed to maintain close ties with its business partners.

Health Foods is also damaged in this situation. It may find new suppliers of bakery products or be able to increase sales of other products. If not, it may not recover its customer base, and this may be the final circumstance that causes this boutique store to fall victim to a chain store operation. See the exhibit "Case Analysis and Solutions."

Case Analysis and Solutions

Bakeries, Inc.: Manufacturer of whole-grain/organic bakery products distributed to retail stores

Exposure	Type of Risk	Potential Solution
One key supplier	Financial	Diversify/Buffer inventory
Small customer base	Financial	Increase advertisement
Litigation—Mille Company and Healthy Foods	Financial/Reputation	Renegotiate contracts with hold-harmless clauses
Reputation	Financial/Reputation	Communication/Media
Survival	Financial/Reputation	Redefine strategy

Mille Company: Processes whole-grain organic flour, selling to Bakeries, Inc.

Exposure	Type of Risk	Potential Solution
New management and culture—employee risk	Social/Political / Legal	Employee meetings/Training/ Change management
Broad number of questionable suppliers	Financial	Quality assurance program
FDA	Social/Reputation/Ethical	Adhere to all regulations
Small market	Financial	Increase consumer awareness/Advertise
Reputation	Financial / Reputation/ Social	Communication—use media outlets/Community involvement
Litigation	Financial/Reputation	Resolve issues/ Renegotiate contracts
Survival	Financial/Reputation	Return to a new simple state

Healthy Foods: Retailer of whole-grain organic foods supplied by Bakeries, Inc.

Exposure	Type of Risk	Potential Solution
One key supplier	Financial	Diversify
Customer loyalty	Financial	Communication/ Advertising
Reputation risk	Financial/Reputation	Communication/ Community involvement
Litigation	Financial/Reputation	Reevaluate business plan

These solutions may not be the only viable options. Other solutions could be exercised if justified by the analysis. In addition, specific circumstances and organizational needs or goals may enter into the evaluation, making an alternative action a better option.

Review Questions

1. Describe the objective of business continuity management (BCM).

2. Compare and contrast risk management and business continuity management.

3. Describe in general terms the objectives of the three internationally recognized standards that promote private-sector preparedness, adopted by the United States Department of Homeland Security.

4. Describe how developing a business continuity plan can help an organization.

5. Describe the role of a business impact analysis (BIA) in business continuity planning

6. Describe the following strategies used in continuity planning:

    a. Active back-up model

    b. Split operations model

    c. Alternative site model

    d. Contingency model'Describe the roles of senior management in establishing a business continuity management (BCM)/business continuity plan (BCP) culture.

7. Identify the four stages of a strategic redeployment plan.

8. Describe the three objectives of the emergency stage of a strategic redeployment plan.

9. Summarize the alternate marketing stage of a strategic redeployment plan.

10. Describe the considerations an organization must address during the contingency production stage.

11. Identify the sole objective of the communication stage.

12. Define supply chain risk management as it applies to the production of goods and provision of services

13. Describe six internal supply chain exposures and vulnerabilities

14. Describe eight external supply chain exposures and vulnerabilities

15. Describe the process for establishing supply chain best practices.

16. Identify the attributes of a good stakeholder crisis communications plan

17. Identify communication that should be directed specifically to internal stakeholders during and following a crisis.

18. Identify communication that should be directed specifically to external stakeholders during and following a crisis.

Application Questions

1. Southern Bend Ranch, located along Texas's Colorado River, is a producer of organic beef and venison. It uses a combination of grass/forage feeding and ranch-grown supplemental organic grain to produce a

uniquely favorable and tender meat, and it is one of only a few producers of this type of meat in Texas.

Southern Bend Ranch sells approximately 85 percent of its beef and venison to one primary customer, Whole Organic Meat Market in Houston. Southern Bend is Whole Organic's sole supplier of beef and venison.

Southern Bend's contract with Whole Organic outlines the parameters in which the beef and venison will be produced as well as the amount of meat that will be supplied. If either of these sets of parameters is not met, the contract defines penalties that Southern Bend Ranch will have to pay. The contract is silent on "acts of God."

The Colorado River, on the southern border of Southern Bend Ranch, has a series of flood-control dams upstream. One spring, the quasi-government entity (QGE) in charge of monitoring the water flow failed to anticipate the effects of a heavy rainfall upstream, including the resulting flooding of the lakes above and between the dams. To prevent flooding the expensive homes surrounding one of the lakes, QGE released water from the lake. As a result, properties farther downstream were flooded. The flooding caused nonorganic pollutants to wash downriver onto part of the ranch.

Southern Bend Ranch informed Whole Organic that its shipments of meat would be cut in half because 50 percent of its herds, grass/forage, and feed had been contaminated by the nonorganic pollutants from the flood. Whole Organic demanded that Southern Bend pay the penalties stipulated in the contract. Southern Bend Ranch countered that because the flood was an act of God, the ranch is not responsible. Lawsuits resulted.

a.   Identify at least four exposures for Southern Bend Ranch.

b.   Identify at least four exposures for Whole Organic Meat Market.

c.   For each exposure listed for Southern Bend Ranch, recommend at least one potential option.

d.   For each exposure listed for Whole Organic Meat Market, recommend at least one potential option.

SUMMARY

An organization can use BCM to address potential threats to its operations. BCM has evolved from emergency preparedness and disaster recovery planning. Although BCM is similar to risk management, the two functions differ in focus and scope. The U.S. Department of Homeland Security has designated three standards of emergency preparedness for private business that address BCM as well as disaster recovery.

BCM is a strategic and operational approach designed to maintain business operations in the event of a catastrophe. Its purpose is to analyze potential risks and determine the most effective solutions the organization may employ to mitigate the risk and resulting damage. An important component of the BCM process is the business continuity plan, which entails these steps:

1. Understanding the business
2. Conducting a BIA
3. Performing a risk assessment
4. Developing the continuity plan
5. Implementing the continuity plan
6. Building a BCM/BCP culture
7. Maintaining and updating the plan

A strategic redeployment plan is a four-stage plan designed to reinforce an organization's resiliency and allow it to survive and flourish following a crisis. The stages are emergency, alternate marketing, contingency production, and communication. Each stage is designed to protect the organization, its stakeholders, its reputation, and its physical assets.

Organizations must achieve a balance between operational efficiency, cost effectiveness, and vulnerability to potential disruptions. They must also accurately assess risk to their supply chain and predetermine measures and countermeasures to maintain production and market share. When the supply chain is affected, organizations must be able to adjust and adapt quickly. Failure to do so may result in loss of market share and brand recognition as well as a reduced capacity to raise capital.

Communicating in a truthful and transparent way throughout a crisis will mitigate organizational risk and benefit the organization in the short term and the long term. During a crisis, stakeholders must be continually engaged and informed so that their concerns are fully addressed. Providing information will increase trust in management and help protect the organization's reputation, allowing for optimum access to capital, markets, talent, suppliers, and customers.

Developing risk mitigation tools involves a review of operations to identify exposures and risks as well as co-dependencies within the supply chain. This review will form the foundation of a risk mitigation plan.

ASSIGNMENT NOTES

1. The material in this section is based partially on Kurt Engemann and Douglas Henderson, *Business Continuity and Risk Management* (Brookfield, Conn.: Rothstein Associates, Inc., 2011), pp. 6–14.

2. Adapted from an unpublished manuscript, Carol A. Fox and Michael S. Epstein, "Why Is Enterprise Risk Management (ERM) Important for Preparedness?" (*Convergys Corporation*, 2009).

3. PAS 56: 2003, Guide to Business Continuity Management, The Business Continuity Institute, March 2003, p. 14.

4. PAS 56: 2003, Guide to Business Continuity Management, The Business Continuity Institute, March 2003, p. 18.

Direct Your Learning ▶▶

Legal and Regulatory Risk

Educational Objectives

After learning the content of this assignment, you should be able to:

▷ Explain how civil law, criminal law, and regulation form the basis for legal and regulatory risk.

▷ Describe the consequences of legal and regulatory risk to an organization.

▷ Explain how each of the following is used to treat legal and regulatory risk:

- Avoidance

- Modification of an event's likelihood

- Modification of an event's consequences

▷ Describe the characteristics of these predominant legal systems:

- Civil law (including Roman-French, German, and Scandinavian)

- Common law

- East Asian

- Hindu

- Islamic

- Socialist-Communist

▷ Distinguish between public international law and private international law.

▷ Describe the legal foundations and the general scope of each of the following commercial liability loss exposures:

- Premises and operations liability

- Products and completed operations liability

- Automobile liability

- Workers compensation and employers liability

Outline

Basis for Legal and Regulatory Risk

Legal and Regulatory Risk Consequences

Modifying Legal and Regulatory Risk

Legal Systems

International Law

Commercial Liability Loss Exposures

Assessing and Treating Legal and Regulatory Risk

Summary

3

Educational Objectives, continued

▶ Given information on an organization's legal and regulatory risk exposures, assess the risk and recommend treatment options for modifying the likelihood and/or consequences.

Legal and Regulatory Risk

BASIS FOR LEGAL AND REGULATORY RISK

Legal and regulatory risk includes uncertainties regarding the financial consequences of legal actions against an organization or noncompliance with statutes and regulations. Legal systems and regulatory requirements vary from one country to another.

The law recognizes that every person or entity has legal interests that are protected by civil law, criminal law, and regulation. Violating one of those interests is the basis for legal and regulatory risk.

The major bases of legal and regulatory risk fall into these categories:

- Torts
- Contracts
- Statutes and regulations

Criminal and Civil Law

Criminal law is a classification of law that applies to acts that society deems so harmful to the public welfare that government is responsible for prosecuting and punishing the perpetrators. This body of law defines offenses; regulates the investigating, charging, and trying of accused offenders; and establishes punishments for convicted offenders. Civil law is a classification of law that applies to legal matters not governed by criminal law and that protects rights and provides remedies for breaches of duties owed to others. Civil law applies to all legal matters that are not crimes and involve private rights.

Society uses criminal law to prescribe a standard of conduct to which all citizens must adhere. A crime can be major (such as murder) or minor (such as a traffic violation). A felony is a major crime involving long-term punishment. A minor crime, or misdemeanor, is punishable by a monetary fine or short-term imprisonment. Summary offenses are crimes that are not felonies or misdemeanors under state law and that usually result in monetary fines rather than imprisonment.

Civil law protects rights and provides remedies for breaches of duty other than crimes. In a civil action, the injured party usually requests reimbursement, in the form of monetary damages, for harm. Written laws, such as statutes and ordinances, specify the nature of crimes and their punishments. Unlike civil law, under which an individual victim can file charges, in criminal law the government decides whether it is in society's best interests to press charges and to prosecute on society's behalf.

In some cases, a single act can constitute both a civil wrong and a crime. For example, a commercial truck driver causes the death of another driver as the result of a traffic accident. Law enforcement authorities may charge the driver with vehicular homicide, a criminal act. The driver and the trucking company may also be subject to civil action by the estate of the deceased party for medical bills, funeral expenses, loss of support, and other damages allowed by law.

Torts

Tort

A wrongful act or an omission, other than a crime or a breach of contract, that invades a legally protected right.

The remedy for a **tort** is usually monetary damages. An organization is liable for any tort it commits through its agents, which can include employees; subordinates; associates; directors and officers; anyone using the organization's property with its permission; and anyone, including volunteers in some situations, acting on the organization's behalf. If its agents commit torts, an organization is generally subject to the same liability as are the individual agents. See the exhibit "Legal Risk—An Example."

Legal Risk—An Example

Traditionally, due to cultural differences, litigation in Japan has been used less frequently than in other parts of the world. However, litigation rates have been increasing there in recent decades. One example is the lawsuits arising from the failure of the Fukushima nuclear power plant following the March 2011 earthquake in Japan. Several hotels and other hospitality-related businesses have filed suits against the utility that operated Fukushima. These suits seek damages for lost business as a result of the power plant failure and concerns about radioactive contamination in the area surrounding the plant. Such actions are a source of legal risk for the power plant operator.

[DA08625]

The wrongful acts that constitute torts fall into three categories:

- Negligence
- Intentional torts
- Strict liability torts

Negligence

Negligence is an unintentional tort. In other words, the wrongdoer (tortfeasor) did not intend the action or the consequences. Instead, the tortfeasor exposed others to unreasonable danger by failing to exercise the duty of care the law requires under the circumstances. The legal responsibility and standard of care established by the law are what a reasonably prudent person would do in similar circumstances. Negligence can be the result of carelessness, ignorance, or accidents.

Intentional Torts

Intentional torts are actions or omissions that the tortfeasor intended, although the consequences of such actions may not necessarily be intended. Examples of legal interests that can be violated by intentional torts include these:

- Physical safety of one's person is an interest that can be violated by intentional torts such as assault or battery.
- Personal freedom of movement is an interest that can be violated by intentional torts such as false imprisonment.
- Protection of property is an interest that can be infringed on by intentional torts such as trespass, nuisance, or conversion.
- Security of reputation is an interest that can be infringed on by intentional torts such as libel or slander.
- Personal privacy is an interest that can be infringed on by intentional torts such as invasion of privacy.
- Economic freedom is an interest that can be infringed on by intentional torts such as false advertising, harassing or intimidating competitors or their customers, or any other action that a court determines exceeds the limits of fair competition.

Strict Liability Torts

Strict liability does not require negligence or intent to harm. Strict liability torts typically arise when an organization engages in certain activities that are considered ultrahazardous or that involve product liability cases. Examples of ultrahazardous activities are blasting, harboring wild or dangerous animals, or manufacturing or selling certain hazardous products.

Contracts

Both businesses and individuals form contracts, which are legally enforceable agreements between two or more parties. A contract may be as simple as the sale of a garden hose or as complex as the sale of an entire organization. Contracts establish the responsibilities of each party involved in the contract. A party that fails to comply with the contract's terms is said to have breached the contract. Individuals and businesses can become liable based on the contract's terms or based on the terms that can be inferred from the contract, known as implied warranties.

Requirements for Enforceability

For a contract to be enforceable, four basic requirements must be met:

- Agreement (including offer and acceptance)—One party makes an offer that the other party accepts. Both parties must mutually understand and agree on the critical terms of the offer and the agreement.
- Consideration—Each party gives up something of value. Commonly, one party exchanges money for the other party's promise to perform some activity.
- Capacity to contract—The parties must have the legal ability to enter into contracts. A contracting party who is not of legal age, sane, or sober does not have the capacity to enter into a contract.
- Legal purpose—The contract must have a legal purpose and must not be opposed to public policy.

Types of Contracts

Implied contract

A contract whose terms and intentions are indicated by the actions of the parties to the contract and the surrounding circumstances.

Express contract

A contract whose terms and intentions are explicitly stated.

Valid contract

A contract that meets all of the requirements to be enforceable.

Void contract

An agreement that, despite the parties' intentions, never reaches contract status and is therefore not legally enforceable or binding.

Voidable contract

A contract that one of the parties can reject (avoid) based on some circumstance surrounding its execution.

Unenforceable contract

A contract that is a valid contract but that because of a technical defect cannot be enforced.

Contracts may be **express contracts** or **implied contracts**. If a woman drives her car into a repair facility and asks the owner to fix it, and the garage owner agrees to do so, an implied contract is formed. The garage owner has agreed to use reasonable means to repair the car, and the woman has agreed to pay a reasonable price for the services. Of course, a good business practice would be for the garage owner to form an express contract with the woman that states the estimated cost of repairs. This would avoid controversy over the interpretation and enforcement of the implied contract.

A **valid contract** is one that meets all of the requirements to be enforceable. A **void contract** is not a contract because it lacks one or more of the requirements of a contract, such as agreement, consideration, capacity to contract, or legal purpose. Therefore, it is not legally enforceable and is without legal effect. A contract to commit a crime, for example, is void and unenforceable because it is for an unlawful purpose. Contracts involving fraud or material misrepresentations are **voidable contracts**.

Minors can form contracts, but the contracts are voidable. Some contracts are **unenforceable contracts**, such as an oral contract to sell land. Such a contract could possess all of the elements of a contract but be unenforceable because the law requires real estate contracts to be in writing.

Statutes and Regulations

In addition to torts and contracts, statutes can impose legal liability on an organization. Statutes are created by federal, state, provincial, or territorial governments and often modify the duties owed to others. In fact, violating the duties imposed by a statute may be used as evidence that the organization breached the duty of care owed to another. Violating a statute also imposes legal liability on an organization regardless of whether the organization committed any tort or assumed any liability under a contract. Statutes are also the basis for most criminal laws.

Examples of statutes that impose legal liability on an organization are tax laws, mail and wire fraud laws, antitrust laws, racketeering laws, and anti-discrimination laws. They also include corporate governance laws such as the Sarbanes-Oxley Public Company Reform and Investor Protection Act of 2002 (Sarbanes-Oxley) in the United States. Sarbanes-Oxley, which applies to publicly traded organizations, requires the principal executive officer and principal financial officer to certify that they have reviewed the corporation's quarterly and annual financial statements. Furthermore, the law requires that the officers certify that the report contains no untrue statements and fairly presents the corporation's financial conditions. These requirements represent a significant source of legal risk for the organization. Similar laws are J-SOX in Japan, the Financial Security Law of France, and the German Corporate Governance Code.

Statutes often do not include all the details necessary for an individual or an organization to abide by the law. To provide these details, governments authorize certain agencies to create regulations. For example, in the U.S., the Environmental Protection Agency (EPA) is authorized to issue regulations for laws protecting the environment. A regulation issued by the EPA might specify the acceptable level of a specific pollutant that complies with the Clean Air Act.

The issuance and enforcement of regulations vary in different regions of the world. For example, the European Union passed trade regulations that ban the import of pirated or counterfeit goods to the member countries. These regulations are binding as law for each of the members. This body of laws continues to grow, and many large organizations have full-time staff whose sole responsibility is to keep the organization in compliance with the applicable statutes.

Apply Your Knowledge

Describe the types of activities that can result in strict liability torts.

Feedback: Strict liability torts typically arise when an organization engages in certain activities that are considered ultrahazardous or that involve product liability cases. Examples of ultrahazardous activities are blasting, harboring wild or dangerous animals, or manufacturing or selling certain hazardous products.

LEGAL AND REGULATORY RISK CONSEQUENCES

The financial and other consequences of legal and regulatory risk can be catastrophic for an organization.

These are among the consequences of legal and regulatory risk to an organization:

- Monetary damages
- Defense costs
- Indirect losses
- Specific performance or injunction

Monetary Damages

The consequence of many criminal acts is incarceration for a specified period of time. Criminal acts can also result in monetary consequences, such as fines.

Failure to comply with statutes and regulations can also result in penalties and fines. For example, under the Sarbanes-Oxley Public Company Reform and Investor Protection Act of 2002 (Sarbanes-Oxley), bonuses or incentive compensation paid to CEOs or CFOs must be repaid if their organizations are determined to have been involved in misconduct requiring a restatement of financial reports. The Dodd-Frank Wall Street Reform and Consumer Protection Act contains similar provisions for repayment of incentive-based compensation of executive officers because of noncompliance with securities laws. Such provisions are often referred to as "clawbacks."

Frequently, a wrongdoer in a civil suit will have to pay compensatory and noncompensatory monetary damages awarded by a court. **Compensatory damages** indemnify those who incurred losses because of a breach of legal responsibility. The two types of compensatory damages are **special damages** and **general damages**.

Courts may also award a sum of money in excess of the amount necessary to indemnify a party for losses. Sometimes called **punitive damages (exemplary damages)**, the purpose of these damages is to modify the wrongdoer's behavior and to set an example so the behavior is discouraged. The amount awarded is intended to be proportionate to the defendant's total assets. However, the amount can be large because a lesser amount might be an insignificant loss that would fail to modify behavior.

Alternatively, before a court verdict is reached, the wrongdoer and the claimant may reach an out-of-court settlement involving payment. Correspondingly, a wrongdoer convicted of a crime may have to pay a fine. The money to pay for these verdicts, settlements, or fines is the basis of the legal or regulatory risk for an organization at fault.

Compensatory damages

A payment awarded by a court to reimburse a victim for actual harm.

Special damages

A form of compensatory damages that awards a sum of money for specific, identifiable expenses associated with the injured person's loss, such as medical expenses or lost wages.

General damages

A monetary award to compensate a victim for losses, such as pain and suffering, that does not involve specific, measurable expenses.

Punitive damages (exemplary damages)

A payment awarded by a court to punish a defendant for a reckless, malicious, or deceitful act to deter similar conduct; the award need not bear any relation to a party's actual damages.

Defense Costs

When an organization faces a civil suit or criminal charge, it must investigate the circumstances and prepare a legal defense. Investigation and defense costs can be the most expensive liability loss for organizations. Cases often require many hours of investigation and legal work to avoid, refute, or mitigate the charges.

Many cases are so technical that expert witnesses are required. Both parties in a technical case typically use expert witnesses, whose fees can be significant. Even the cost of reproducing pertinent documents or obtaining witnesses can be significant. Beyond the substantial legal fees, the defendant is usually responsible for paying all costs imposed by the court, including jury fees, filing fees, and premiums on court bonds.

Even if an organization has not committed a legal wrong, it can suffer a liability loss in the form of defense costs. A claimant might, for any reason, file an unfounded claim against an organization. This creates a liability loss because the organization must spend money to respond to the claim.

Indirect Losses

As a consequence of the direct liability losses, several other net income losses are possible because of the filing of a claim against an organization. For example, having a director or an officer of a corporation face a criminal indictment, whether or not it results in a conviction, can cause substantial harm to a corporation's reputation. A loss of reputation eventually results in loss of revenue or market share.

The subprime mortgage crisis in the United States saw several lenders required to pay monetary damages to customers who were charged unfairly high interest rates or excessive loan fees. As a result of the negative publicity surrounding such actions, many of these mortgage companies either were acquired by other firms or went out of business. Such additional indirect costs can be weighted several times higher than the direct loss costs.

Specific Performance or Injunction

In a breach of contract claim, a court might order **specific performance**. For example, a construction firm might have breached a contract by failing to erect a structure. A court may order the construction firm to complete the structure specified in the contract.

A court can also order a party to refrain from engaging in a particular activity. This is called an **injunction**. For example, a firm might burn construction waste, thereby spreading noxious fumes to adjoining properties and making the occupants ill. A court may prohibit the firm from burning its rubbish at the construction site.

Specific performance
A court-ordered equitable remedy requiring a party to perform a certain act, often—but not always—as a result of breach of a contract.

Injunction
A court-ordered equitable remedy requiring a party to act or refrain from acting.

Both specific performance and injunction can result in financial consequences because of associated attorneys' fees and court costs.

MODIFYING LEGAL AND REGULATORY RISK

Legal and regulatory risk is categorized as hazard risk arising from liability risk exposures.

Overview of the Procedure

The potential negative aspects of legal and regulatory risk can be treated in these ways:

- Risk avoidance
- Modifying the likelihood of an event
- Modifying the consequences of an event

These are not the only treatment options for legal and regulatory risk. For some situations, risk sharing (transfer) or retaining the risk may be appropriate.

Risk Avoidance

There are two types of avoidance: stopping a current activity or never starting the activity. When an organization stops a current activity, the probability of any future liability is zero. However, the organization may continue to experience liability claims from previous activities. For example, a manufacturer that stopped making a defective product is still liable for losses caused by the products it manufactured and distributed in the past.

When an organization decides not to undertake an activity, it will not experience any liability claims related to that activity. Avoidance is usually used only in high probability-high severity situations. Although this risk treatment technique does reduce to zero the likelihood of the loss occurring, it is frequently a last resort because when an organization does not engage in the activity, it can never obtain the potential rewards. In other words, using avoidance as a risk treatment technique prevents liability losses, but also prevents any possibility of gain from the activity.

Modifying the Likelihood of an Event

Modifying the likelihood of an event arising from legal and regulatory risk is often called **loss prevention** by some risk management professionals. This risk treatment method can be applied to these bases of legal and regulatory risk:

- Torts
- Contracts
- Statutes

Modifying the Likelihood of Tort Liability

The risk management professional can consider contractual removal or limitation of tort liability and hazard control as a means of modifying the likelihood of litigation against an organization.

One way to prevent the likelihood of litigation is by removing or limiting the organization's legal obligations to others. Several different clauses can be added to contracts to remove or limit liability, including these:

- Waivers—A known right can be voluntarily relinquished through a waiver. For example, for a subcontractor to win a bid for a construction contract from a general contractor, the general contractor may require the subcontractor to obtain a written waiver of the subcontractor's insurer's right of subrogation.

- Hold-harmless agreements—These are contractual provisions by which one party (the indemnitor) agrees to assume the liability of a second party (the indemnitee). Hold-harmless agreements are commonly found in leases that require tenants to hold landlords harmless from claims made by third parties who are injured by the tenants' negligence. Construction contracts also contain hold-harmless agreements.

- Exculpatory agreements—These contractual provisions enable a party to avoid liability for negligence or a wrongful act. The participant in an activity signs a "release of liability" agreement for activities specified in the contract. For example, Jim is a risk management professional employed by a dude ranch that allows tourists to ride horses around the ranch's surrounding area. Laurie pays the ranch owner so she can ride a horse there, and Jim has Laurie sign a contract releasing the owner from any liability associated with her riding the horse. Under the exculpatory agreement in the contract, Laurie agrees not to sue the ranch owner for any injuries she might sustain, even those resulting from the owner's or an agent of the owner's negligence. The exculpatory agreement relieves the owner and the owner's agents of liability to Laurie.

But what is it?

- Unilateral notices—Liability can be limited if unilateral notices are posted so that they are physically apparent, expressed in language the other party understands (which is a concern if the other party does not speak the language used), and reasonable in extent (not forever or applicable to every possible risk). However, the lack of mutual consent, or absence of a freely bargained exchange of values, also limits the legal effectiveness of unilateral notices such as signs posted on walls, notices on backs of ticket stubs, or limitations on product warranties.

Hazard

A condition that increases the frequency or severity of a loss.

Hazard control is another method to modify the likelihood of legal risk. Hazard control involves implementing risk control measures that eliminate or reduce hazards. A key aspect of risk control for tort liability is hazard control for the risk exposures covered under an insurance policy, such as premises and operations, products, and completed operations. The specific hazards related to these liability risk exposures vary by organization.

For premises and operations, these are the risk control areas of particular concern to a risk management professional:

- Parking lots
- Building entrances and exits
- Walking surfaces
- Merchandise displays and counters
- Escalators, elevators, and stairways

Proper maintenance and housekeeping in these areas can reduce the chance of injury and subsequent litigation.

The products and completed operations liability risk exposure varies by the type of product manufactured, distributed, or sold; or by the type of operation completed. However, there are sound general risk control measures that organizations should consider regardless of the type of product or completed operation. These include proper design and testing of products, quality control, and clear instructions or technical manuals.

Modifying the Likelihood of Contractual Liability

Organizations enter into a variety of contractual agreements that subject the organization to a wide range of legal responsibilities. Examples include leases, purchase orders, sales contracts, shipping agreements, exculpatory agreements, and hold-harmless agreements.

A primary measure to reduce the likelihood for contractual liability is to have most if not all contracts reviewed by counsel, preferably before they are signed. In addition, contractual liability can be prevented through other measures, such as using written contracts rather than oral contracts that rely on memory and word of mouth. This is true even in long-term business relationships. Care must be taken when committing an agreement to writing that the contract accurately reflects the intentions of both parties. Terms that are vague or ambiguous may be used against the party who drafted the agreement.

Modifying the Likelihood of Statutory Liability

Risk management professionals can help prevent statutory liability by understanding statutory compliance requirements applicable to their organizations. This understanding can be gained from information acquired from several sources. One source is internal experts who are knowledgeable about statutory requirements. If the organization does not have such persons on staff, it may turn to an external expert or consultant with this expertise. Another source is trade associations, which often provide training courses to educate their members about compliance issues. Additionally, legal libraries, both physical and online, can provide the needed information.

Once this information is obtained, these same sources may help determine how to fulfill the statutory obligations. Once a plan is devised about how to fulfill those obligations, responsibility must be assigned to ensure that the organization stays in compliance. The risk management professional must be vigilant in monitoring the activities of those assigned with compliance responsibilities.

Compliance with corporate governance statutes must be directed by senior management and the corporate board of directors. Directors and officers must place the interests of the corporation above their own and must be alert for signs that this standard is not being met. A board of directors cannot be a rubber stamp for management; it must maintain its independence and devote sufficient time and resources to understanding the firm's operations. Open, clear, and concise communication among directors and officers is an important factor in preventing or reducing losses. Directors and officers must have a clear understanding of the corporation's charter and bylaws, as well as securities laws and antitrust laws, and they must avoid taking actions that would violate any of these. Executive compensation packages should provide incentives for long-term results to reduce the likelihood of noncompliance with regulations and promote ethical decision making.

A corporate code of conduct is also an important technique to modify the likelihood of statutory liability. This code provides all employees with the organization's mission and commitment to ethical behavior and outlines applicable policies and the importance of regulatory compliance. In global organizations, the code of conduct must reflect the various legal and regulatory environments of all of the jurisdictions in which the organization conducts business. For example, several retail companies have been criticized for using child labor in overseas factories that produce goods for the United States market. Corporate codes of conduct for such companies vary regarding this issue with some companies indicating a minimum age for employees while others forbid hiring children regardless of jurisdiction. Other codes state only that the organization must comply with the applicable local laws regarding minimum age of employment.[1]

Modifying the Consequences of an Event

In addition to risk avoidance and modifying the likelihood of an event, risk treatment involves modifying the consequences of an event. For hazard risk, this risk treatment technique is often referred to as **loss reduction**. The purpose of this technique is to decrease the severity or effect of an organization's losses. As with modifying the likelihood of an event, modifying the consequences of an event can be applied to these bases of legal and regulatory risk:

- Torts
- Contracts
- Statutes

Modifying the Consequences of Tort Liability

Two methods to modify the consequences of tort liability are the development of defenses and participation in settlement negotiations.

Developing defenses is an important step in the litigation process. The risk management professional should rely on legal counsel's expertise to develop the most effective defense strategy. However, the risk management professional should be aware of the advantages and implications of these five widely used defenses:

- Legal **privilege**—In certain situations, an organization's actions do invade others' legally protected interests and do cause harm, but those actions are legally excused because the organization has the right to invade another's interests to promote or protect one's own, greater interests. In resolving conflicts, common law establishes priorities among competing rights, particularly regarding actions that would otherwise constitute torts. For example, the law generally places more importance on protecting persons than on protecting property and more importance on preserving peace and order than on protecting privacy.

- **Immunity**—Certain entities, such as governments and governmental officials, charities, young children, and the insane, have traditionally not been subject to lawsuits arising out of contract and tort law. Generally, children and the insane are incapable of the intent or lack the mental abilities usually presumed by legal liability. Governments and their officials have immunity when conducting regulatory activities so agents of the state can act without fear of legal retribution. Charities may be immune from suit so that their resources, largely donated for humanitarian purposes, will not be drained.

- **Comparative negligence**—The degree of the defendant's and plaintiff's negligence may affect the court decision, the size of the verdict, or the severity of the punishment. In most cases, the responsibility may be proportionally shared between the plaintiff and defendant.

- **Last clear chance doctrine**—In some instances, the injured party had the ability to avoid loss or injury, but chose to act in a manner that did not

Loss reduction

A risk control technique that reduces the severity of a particular loss.

Privilege

A rule of law allowing a person to refuse to disclose confidential communications.

Immunity

A defense that, in certain instances, shields organizations or persons from liability.

Comparative negligence

A common-law principle that requires both parties to a loss to share the financial burden of the bodily injury or property damage according to their respective degrees of fault.

Last clear chance doctrine

A defense to negligence that holds the party who has the last clear chance to avoid harm and fails to do so solely responsible for the harm.

avoid risk. For example, a pedestrian crossing a street at a red light may have the last clear chance to observe traffic and step out of harm's way, so the driver of the vehicle that strikes the pedestrian could be relieved of some, if not all, of the fault for causing the injury.

- Assumption of risk—If the plaintiff had a sufficient understanding of the risk and, as a reasonably prudent person, voluntarily accepted the risk, the plaintiff is considered to be in complete control of his or her actions. The defendant should not be held liable for the plaintiff's damages. While no one has perfect information, a plaintiff can argue that the defendant had superior knowledge and failed to disclose the complete risks to the plaintiff.

Another method to modify the consequences of tort liability is participating in settlement negotiations. An organization's risk management professional (and perhaps, for major claims, its senior management) should take an active interest in lawsuit negotiations. Before a final verdict, settlement negotiations might offer opportunities to resolve the suit more favorably than would the court. Therefore, regardless of whether any negotiations are handled by the organization's or by the insurer's legal counsel, the organization's risk management professional or other responsible executive should advise the lawyers in designing or appraising the acceptability of various settlement offers. Without such guidance, the attorneys might fail to recognize or might reject a possibly advantageous settlement offer.

The organization's role in these settlement negotiations is to participate in, advise, and guide. However, the attorneys should ultimately direct the settlement negotiations. If the suit is not covered by insurance, the organization's own legal counsel should direct the negotiations. If an insurance policy applies, this policy will almost always give the insurer the right to control the litigation, including settlement negotiations. In either case, however, the organization's risk management professional and/or senior management should ensure that counsel is aware of the organization's goals in any settlement and should be available to assist in settlement negotiations.

Modifying the Consequences of Contractual Liability

Measures that can be taken to reduce the loss associated with contractual liability include these:

- Select a favorable jurisdiction—Usually, a clause negotiated into a contract specifies which state's law will govern the contract's interpretation. If the contractual parties are domiciled in the same state, that state's law applies.
- Include limits of liability—This measure tries to anticipate legal claims and to limit an organization's legal responsibility. The limit can range from zero to a specified amount.
- Include a liquidated damages provision—This provision limits the amount for which one party might otherwise be liable. These agreements

are usually entered into before either party begins to perform under the contract.

- Include a valuation clause—A valuation clause can be included in a contract for the transportation or bailment of property to specify the valuation of the property in the event that it is lost, stolen, or damaged.
- Evaluate duty to mitigate—The party that claims the other party breached the contract still has a duty to mitigate or use good faith efforts to reduce the severity of its losses. As a defense, the breaching party can claim that the nonbreaching party failed to fulfill this duty to mitigate and therefore suffered greater loss than was necessary.

Modifying the Consequences of Statutory Liability

Few defenses are available to an organization to reduce the fine or penalty it faces when it violates a statute, which is why most organizations work diligently to prevent violations. A defense commonly pled by organizations in these cases is that the statute was unconstitutional or was too vague or ambiguous to be enforceable. If the statute has already been tested on this defense and upheld by a higher court, it will likely not be effective.

Apply Your Knowledge

The risk management professional for a manufacturer of power tools is reviewing the organization's products liability risk exposures. Describe the risk control measures the organization can use to modify the likelihood of tort liability related to injuries caused by its products.

Feedback: These risk control measures should be considered to modify the likelihood of tort liability:

- Proper design of power tools to avoid misuse or injury
- Testing of all products during production and prior to distribution
- Implement quality control procedures
- Provide clear instructions or manuals for the proper use of the power tools

LEGAL SYSTEMS

Although no two countries have identical legal systems, many nations share legal approaches and concepts. Additionally, some countries classified within one system have incorporated legal concepts found traditionally within other systems. This section provides information about the development of different legal systems to give insurance professionals a basic understanding of the differences they might encounter in the international legal environment.

In a majority of countries, the legal systems fall into these two major categories:

- Civil-law system
- Common-law system

The civil-law tradition developed within these three distinct subsystems:

- Roman (and French)
- German
- Scandinavian (Nordic)

Other predominant legal systems include the East Asian, Hindu, Islamic, and Socialist-Communist systems.

Civil Law

Civil law, or Roman-Germanic law, uses comprehensive codes and statutes to form the backbone of a legal system. This system relies heavily on legal scholars to develop and interpret the law. The civil-law system is the most influential system in the world. More countries use its subsystems, in one form or another, than any other legal system.

It is the dominant legal system of western Europe, almost all of Latin America, and parts of Africa and Asia. Additionally, the civil-law system can be found in parts of some traditionally common-law countries (for example, Louisiana in the United States, Quebec in Canada, and Puerto Rico). However, these legal systems can vary a great deal from one country to another in their legal institutions, processes, and rules.

In the civil-law system, a judge is a civil servant whose function is to find the correct legislative provision within a written code of statutes and apply it to the facts presented in a case. Judges perform little interpretation of a code, and their opinions do not determine their thought processes on legal issues.

The civil-law courts usually are divided into two or more separate sets, each with its own jurisdiction over different issues, with a different hierarchy, judiciary, and procedures.

The typical civil-law case usually is divided into these three stages:

- The preliminary stage involves submission of pleadings and appointment of a hearing judge.
- At the evidence stage, a hearing judge takes evidence and prepares a written summary of the proceedings.
- At the decision stage, the presiding judge decides the case based on the record provided by the hearing judge, the counsels' briefs, and arguments.

The civil law system does not have the common-law system's jury trial; instead, a series of isolated meetings, written communications, motions, and rulings help decide the case. Civil-law countries have varying time frames for these events; some countries' procedures proceed very quickly, and others proceed very slowly.

Roman-French Law

The French civil code of 1804 consolidated the contrasting concepts of law by decree and law by custom. Although a magistrate is the final arbiter of a private law dispute, a court can rely on appointed experts, who have wide-ranging powers to investigate and present evidence to support an opinion rendered by a court. A magistrate usually will not reject an expert's opinion.

However, in France and Italy, a party can appeal a primary court's opinion, although courts in those countries tend to have extremely heavy backlogs. Under these circumstances, the examination of detailed factual or legal issues can be difficult because, with the passage of time, memories fade and some witnesses become difficult to find.

The French civil code was the basis for codes in the Netherlands, Italy, Portugal, and Spain. Haiti also adopted the French Code, and Bolivia and Chile adopted it for the most part. In turn, Ecuador, Uruguay, Argentina, and Colombia used the Chilean code as the model for their own legal systems. Puerto Rico and the Philippines used the Spanish code as their legal systems' model.

German Law

Germany's location in the center of Europe has greatly influenced its political and social history. Many scholars consider the German civil law system as the most developed and influential of all the civil-law subsystems.

The German private law, or *Bürgerliches Gesetzbuch* (BGB), is the civil code that took effect in 1900. Unlike the French code, which was designed for laypersons to read, the BGB was developed for legal professionals to read and was too technical for laypersons. The German civil law influenced the U.S. legal education system; the American Law Institute's (ALI) restatements, or authoritative treatises, on law; and the development of the Uniform Commercial Code (UCC).

The original German code emphasized the rights of people to enter into contracts freely and dealt with the enforceability of all kinds of contracts. Similarly, the German code requires a finding of fault on the part of a wrong-doer in a tort suit. Although some elements of those concepts still exist, the availability of insurance as a risk- and damage-spreading mechanism has caused the German code to expand individual obligations and potential culpability.

Compensation for damages without culpability has effectively created a "cradle-to-grave" safety net as part of a wide social compact in Germany. For example, German statutes grant compensation for certain types of accidents, regardless of culpability, including railway, traffic, aircraft, electrical, gas, and nuclear power station accidents.

The German and Swiss codes, along with the French code, influenced code developments in Brazil, Mexico, precommunist China, and Peru. Additionally, Japan used the German code in the development of its own code, and Turkey used the similar Swiss code in developing its legal system.

Scandinavian Law

The Scandinavian (Nordic) legal system is both a civil-law system and an independent system. The legal systems in the Scandinavian countries are based neither on large bodies of codified regulations, like those of the French and German systems, nor on case (common) law.

The Scandinavian legal systems evolved from a long-established history of customary law. Elements of law by decree developed as a result of Germanic and Russian influences. Additionally, the Scandinavian countries have codified historical business practices as statutes. In tort law, as distinguished from contracts, damages contain a punitive element beyond just and fair compensation.

The development of a virtually distinct legal system in Scandinavian countries resulted from the historically close links among those countries. For example, Finland was part of Sweden for hundreds of years until it became part of Russia, then eventually gained independence. Norway, now independent, was part of Denmark.

Common Law

In the common-law legal system, a judge interprets the facts of a case, examines precedents (prior judicial rulings in similar cases), and makes a decision based on the facts in the current case. Precedents are guides, not rigid frameworks for all decisions. This system tends to be fact-intensive, relying on the judge's reasoning for a final decision.

England and most of the former British colonial countries, including Australia, Canada, India, and the U.S., use the common-law system. Japan's law combines the civil- and common-law systems, particularly relating to corporate law, which resulted from U.S. influence in post-World War II Japan. East Asian legal systems also influenced Japan's legal system. Other examples of blended common-law systems are Canada and the U.S. Both the province of Quebec and the state of Louisiana have state legal systems based on French civil law.

East Asian Law

East Asian countries have a common background profoundly influencing their legal developments over the centuries. China has a dominant presence in East

Asia. Although both Korea and Japan have different legal systems, they both reflect the Chinese influence.

Until the 19th century, Japan's civil code was based on the developing German civil code. However, this imported legal code did not supplant the local customary law already existing in Japan. Even today, a tradition of informal compromise, contrasted with individual parties' asserting their rights in negotiations, remains a strong characteristic of the East Asian countries' approach to contract disputes. Japan today has relatively few attorneys, judges, and lawsuits.

Other Asian countries have relied on both civil and common law to varying degrees. French colonialism influenced the legal systems of the southeast Asian countries Laos, Cambodia, and Vietnam for many years. By contrast, England's common-law system influenced the legal systems of Singapore, Malaysia, and Brunei. U.S. influence was prevalent in post-World War II Japan and in the Philippines after the Spanish-American War.

Hindu Law

Hinduism provides religious and philosophical rules in India and some surrounding countries. The Hindu legal system is perhaps the oldest in the world. The customs and laws of Hinduism have applied separately and distinctly to the members of four major caste groups: Brahmans (priests), Kshatriyas (warriors), Vaishyas (tradesmen), and Sudras (servants and artisans). Movement from one caste to another historically was not permitted, even with professional or political success, although laws have attempted to eliminate the rigid caste system. Legislation in India has voided all the rules of the caste system when they conflict with social justice.

By the early 1800s, most of India was under the control of the British, whose policy in settling colonies was to retain existing law, allowing Hindu law to become the official system for the Hindu population. The effect of British rule on Hindu law was the development of legislation, the judiciary, and the legal education system. A statutory code of commercial, criminal, and civil procedure has replaced the Hindu law of contracts and property. However, India's legal system still reflects remnants of the caste system.

Islamic Law

The Islamic legal system is used in countries whose citizens are almost entirely followers of the Islamic religion. This legal system is based on the foundations of the *Book of the Qur'an* (*Koran*) and includes almost all of the countries of the Middle East and northern Africa, southern Asia, southeastern Europe, and parts of southeast Asia.

More Islamic countries are members of the United Nations than countries whose majorities follow any other religion. Islam is the second most prevalent religion in the world, with approximately 1.2 billion followers.

With the end of World War I and the collapse of the Ottoman Empire, Europeans regained control of most of the territories that Islamic warriors had captured in previous centuries. In the decades following World War II, many Islamic peoples attempted to gain their independence, often from European countries. Internal debates, still ongoing, centered on whether states should be theocracies or secular states that follow Islamic law.

The primary system of law within the Islamic countries is the *Shari'ah*, with a secondary system of jurisprudence called the *fiqh*. The *Shari'ah* consists of the two primary sources of Islamic law from which all legal principles derive, the *Qur'an* and the *Sunnah*. The *fiqh*, or Islamic jurisprudence, is the process of applying *Shari'ah* principles to both real or hypothetical cases.

The *Qur'an*, the highest source of law within Islam, gives followers of Islam the authority to make law and render opinions. The *Sunnah* forms a second tier of the *Shari'ah* and mandates the standard of conduct people are to follow to comply with the *Qur'an*.

The *Qur'an* is a religious book, not a legal code or book of law, but it serves as the foundation for the Islamic legal system. It contains specific precepts about ethics, crime, business transactions, domestic relations, inheritance, and war. The *Qur'an* differs from a code of law in that it does not mention the legal consequences of the disregard of its rules.

The *faqh* refers to the body of laws developed from the *Shari'ah*. Five schools of *faqh* (*faqh madhhabs*) exist today. Four are within the *Sunni* sect of Islam. The fifth school is within the *Shai* (*Shiite* or *Shiah*) sect of Islam. At times, conflict has divided the different *faqh madhhabs*. Identifying with a different school or attempting to change affiliation can be considered heresy. Additionally, at times judges prohibit intermarriage between the different *faqh madhhabs*.

Approximately 90 percent of all Muslims identify themselves as *Sunni*, with the balance being *Shai*. The *Shai* live primarily in Iran, southern Iraq, Syria, and Lebanon and believe that the leader of the Islamic religion should be a direct descendant of Muhammad. *Sunni* Muslims do not have this requirement. A significant difference between *Shai* and *Sunni* is that *Shais* also believe that individual reasoning (*ijtihad*) is a legitimate source of Islamic law.

Socialist-Communist Law

The socialist system originated with the Marxist overthrow of czarist Russia in the October Revolution in 1917, which created the Soviet Union. Before the revolution, Russia was a civil-law country.

The result of the Marxist takeover was the imposition of socialist ideology over the civil-law system that already existed. The central idea of the system was the emphasis on the state's interest over that of individuals. Russia developed new codes that reflected the Marxist ideas that the laws should serve the interests of socialism.

Private-sector business legal principles, such as contracts, commercial law, torts, property, and bankruptcy, are of little use within a socialist system. Public law replaces private-sector legal principles. For example, because the government owns all property and production, all contract law is public. In a socialist country, the socialist political party controls and influences the entire legal system, including the courts. All decisions from the courts, although independent in nature, are subject to party control or revision.

Western civil- and common-law systems heavily influenced the law in Russia. Asian socialist-communist countries discovered problems applying the Soviet-style legal principles in their societies. The communist People's Republic of China, for example, abandoned the legal principles introduced to them by the Soviets and developed a more informal system more similar to East Asian traditions.

With the fall of the Soviet bloc in the 1990s, former eastern European bloc countries abandoned the socialist-communist legal system in favor of a civil-law system. Many changes were profound, with legislatures endorsing basic free market principles. The actual changes varied by country. Today, Russia is a civil-law country. However, the Russian government often changes the legal applications of civil law with regard to individuals and businesses.

Several other communist-ruled or communist-influenced countries, such as Cuba, North Korea, Vietnam, and the People's Republic of China, still use the Soviet-based legal system. The People's Republic of China now permits a private economy and has adopted it as part of the Constitution of the People's Congress. China's dominant constitutional principles still require observance of socialist doctrine. China also has adopted civil-law type of codification, the General Principles of Civil Law, and is developing an ever more extensive codification.

INTERNATIONAL LAW

In any legal dispute arising between parties from different countries, public and private international law must be considered.

Those resolving international disputes between individuals or corporations first apply any applicable public international law, such as an international treaty, that governs the dispute. If no international treaty applies, then any relevant laws of the involved countries are applied to the dispute in accordance with the principles of private international law.

Public International Law

Public international law concerns the interrelation of nation states and is governed by treaties and other international agreements.

Public international law

A law that concerns the interrelation of nation states and that is governed by treaties and other international agreements.

International treaties agreed to by a business's country of origin govern some international business transactions. These treaties may be between two countries, or they may be multilateral treaties among many countries.

The North American Free Trade Agreement (NAFTA) is a trilateral treaty governing all business interactions involving Canada, Mexico, and the U.S. Other treaties, such as the World Trade Organization's General Agreement of Tariffs and Trade (GATT), involve more than one hundred countries as signatories.

These international agreements affect member countries by requiring that they amend their national laws to comply with the agreements' requirements. For example, countries that signed GATT agreed to adjust their tariff rates on imported goods from other GATT member countries. However, these agreements are not limited to trade and tariffs. For example, NAFTA includes investment provisions, and the World Trade Organization's Trade-Related Aspects of Intellectual Property Rights Agreement ensures that the laws of member countries set basic standards for the protection of intellectual property.

Private International Law

Private international law involves disputes between individuals or corporations in different countries and is also referred to as conflicts of law. It involves questions about which laws apply in settling the disputes and how they apply. It determines which jurisdiction's law applies to the business transaction in question, which country's court hears a dispute, and whether other countries will enforce the foreign decision.

Private international law
A law that involves disputes between individuals or corporations in different countries.

In any legal dispute arising between parties from different countries, these two issues must be considered:

* Whether a court in one country will recognize the decision of another country's court
* Whether a court has the right to hear the legal dispute

The first issue is referred to as comity, the practice by which one country recognizes, within its own territory or in its courts, another country's institutions. Comity can also apply to the rights and privileges acquired by a citizen in a country. Many experts believe that comity is the basis for all private international law.

The second issue is referred to as jurisdiction. Just as in domestic cases, one of the basic questions of international law is whether a court has the right (jurisdiction) to preside over a particular case.

More specifically, courts in international cases must determine whether they have jurisdiction over the person or entity (*in personam* jurisdiction) and over the subject matter (*in res* jurisdiction) and if they have jurisdiction to render the particular judgment in the case.

In international cases, personal jurisdiction is based on whether the person or entity is present in the country or has committed the act in question in that country.

A significant issue frequently arising in international law is whether one country's courts have jurisdiction over either another country's citizen or a corporation with its place of business in another country. Jurisdictional issues are increasing in importance and complexity as governments try to control the increase in international business.

For example, one country's jurisdiction over Internet commerce originating in another country raises complex jurisdictional questions. Other cases involving jurisdictional issues include the U.S.'s attempt to prevent U.S. residents from purchasing prescription drugs from other countries, China's claim to all Chinese-language domain names and its blocking of certain Web sites, and some European courts' claiming authority over Web sites from outside their countries' borders.

Cyber issue w/ jurisdiction on international cases

COMMERCIAL LIABILITY LOSS EXPOSURES

Commercial liability loss exposures are potential losses that can arise when an organization is held to be financially responsible to another individual or organization for bodily injury or property damage.

Commercial liability loss exposures can be categorized in many ways, depending in part on the purpose of the categorization. The exhibit depicts a broad categorization that reflects insurance practices. See the exhibit "Major Categories of Commercial Liability Loss Exposures."

Major Categories of Commercial Liability Loss Exposures

- Premises and operations liability
- Products and completed operations liability
- Automobile liability
- Workers compensation and employers liability
- Management liability
- Professional liability
- Environmental liability
- Marine liability
- Aircraft liability

[DA04739]

Several of the primary exposures are discussed here:

- Premises and operations liability
- Products and completed operations liability
- Automobile liability
- Workers compensation and employers liability

Premises and Operations Liability Loss Exposure

The premises and operations liability loss exposure relates to liability arising from bodily injury or property damage caused either by an accident that occurs on an organization's owned, leased, or rented premises or by an accident that arises out of the organization's ongoing (as opposed to completed) operations but occurs away from the premises. An organization's liability for such accidents is usually based on negligence—that is, the organization's failure to exercise the appropriate degree of care owed to some person under the circumstances.

Under the common law, owners and occupiers of land owe different duties of care to others on the premises, depending on their reasons for being on the premises. For example, an owner or occupier would owe a greater degree of care to a business guest or a customer than to an adult trespasser. Many jurisdictions have abandoned these common-law rules in favor of a reasonable care standard for owners and occupiers that applies under the circumstances to anyone who might be on the premises.

In some cases, premises and operations liability can be based on strict liability. For example, a blasting contractor could be held strictly liable for unintentional damage to buildings near the blasting operations. It can also apply to liability assumed by a land owner or occupier under hold-harmless agreements in contracts such as leases of premises, maintenance agreements, and construction contracts.

The premises and operations liability loss exposure includes bodily injury or property damage claims arising out of the use of mobile equipment (such as bulldozers and cranes). However, liability arising from the ownership, maintenance, or use of automobiles is treated as a distinct loss exposure, as is watercraft (vessel) liability and aircraft liability. Liability for employee injury or illness, whether based on obligations under workers compensation laws or based on common-law principles, is also regarded as a distinct loss exposure.

Products and Completed Operations Liability Loss Exposure

Liability for products and liability for completed operations are often treated as components of one loss exposure. However, products liability and completed operations liability each have distinguishing characteristics.

Products Liability

Products liability arises out of the manufacture, distribution, or sale of an unsafe, dangerous, or defective product and the failure of the manufacturer, distributor, or retailer to meet its legal duties to the user or consumer of the product.

Products liability lawsuits may be based on a variety of recovery theories, including negligence, misrepresentation, fraud, deceit, and breach of warranty. In actions for products liability, the plaintiff must prove that the defendant failed to take reasonable care in the design, manufacture, distribution, or sale of the article that caused the injury.

Since the 1960s, many products liability lawsuits have been based on strict liability in tort. In contrast to negligence actions, under strict liability in tort, the conduct of the manufacturer, distributor, or retailer is irrelevant, and the focus is on the safety of the product itself. The plaintiff must prove three elements:

*   The product was defective when it left the manufacturer's or supplier's custody or control.
*   The defective condition made the product unreasonably dangerous.
*   The defective product was the proximate cause of the plaintiff's injury.

Although products liability actions based on strict liability in tort are typically directed at the manufacturer of the defective product, the plaintiff can seek damages from any entity that qualifies as a seller, including a distributor or retailer.

Completed Operations Liability

Completed operations liability is the legal responsibility of a contractor, repairer, or other entity for bodily injury or property damage arising out of the entity's completed work, as in these examples:

*   Several months after a heating contractor installed a new boiler in an apartment building, the boiler exploded because the contractor had installed it negligently. The explosion damaged the apartment building and injured a tenant. Both the building owner and the tenant sued the contractor for damages.
*   A family was hosting a picnic in their backyard. A wooden deck completed a few weeks earlier by a contractor collapsed under some guests, who were injured. They sued the decking contractor for damages.
*   A repair shop overhauled a production machine belonging to a manufacturer. After the machine was returned to service, it malfunctioned and injured an employee of the manufacturer. The employee sued the repair shop for damages.

Under the common-law accepted work doctrine, a contractor could not be held liable for negligent performance of completed work once the owner had accepted the work. Over time, courts formulated several exceptions to this doctrine, holding contractors liable even after the work was accepted if the contractor knew of a danger or deliberately concealed a defect in the completed work. Eventually, many courts abandoned the accepted work doctrine altogether and permitted a right of action to anyone injured through the contractor's negligence. Some courts have even applied the strict liability in tort rule in much the same way as in holding the product manufacturer liable to the ultimate consumer or user.

Automobile Liability Loss Exposure

Automobile liability is legal responsibility for bodily injury or property damage arising out of the ownership, maintenance, or use of automobiles.

Under the common law, ownership of an auto does not in itself make the owner liable for injury or damage caused by someone else's negligent operation of the vehicle. Several states have passed laws making an auto owner liable for damages arising from any person's operation of the auto with the owner's express or implied permission.

Auto liability loss can also arise from negligent maintenance of a commercial auto. For example, negligent servicing of brakes, tires, or steering apparatus may be the proximate cause of a truck's running into another vehicle.

Anyone who is injured or whose property is damaged as a result of the negligent use of an auto has a right of action against the operator. In addition, any person or organization legally responsible for the operator's conduct can be held jointly liable. For example, an employer can be held jointly liable for its employee's negligent operation of an auto during the course of employment. However, when an employee substantially deviates from the scope of employment, the employer is not usually liable. For example, if a truck driver deviates from a prescribed route in order to spend the night at the home of a relative, the employer would not be responsible for an accident that occurs while the driver is on the way to the relative's home.

Liability for Operation by Others

A person who negligently furnishes a defective auto to another person may be held liable to a third person injured as a proximate result of the defect. Some courts have recognized an exception to the general rule in cases involving a used auto sold "as is," on the theory that the buyer understands (or can reasonably be expected to understand) that the used auto has not been inspected for defects and should be inspected by the buyer before being put into use.

Similarly, a person who negligently entrusts an auto to a person who is unskilled in its operation or otherwise incompetent to operate it may be held directly liable for resulting injuries. To establish liability for negligent entrustment, the plaintiff must show that the party entrusting the vehicle knew or should have known of the driver's incompetence, inexperience, or reckless tendencies.

Auto No-Fault Laws

The goal of auto no-fault laws is to provide stated benefits for all persons injured in auto accidents without a need to prove fault. In the United States, nearly half the states have some form of no-fault system in operation.

Provisions in the no-fault laws vary widely. About half of the no-fault states preserve the tort system but require insurers to offer, or require all auto registrants to purchase, personal injury protection (PIP) insurance that provides specified first-party benefits for medical expenses, loss of income, or death resulting from auto accidents. These states are said to have "add-on" no-fault plans.

The remaining states have "modified" no-fault plans that restrict the right to sue for torts in motor vehicle cases and require all auto registrants to purchase specified PIP benefits. Some of the states in this category have a "verbal threshold" that defines the seriousness of the injuries (for example, total or partial loss of a bodily member or bodily function, permanent disability or disfigurement, or death) beyond which the right to sue is allowed. The remaining states with modified no-fault plans set a monetary damages threshold that, if exceeded, allows auto accident victims to sue.

A few of the no-fault states give auto owners the choice to either retain the right to sue or to accept some limitations on their right to sue. Those who accept limitations on their right to sue are charged lower auto liability insurance premiums.

Because the right to sue is not entirely eliminated, organizations that use autos still should obtain auto liability insurance or adopt some other risk management technique for handling their auto liability loss exposure. In addition, each state has either an auto financial responsibility law or a compulsory liability insurance law requiring motorists to carry minimum amounts of auto liability insurance.

Workers Compensation and Employers Liability Loss Exposure

An employer's responsibility to pay claims under workers compensation statutes is a common example of liability imposed by statute. In the context of this discussion, the term "workers compensation statutes" includes the various state workers compensation statutes as well as federal statutes, such as the U.S. Longshore and Harbor Workers' Compensation Act, that have essentially the same effect as the state laws with regard to certain classes of employees.

In addition to payments required by workers compensation statutes, an employer may also be held liable for occupational injuries or illnesses of its employees as a result of either tort suits or hold-harmless agreements to which the employer is a party.

Employees' Tort Suits Against Employers

The typical workers compensation statute is intended to provide an "exclusive remedy" for occupational injury or illness to all employees subject to the law. Exclusive remedy means that the only remedy available to an injured employee under workers compensation is to recover, on a no-fault basis, the benefits required by the applicable statute.

In practice, various exceptions, such as these, allow a covered employee (or a spouse or family members) to make a tort claim against the employer:

- Claims for employee injury caused intentionally by the employer
- Claims by the employee's spouse for loss of consortium as a result of employee injury caused by the employer's negligence or other torts
- Claims for injury resulting from the employer's negligence or torts while acting in some capacity other than employer

Workers compensation statutes exempt some types of employees—for example, farm workers, domestic workers, occasional laborers, real estate agents, and employees who are members of the employer's own family. These employees retain the right to make tort claims against their employers for occupational injury or illness resulting from the employer's wrongful acts or omissions.

Hold-Harmless Agreements

An employer's liability for the injuries of employees can also be assumed under contract. An employer who agrees to indemnify another party against certain types of claims may be agreeing (sometimes unknowingly) to indemnify the other party for claims made by the employer's own employees against the other party. See the exhibit "Liability for Employee Injury Assumed Under Contract."

> ### Liability for Employee Injury Assumed Under Contract
>
> Miguel, a building contractor, agreed in his construction contract with Emma to indemnify her for any bodily injury or property damage claims made against her in connection with his work at her premises.
>
> Carl, one of Miguel's employees, was injured because of a dangerous condition at the building site for which Emma was responsible. Although he was eligible for workers compensation benefits, Carl made a negligence claim against Emma because he believed that the damages recoverable in a tort suit would be greater than workers compensation benefits. Workers compensation statutes do not prohibit covered employees from suing persons other than their employers for occupational injuries or diseases.
>
> Apart from his regular workers compensation obligations, Miguel was legally obligated by contract to indemnify Emma for damages resulting from Carl's suit. This case illustrates how an employer (or the employer's insurer) can end up paying for injury to the insured's own employee despite the fact that workers compensation is considered to be the exclusive remedy for on-the-job injuries of employees.

[DA04741]

ASSESSING AND TREATING LEGAL AND REGULATORY RISK

Knowing how to apply legal and regulatory risk assessment to the facts of a case is an important skill. By carefully considering the facts provided and answering the Knowledge to Action questions, this activity should help you make the transition from knowing risk assessment considerations to knowing how to apply that knowledge.

Case Facts

You are the risk management professional for a property development company that owns several large shopping malls and two hotels. You are in the process of renegotiating the liability insurance program that is due for renewal in three months. As part of this process, you must assess the organization's legal and regulatory risk and determine risk treatment options.

Overview of Steps

Your work includes these two steps:

- Risk assessment
- Risk treatment

Risk Assessment

Risk assessment includes risk identification and risk analysis. As part of risk identification, the risk management professional should consider the causes and sources of risk.

Knowledge to Action

Which one of these sources of legal liability includes wrongful acts classified as torts?

a. Contracts

b. Statutes

c. Negligence

d. Regulations

Feedback: c. Negligence is the source of legal liability that includes the wrongful acts classified as torts.

The risk management professional should also identify commercial liability loss exposures. The organization can be held financially responsible for injuries to individuals or organizations for liability arising from these loss exposures.

Knowledge to Action

Describe the premises and operations liability loss exposure for this property development company.

Feedback: The premises and operations liability loss exposure relates to liability from bodily injury or property damage caused by an accident that occurs on the organization's owned, leased, or rented premises. The organization's liability is usually based on its failure to exercise the appropriate degree of care owed to others.

The property management company contracts with a security firm to handle all security matters at its malls and hotels.

Knowledge to Action

Describe the requirements for a contract to be enforceable.

Feedback: These are the four basic requirements for an enforceable contract:

• Agreement—One party makes an offer that the other party accepts.

• Consideration—Each party gives up something of value.

- Capacity to contract—The parties must have the legal ability to enter into contracts.
- Legal purpose—The contract must have a legal purpose.

As part of risk analysis, the risk management professional should consider the consequences of risk events.

Knowledge to Action

A customer trips getting on an escalator at one of the malls owned and operated by this property development company. The customer suffers significant injuries and initiates a civil suit against the company.

Describe the types of monetary damages the company may have to pay if found negligent in this case.

Feedback: A wrongdoer in a civil case will have to pay compensatory damages to the injured customer. Compensatory damages include special damages for expenses such as medical costs or lost wages and general damages for losses such as pain and suffering.

Risk Treatment

Risk treatment involves considering ways to modify the consequences of identified risks. The likelihood of litigation can be modified through contractual limitation of tort liability.

Knowledge to Action

Explain how the property development company could use hold-harmless agreements to remove or limit liability from its tenants.

Feedback: The property development company could use hold-harmless agreements in the leases with stores and other tenants in the malls. Such agreements would require these tenants to hold the property management company harmless from claims made by third parties who are injured by the tenants' negligence—for example, if a customer in a restaurant within the mall were to be injured as the result of falling on a spill that had not been cleaned up by restaurant staff. The property management company's liability would be limited related to the customer's injuries based on the hold-harmless agreement.

Hazard control is another method to modify the likelihood of legal risks. It involves implementing risk control measures within the operation.

Knowledge to Action

Describe some of the risk control areas that would be of particular concern to the risk management professional for the two hotel operations.

Feedback: For the hotels, the risk management professional would consider housekeeping and maintenance in the parking lots, building exits and entrances, and all walking surfaces. Stairways, elevators, and escalators are another risk control area to be considered.

The property management company enters into many contracts throughout the year, and the risk management professional is considering measures to reduce the consequences of contractual liability.

Knowledge to Action

Which one of the following is a measure that can be taken to reduce the loss associated with contractual liability?

a. Comparative negligence

b. Legal privilege

c. Risk avoidance

d. Liquidated damages provision

Feedback: d. A liquidated damages provision limits the amount for which the management company might otherwise be held liable.

Another area of concern for the risk management professional is compliance with statutes and regulations in the various jurisdictions where the organization operates.

Knowledge to Action

Describe the measures the risk management professional should take to assist the organization in modifying the likelihood of statutory liability.

Feedback: To modify the likelihood of statutory liability, the risk management professional must understand the statutory compliance requirements that apply to the shopping mall and hotel operations. Internal experts or external consultants can assist with this process. Legal libraries can also provide information on statutory requirements.

Review Questions

1. Identify the categories of the major bases of legal and regulatory risk

2. Distinguish between criminal law and civil law

3. List the three categories of wrongful acts that constitute torts

4. Explain how legal liability can arise from contracts

5. Describe the requirements of agreement for an enforceable contract

6. Explain how statutes modify the duties that organizations owe to others.

7. Identify the consequences of criminal acts

8. Identify the two types of monetary damages that may be awarded in a civil suit

9. Explain why defense costs can be the most expensive loss for an organization

10. Describe the use of an injunction in a civil suit.

11. Identify the ways to treat the negative aspects of legal and regulatory risk

12. Describe the circumstances for which avoidance may be used as a risk treatment technique.

13. List the clauses that can be added to contracts to remove or limit liability.

14. Explain how unilateral notices can limit the likelihood of tort liability.

15. Explain how hazard control can be used to modify the likelihood of legal risk.

16. Describe the risk control areas a risk management professional should be concerned about for premises and operations risk exposures.

17. Describe the measures to reduce the likelihood of contractual liability.

18. Explain how a corporate code of conduct reduces the likelihood of statutory liability.

19. Identify the five defenses that are widely used in the litigation process.

20. Explain how participating in settlement negotiation can modify the consequences of tort liability.

21. Describe a defense used by organizations to modify the consequences of statutory liability.

22. Identify the two major legal systems.

23. Name the three stages of a typical civil-law case.

24. Describe the common-law legal system.

25. Explain why private-sector business legal principles, such as contracts and bankruptcy, are of little use within the socialist legal system.

26. Contrast public and private international law.

27. Define comity as it relates to private international law.

28. Explain the three areas of jurisdiction that courts in international cases must determine before presiding over a particular case.

29. The premises and operations liability exposure relates to liability for

bodily injury or property damage caused by accidents arising from two sets of circumstances. Describe them.

30. Name the three elements a plaintiff must prove in order to recover in a products liability suit based on strict liability in tort.

31. Briefly describe common law and statutory law approaches to imposing auto liability solely on the basis of auto ownership.

32. Explain what a plaintiff must show to establish an auto owner's liability for negligent entrustment.

33. Explain how under an auto no-fault law, a verbal threshold differs from a monetary damages threshold.

34. Describe the situations in which an employer might be sued by an employee (or family members of an employee) for work-related injury.

Application Questions

1. Snowplow Operator clears one foot of snow from the parking lot of Office Building without being asked to do so. Snowplow Operator submits an invoice, which Office Building refuses to pay.

   a. Describe the elements of an enforceable contract.

   b. Explain which element of an enforceable contract is missing for Snowplow Operator.

2. Alderton Trampoline Company (Alderton) makes trampolines for residential use. What risk control measures might Alderton use for its products

3. Waxton Road Building Contractor (Waxton) wants a bonus that rewards rapid completion included in its contract with the highway department. In addition to the bonus provision, explain how might the highway department further encourage Waxton to be on time?

4. The risk manager for a chain of grocery stores is in the process of assessing the organization's legal and regulatory risks. As part of this process, risk treatment options must also be considered.

   a. Describe the types of wrongful acts that constitute potential torts for this organization.

   b. Explain how the risk manager could use modifying the likelihood of an event as a risk treatment method for torts.

SUMMARY

Torts, contracts, statutes, and regulations form the basis of legal and regulatory risk. The financial consequences of litigation, breach of contract, or non-compliance with laws and regulations can be a substantial source of risk to an organization.

The consequences of legal and regulatory risk to an organization can take several forms, such as monetary damages, defense costs, indirect losses, and specific performance or injunction.

Risk avoidance, modifying the likelihood, and modifying the consequences are risk treatment methods for legal and regulatory risk. These methods can be applied to torts, contracts, and statutes.

Countries share legal approaches and concepts, which can be grouped into predominant families of law. In general, countries adopt legal systems that are either civil-law systems or common-law systems.

International law comprises public international law, which governs the interaction of nation states, and private international law, which governs disputes between individuals or corporations in different countries.

Liability loss exposures can be categorized in many ways that reflect insurance practices. Such categories include these:

- Premises and operations liability
- Products and completed operations liability
- Automobile liability
- Workers compensation and employers liability

You should now understand how to assess an organization's legal and regulatory risk exposures and recommend treatment options for modifying the likelihood and consequences of those risks.

ASSIGNMENT NOTE

1. Corporate Codes of Conduct, International Labour Organization, www.actrav. itcilo.org/actrav-english/telearn/global/ilo/code/main.htm (accessed February 9, 2012).

Direct Your Learning ▶▶

International Insurance

Outline

Insurers' Global Expansion

Methods of Engaging in International Business

Overview of International Insurance

Regulatory Compliance

Reverse Flow Business

International Insurance Solutions

Selecting International Insurance Solutions

Structuring an International Insurance Program

Captives and Multinational Insurance Programs

Summary

Educational Objectives

After learning the content of this assignment, you should be able to:

▷ Describe the strategic reasons, considerations, and approaches for insurers to expand their operations globally.

▷ Describe each of the methods a company can use to engage in international business, including key issues involved in each method:

- Foreign trade

- Foreign contractual relationships

- Foreign direct investments

▷ Explain how each of these factors, which vary by country, can affect a company involved in international business:

- General business-related laws and regulations in foreign countries

- Extraterritorial laws of the United States

- Insurance laws, systems, and market offerings

- Culture, customs, and language

▷ Describe each of these types of regulations that must be complied with when developing and administering an international insurance program:

- Regulations regarding nonadmitted insurance

- Regulations regarding compulsory coverages

- Regulations regarding mandatory participation in government insurance programs

- Regulations regarding permissible insurance activities

- Regulations regarding premium taxes

- Other regulations

4

▷ Describe reverse flow business in terms of the following:

- The methods of writing reverse flow business

- Underwriting considerations for reverse flow business

- The producer's role in writing reverse flow business

▷ Describe the characteristics, advantages, and disadvantages of each of these international insurance solutions:

- Territorial endorsements to United States policies

- International package policies

- Coverage from nonaffiliated local insurers ("local placements")

- Controlled master programs (CMPs)

▷ Given scenarios describing an organization's international loss exposures, select the most appropriate international insurance solution(s) from among the following:

- Territorial endorsements to United States policies

- International package policy

- Coverage from nonaffiliated local insurer(s) (local placements)

- Controlled master program

▷ Describe the options for structuring an international insurance program.

▷ Describe how a captive insurance company can be used to benefit a multinational insurance program.

International Insurance

INSURERS' GLOBAL EXPANSION

Global competition is now a factor in virtually every industry. Advances in communication and transportation, international trade agreements to lower trade barriers, and growth in emerging markets have led many businesses to expand into global markets. Global investment and expansion in the insurance industry, both by insurers based in the United States entering foreign markets and by foreign insurers entering U.S. markets, have increased significantly in recent years and are likely to continue to do so.

Insurers are increasingly expanding operations to foreign markets. These four topics provide a basic understanding of why and how insurers engage in global expansion:

- Trends in global expansion
- Strategic reasons for global expansion
- Global market considerations
- Approaches to global expansion

Trends in Global Expansion

Global commerce has been growing since the end of World War II. During the past two decades, this growth accelerated as a result of numerous trade agreements throughout the world, advances in transportation and communication, the influence of the Internet, and financial innovation. The insurance market, like the markets in other industries, has become a global market where U.S. insurers compete in many other countries and where insurers domiciled in other countries compete in the U.S.

The U.S. experiences a trade deficit in global insurance trade that has increased steadily since 1995. In 1995, the deficit was approximately $1 billion, less than 1 percent of the U.S. global insurance trade. In 2006, the deficit was about $24.3 billion, almost 10 percent.[1] In 2006, foreign-owned insurers wrote 13.6 percent of the nonlife U.S. insurance premiums, and U.S. insurers ceded 53.1 percent of reinsurance premiums to foreign-domiciled entities.

Meanwhile, the U.S. also continued to increase exports of insurance with a 19 percent increase in 2006 (reinsurance comprised 60 percent of this total). However, in the same year, imports of insurance into the U.S. increased by 18 percent (reinsurance comprised 90 percent of the total).[2]

These statistics express the increased global competition within the international insurance industry. While there is greater competition for U.S. insurers from foreign insurers within the U.S. market, growth of the U.S. market has been slowing. From a low rate of growth of 2.1 percent for all insurance premiums (life and nonlife), to a decline of 7.8 percent in 2009, the U.S. market offers low growth potential along with increased competition.

As indicated in the chart in the exhibit, almost all of the premium growth in property and casualty insurance is occurring in emerging markets. For example, the Chinese nonlife market grew by 18.6 percent in 2009. There is, therefore, a growth opportunity for U.S. insurers in global markets, especially in emerging markets. See the exhibit "Global Insurance Markets—2009."

Global Insurance Markets—2009

	Nonlife Premiums USD billion	Change versus 2008
Industrialized Countries	1486	-0.6%
United States	647	-1.8%
Germany	127	1.0%
Japan	107	-2.0%
United Kingdom	92	-3.1%
France	89	0.9%
Italy	54	-2.5%
Hong Kong	3	6.1%
Emerging Markets	249	2.9%
Latin America and Caribbean	67	4.3%
Central and Eastern Europe	67	-7.5%
South and East Asia	75	13.9%
Middle East and Central Asia	22	4.7%
Africa	17	0.4%
World	1735	-0.1%

swissre.com/media/media_information/pr_sigma2_2010.html [DA06391]

Strategic Reasons for Global Expansion

Key strategic reasons why insurers pursue global expansion are revenue growth, financial stability, and building global competitiveness.

Revenue Growth and Financial Stability

Revenue growth is the primary reason that insurers look to global expansion. Some insurance markets, including the U.S., are considered mature markets, meaning that there are few new potential customers. In a mature market, competition for market share results in shrinking profit margins and companies will look for new opportunities for revenue growth. However, worldwide nonlife premium growth increased from $671 billion to more than $1.7 trillion between 1991 and 2009. Therefore, global markets, especially those in emerging economies (developing countries where the economy is growing rapidly) offer such growth opportunities.

Global expansion, particularly into emerging economy markets, also allows insurers to diversify operations and risks. Expanding into foreign markets has the benefit of allowing insurers to achieve these objectives:

- Greater stability during economic downturns—Spreading risks worldwide helps to counter the effects of economic downturn in a particular country. Furthermore, even in a worldwide recession, the potential for growth in emerging markets can offset loss of income from declines in premiums and investment returns. For example, in 2009, nonlife premiums dropped in the developed countries of the U.S., United Kingdom, and Japan, but increased in emerging markets.
- Diversification of risk—Spreading risk over a larger and more diverse base minimizes the impact of heavy losses in any one segment of the operation. This has long been the business model of international reinsurers who spread the risk of extreme natural catastrophes through globalization.

Global Competitiveness

Global expansion can increase an insurer's competitiveness in several ways. Through the growth from global expansion, an insurer may achieve economies of scale and efficiencies that allow it to compete more effectively in its domestic market as well as in the global market.

A global expansion strategy also provides an insurer with the technology and strategic resources to quickly expand into additional foreign markets or offer additional products when there is an opportunity. If an insurer waits to begin expansion until a market is developing, that insurer may lag behind other organizations that were more nimble in their ability to enter that market.

Insurers may also choose to expand in order to remain competitive in a specific specialty market. For example, an insurer specializing in mining risks or oil exploration may be better able to compete if it markets such coverage globally.

Global Market Considerations

Many companies pursue international growth strategies to build long-term financial strength. However, the decision to operate globally involves many variables. Management needs to determine the global markets to target, what products could be sold in other countries, what distribution channels should be used, and how regulations and government restrictions might affect global operations. Making these determinations is essential for an insurer to decide whether operating globally would improve its competitive advantage.

There are three key areas for an insurer to evaluate in making a strategic decision about expansion into a global market:

- Market analysis
- Economic considerations
- Political risks

Market Analysis

When a company is considering global expansion, it must analyze the insurance market in the country it plans to enter. Financial requirements, including capital and surplus, need to be evaluated. The company must also assess whether the potential return is worth the amount of capital that will need to be committed. Other factors include the ease of entry and the difficulty of withdrawal from the market. The competition from other insurers will also be included in this analysis. The insurer will consider whether it has any competitive advantage that it can use to provide leverage in the country where it plans to expand, such as a product offering that fits well in the market.

Distribution channels, the availability of producers, and underwriting practices are additional factors to analyze as well as whether these practices are compatible with the insurer's marketing and underwriting philosophy.

Other factors include cultural and language differences, and whether the insurer has the staff or can hire and manage the appropriate staff to overcome any linguistic or cultural barriers.

Economic Considerations

Insurers evaluating global expansion must also consider the host country's economic environment. Important considerations include the level of economic stability, monetary policies, the prevailing attitude toward foreign investors, and the potential for exchange-rate volatility. Other economic factors such as the country's gross domestic product or national income are also important, as is specific information including regulation, taxation, and premium tax requirements. Insurers will want to evaluate whether the country's economy is growing and whether there are any significant risks to economic growth on the horizon. For example, some countries that were growing rapidly may experience high levels of private and public debt that will restrain future growth potential.

Insurers need to have information regarding average personal income, disposable income, and the prevailing wages for various occupations in any country that is a potential market. This information is important, along with other demographic factors, to determine how many of the country's residents are potential consumers. Insurers also need to understand the wages they would need to pay employees in that country. Additionally, insurers considering expansion need to understand the laws and regulations that may affect them as potential employers.

Political Risks

Political risks are uncertainties faced by companies doing business in foreign countries that arise from the actions of host-country governments. These risks are greater in developing or emerging countries than in established countries with stable governments. Serious concerns include kidnap and ransom, terrorism, civil unrest, acts of war, revolution, and changes in government. Foreign nationals and their businesses can be at great risk in unsettled parts of the world. When considering global expansion, insurers often work with consultants who provide country reports or political risk scores to determine what political risks are present and how dangerous those risks are for foreign businesses.

Of greatest financial concern is the potential for the confiscation of business assets by a foreign government or other interference with the rights of ownership of corporate assets, such as confiscation of inventory. Expropriation occurs when a foreign government takes property without compensating its owners. This occurred in Cuba during the 1960s, when many U.S. firms had business properties and inventory expropriated as part of Cuba's regime change. This can also occur when a cash-strapped government seeks to seize businesses that generate high returns.

Foreign governments might also nationalize a business and compensate the owners, usually at a lower rate than the market value of the assets. For example, in 1956 the government of India enacted legislation to nationalize insurance, resulting in the takeover of all insurers including several foreign companies.

Companies are also concerned when countries treat local businesses more favorably than foreign businesses regarding taxes, government contracts, or access to required financing. Insurers will also evaluate the nature and extent of regulation. Several countries prohibit nonadmitted insurance or have laws requiring insurance to be written by local insurers for designated classes of business. For example, China requires insurers to be licensed by the China Insurance Regulatory Commission (CIRC) before they can write insurance in China.

Approaches to Global Expansion

Insurers who, after careful consideration, decide to expand into a global market may decide to form an alliance or joint venture with an existing insurer in that country, to merge with another insurer, to begin a new operation, or to acquire an existing foreign company.

Strategic alliance

An arrangement in which two companies work together to achieve a common goal.

Joint venture

A business association formed by an express or implied agreement of two or more persons (including corporations) to accomplish a particular project, such as the construction of a building.

- **Strategic alliance**—Strategic alliances have the advantages of bringing together separate areas of expertise and of gaining a host-country participant, who can access local markets and who is familiar with local laws, regulations, and customers. Such an alliance can provide a low-risk approach to quickly entering a new market. Strategic alliances include international licensing agreements (contractual agreement allowing one party to use another party's distribution system or trademark), and co-marketing/co-development agreements.

- **Joint venture**—A joint venture is a specific type of strategic alliance that involves shared ownership, shared responsibilities, and often joint management of the foreign venture. A joint-venture agreement brings together two companies to form a new organization that is legally separate and distinct from the parent companies, with its own management and directors. The most common form of joint venture occurs when a domestic company joins with a company from the country in which the operation is located. Joint ventures with governments or state-owned industries are referred to as public-private ventures and are common in India, China, Russia, and the former Soviet republics. Joint ventures allow companies to enter markets (both geographic and product markets) that would otherwise be beyond the reach of an individual company. For example, insurers wishing to expand into India commonly enter into joint venture agreements because India's law caps foreign direct investment for insurance.

Merger

A type of acquisition in which two or more business entities are combined into one.

- **Merger**—The advantage to merger is the ability to combine resources and reduce overhead expenses, allowing the new company to be more successful than the sum of the parties to the merger. International mergers carry a high degree of risk and are complicated by compliance with the regulations and antitrust laws of more than one country.

Subsidiary

A company owned or controlled by another company.

- Wholly owned **subsidiary**—Acquisition of, or formation of, a wholly owned subsidiary allows for direct ownership and control of assets in a foreign country. This presents the highest degree of business, political, and economic risk. Operating a subsidiary in a foreign country requires more capital than other methods of entering a foreign market, such as a joint venture, but also gives the domestic company greater control over operations. Acquiring an existing company generally results in faster entry into a market. However, establishment of a new company gives an insurer the greatest level of control over foreign affiliates because the parent company makes decisions about management, distribution channels, product mix, and other organization issues.

METHODS OF ENGAGING IN INTERNATIONAL BUSINESS

As more businesses seek to participate in international business, the insurance or risk management professional needs to know the different methods by which a company may get involved, as well as the key issues each method involves.

An organization can engage in international business through any of these methods, each of which involves different levels of investment and business risk:

- Foreign trade
- Foreign contractual relationships
- Foreign direct investments

Foreign Trade

Foreign trade is the importing and exporting of a product from one country to another. It is the most common method used to participate in international business, and, compared with other methods, is the one that requires the lowest level of investment and entails the least amount of **business risk**.

Key issues for organizations involved in foreign trade include both regulatory compliance and the formation of international sales contracts. Export and import controls imposed by the United States government are important regulatory concerns, while international sales contract concerns include terms of sale and methods of payment.

Business risk

Risk that is inherent in the operation of a particular organization, including the possibility of loss, no loss, or gain.

Export Controls

Any kind of good that is sent from the United States to another country is an export. The form of transfer—shipment by carrier, mail, airplane courier, or facsimile—is subject to governmental controls. Any item, even if it leaves the country only temporarily or is not for sale (for example, a gift), is subject to control.

Most exports do not require a license and are sent to other countries under the No License Required (NLR) designation. Some goods require a Commerce Export License, which must be obtained from the Bureau of Industry and Security (BIS). BIS is responsible for implementing and enforcing the Export Administration Regulations (EAR), which regulate the export and re-export of most commercial items. These goods are often referred to as dual-use items, because they have both commercial and military applications.

Any goods may be subject to a classification system determined by the U.S. Department of Commerce. The Department of Commerce assigns a specific alphanumeric code to goods known as an Export Control Classification

Number (ECCN); all ECCNs are listed in the Commerce Control List (CCL). The classification of the good determines its licensing requirements.

Once the classification is determined, the country of destination and end user are reviewed. Depending on the geopolitical climate, some classifications of goods may be prohibited from sale. Other types of goods are classified as EAR99, not subject to the CCL. Generally these items do not require a license in many situations.

The EAR does not control all goods, services, and technologies; other U.S. government agencies regulate more specialized items.[3] The Office of Foreign Assets Control (OFAC) of the U.S. Department of the Treasury administers and enforces economic and trade sanctions as determined by U.S. foreign policy and security objectives. OFAC operates under Presidential national emergency powers as well as authority granted by legislation. OFAC imposes controls on transactions and can freeze assets under U.S. jurisdiction.

OFAC may prohibit trade or financial transactions and other dealings by U.S. entities based on national policy and national security goals. Prohibitions vary and must be reviewed. OFAC may provide for a general license authorizing certain transactions, or it may provide a specific license on a case-by-case basis, depending on the circumstances.

Insurers participating in worldwide insurance markets through global insurance policies can insure global risks without violating U.S. sanctions law by inserting policy language that explicitly excludes risks violating U.S. sanction laws. For example, such a clause in an ocean marine cargo policy would read, "…whenever coverage provided by this policy would be in violation of any U.S. economic or trade sanctions, such coverage shall be null and void." This type of exclusion prevents OFAC compliance problems and ensures that insurance and risk assumption will not be extended to sanctioned countries, entities, or individuals.

If the insurer cannot use the exclusionary language, OFAC also allows for an insurer to apply for a specific OFAC license in order to compete in international insurance markets. A separate license is required for an insurer to pay claims arising under any authorized global policy. OFAC regulations supersede all state regulations, regulating an insurer's ability to decline policies, cancel policies, or withhold claim payments.

Import Controls

The U.S. regulates the import of goods by using one or a combination of four techniques:

- Tariffs
- Quotas
- Licenses
- Prohibited imports

Many goods are imported into the U.S. because it is cheaper to manufacture them in another country. Tariffs are a tax, or duty, assessed on goods imported into the U.S. The tariff is *ad valorem*, a percentage of the price added to the sales price of the goods. The tariff increases the item price for the U.S. consumer, which may make a similar good produced in the U.S. more attractive to the American consumer. The tariff helps to eliminate the cost advantage of the imported good, protecting its American manufacturers and distributors.

Import duties are collected by the U.S. Customs Service. Goods are unloaded from carriers and stored in warehouses until the shipments are examined. Formal entry into the U.S. is made through the presentation of documentation describing the goods for classification so that the correct import duties are assessed.

Quotas are limits on the amount of a good that may be imported into the U.S. Often the good can be manufactured or otherwise produced at a cheaper cost. The imported good, if brought into the U.S. for sale in the quantity American consumers would buy, may provide sufficient supply at a price that precludes American producers from competing. Limiting the amount of a good that is already made in the U.S. protects the American producer.

Licensing, the third method of control of imports, is granted by a country's government. By requiring a license to conduct business, the government ensures that a good will be imported into the country on more favorable terms than if domestic companies competed for the goods for use or resale.

Prohibited imports are goods that are illegal to be imported and sold in the U.S. Obvious examples of prohibited imports are marijuana and cocaine.

International Sales Contracts

International trade is facilitated by agreements between trading partner countries. The United Nations Convention of Contracts for the International Sale of Goods (CISG) provides for a uniform code for international contracts. Similar to the Uniform Commercial Code (UCC), which provides uniformity for commerce within the U.S., CISG provides rules for writing international contracts and transfer of goods under the contracts.

While the same sales contract may not be used by parties for all transactions, the contract terms should clearly define the venue by which any disputes would be decided (choice of law) and the method, timing, and currency of payment. The contract may define whether the goods are to be sold directly to consumers in the foreign country or whether any distributor(s) will be selected. Warranties for the goods may also be addressed in the contract.

Choice of law specified in the sales contract will address most issues regarding differences in contract law because the country, as well as the local jurisdiction (such as state, province, or municipality), is specified in the contract. The method of payment ensures compliance with import and export financial regulations. Timing determines cash flow and delivery dates. Choice of currency addresses the risk associated with inflation and currency fluctuations on the international market.

Often, international sales contracts will include a *force majeure* (French for "superior force") clause. Essentially, incorporating this clause in the international contract frees all parties from obligation when an extraordinary event or circumstance beyond the control of the parties (such as war, strike, riot, earthquake, or volcanic eruption) prevents one or both parties from fulfilling their obligations under the contract.

Selling Terms

The selling terms agreed to by the seller and buyer and referenced in the contract of sale are a key issue in foreign trade.

The selling terms in a contract of sale typically follow standards expressed in either the *Revised American Foreign Trade Definitions (RAFTD)* or the *Incoterms*. The *RAFTD* were adopted by a joint committee consisting of representatives of the Chamber of Commerce of the United States of America and other U.S. trade associations. The Incoterms, developed by the International Chamber of Commerce, are now more widely used in international trade than the *RAFTD*.

The details of all the various selling terms defined in the *RAFTD* and *Incoterms* are beyond the scope of this discussion. However, an example will illustrate how selling terms can affect the respective duties of the seller and buyer in an international sale of goods.

Assume that a French company purchases American-manufactured cloth-covered folding chairs. The chairs are shipped in a metal intermodal container carried on an oceangoing vessel from Philadelphia, Pennsylvania, to Le Havre, France. During the voyage, the goods are damaged by salt water when the container breaks because of a severe storm. The selling terms stipulated in the contract of sale will determine which party (the buyer or the seller) will bear the financial consequences of the loss.

If the selling terms are Free On Board (FOB) Philadelphia, the American firm (the seller) assumes all risk and costs incurred to place the goods safely aboard the vessel named by the buyer. Once the goods are on board the vessel, the French company (the buyer) assumes the risk of loss or damage and must both pay the transportation costs (freight) and obtain cargo insurance if it wishes to insure the shipment.

If, instead of FOB selling terms, the selling terms are Cost, Insurance, and Freight (CIF) Le Havre, the seller's and buyer's responsibilities for loss are essentially the same as under FOB terms. However, under CIF terms, the seller must arrange and pay for ocean transportation to the named port and purchase cargo insurance covering the goods until they reach their destination. Thus, in the example, the buyer would still bear the risk of loss during the ocean voyage, but the cargo insurance purchased by the seller would indemnify the buyer.

In addition to addressing who bears the risk of loss, who pays freight costs, and who pays for insurance, selling terms also address issues such as these:

- Seller's duty to provide the goods and the commercial invoice in conformity with the contract of sale
- Seller's duty to assist the buyer in obtaining an export license or other authorization needed to export the goods
- Seller's duty to place the goods at the disposal of the buyer at the named place of delivery or on board a vessel named by the buyer
- Buyer's duty to pay the price stated in the contract of sale
- Buyer's duty to obtain any import license or other authorization needed to import the goods
- Buyer's duty to take delivery of the goods as agreed

Methods of Payment

Despite the selling terms, the seller is actually exposed to loss until it receives the buyer's payment for the goods. The buyer might be unable to make its payment, or may refuse to pay because the goods are damaged or do not meet the specifications agreed upon. The seller usually will define the method of payment in the sales contract. These are four possible methods of payment:

- Cash in advance—Funds deposited prior to receipt of the goods. This is a double disadvantage to the buyer. First, the buyer loses the time advantage of the funds, which is the use of the funds for other investment opportunities. Second, if the seller fails to ship the goods, the buyer may have difficulty recovering the funds.

- Open account—A rotating charge account under which the buyer settles the account at determined intervals. An open account is usually established only if there is a long-term relationship between buyer and seller.

- Draft—A written order by a first party, called the "drawer" (the seller), to the second party, called the "drawee" (the buyer), to pay funds to a third party, called the "payee," or to the bearer of the draft. The seller uses the draft drawn on the customer and sells it to the bank; the bank then discounts the draft. In consideration of the discount charge, the bank uses its money to finance the shipment. The seller is paid the discounted value of the sale and does not have working capital tied up waiting for payment. If the drawee (buyer) refuses to pay, the bank has recourse against the seller. So, until the buyer pays the draft, the seller is still exposed to loss if the goods are lost or damaged in transit.

- Letter of credit (LOC)—The buyer establishes credit with a local bank, which then contacts a bank in the seller's country, establishing a credit in favor of the seller. The seller then receives a letter of credit in confirmation of the credit. If the seller is domiciled in the U.S., the letter of credit is called an "export letter of credit." If the buyer is domiciled in the U.S., the letter of credit (in favor of the foreign seller) is called an "import letter of credit." The LOC specifies what the seller must do to access the credit. If the LOC requires an insurance certificate or policy, the certificate or policy must be prepared exactly as stipulated. When the seller comes to use the credit, the seller follows the same procedures as though drawing a draft on the buyer and presents the documents to the bank that issued the credit. The seller immediately receives money from this bank, and if the letter of credit is properly drawn, there is no recourse against the seller. Letters of credit that have this no-recourse feature are called "irrevocable letters of credit." Revocable letters of credit are rarely used. The revocable letter merely states the manner in which payment is to be made. It provides no protection for the seller because it can be canceled or amended without notice to the seller.

Foreign Contractual Relationships

A second method for conducting international business is through the use of foreign contractual relationships. In comparison with foreign trade, foreign contractual relationships increase business risk and resource commitment. Two main types of foreign contractual relationships are product licensing and franchising.

Product Licensing

Product licensing is permission granted by one company to another to manufacture its product or to use its distribution facilities or technology. The licensing of products between different countries can occur for three primary reasons:

- A company may decide that selling its product in the second country is economically unfeasible because of labor costs, transportation costs, or regulations.

- A company may decide that it does not have the time or resources to produce the product in another country.

- A company may lack sufficient knowledge about the country's legal, political, social, and business environments.

Licensing technology includes granting the right to use, under specified conditions, the company's intellectual property, such as copyright, trademark, or patents. For example, a common license agreement provides for licensing computer software. A company does not buy the software program in a legal sense, but buys the right to use the program and agrees to do so under set conditions.

Just as software firms are concerned about the illegal use of their products, one of the major considerations for any firm granting a license to a foreign firm is protecting its assets. Before entering into any agreement, the domestic company assesses the trustworthiness of the foreign company it is dealing with and the foreign company's ability to meet the financial requirements of the licensing agreement.

Thoroughly understanding the foreign legal environment regarding copyright, trademark, and patent protection is necessary. A company should consult a lawyer who is an expert in the intellectual property field about global intellectual property legal issues.

Franchising

Franchising occurs when one company assigns to another the right to supply its products or services within a market. A franchise is a contract entered into for a specific time period. The franchisee (who receives the franchise) pays a royalty to the franchisor (who grants the franchise) for the rights assigned, in addition to other possible considerations. The franchisor provides training, technical assistance, specialized equipment, advertising, and promotion as stated in the agreement.

In franchising, the company image and its name are the franchisor's assets. The franchisor allows the franchisee to use its image and certain assets.

An important aspect of franchising is the control over the use of the company's name and the quality of the product or service. For example, many franchisors retain control over all advertising and pricing of products in the markets. Some companies control the risk of improper use of the corporate name or the risk of poor product or service quality by withholding vital technology or required component products. For example, a hotel chain can maintain control of its reservation system, or a grocery cooperative can maintain control of all product distribution.

Foreign Direct Investment

A third method to conduct foreign trade is foreign direct investment, which occurs when a company in one country acquires control over assets located in another country. This type of investment also anticipates managerial control of the assets acquired in the foreign market. This arrangement contrasts with foreign portfolio investment, which occurs when a company purchases foreign stocks, bonds, or other financial instruments. Foreign direct investment usually takes one of two forms, known as subsidiaries and joint ventures.

Subsidiaries

A subsidiary is a company owned or controlled by another company. A subsidiary might be subject to the parent company's complete or partial control. Generally, a company is not a subsidiary unless another company controls 50 percent or more of its shares.

A distinguishing characteristic of a subsidiary, as opposed to a joint venture, is that a subsidiary issues stock. The stock can be 100 percent owned by the parent company, or some of the shares can be publicly traded in the foreign market. In fact, joint ventures are often subsidiaries in which the partners each own a percentage of the stock. In many foreign markets, the government requires a company to form a subsidiary to bring the parent firms and subsidiaries under the local laws of incorporation. These local laws can require both the subsidiary and the parents to comply with local financial reporting and disclosure.

The fully owned subsidiary provides a company with the highest level of control over operations, but presents the highest level of business risk, commitment of capital, and managerial control. With higher risk, a company expects to achieve higher returns. For a company experienced in international operations, this trade-off between risk and return can be acceptable and even desirable.

The time required for a company to enter a foreign market using a subsidiary varies, depending on the entry technique the company chooses or requires. Acquiring an existing company in the foreign market can usually occur relatively quickly. Conversely, if a company develops its subsidiary from the ground up, it might take years to become relevant in the foreign market. This latter approach probably gives the company the greatest control over its foreign affiliates, because the parent company would develop the local management, distribution channels, and product mix. However, this approach also requires a larger investment of resources and time.

Joint Ventures

In the international trade context, a joint venture involves shared ownership and control of a foreign operation. Joint ventures allow a company to enter either a geographic or product market and to acquire technology or revenue that would not otherwise be within reach.

The most common joint arrangement involves a company joining forces with a second company to operate a joint venture in the second company's country. Less common are joint ventures formed by companies from two different countries to operate in a third country. Additionally, companies rarely enter into joint ventures with more than three partners.

Like subsidiaries, joint ventures increase companies' business risk and commitment of resources. A company might have to invest substantial capital or share proprietary technology with its joint venture partners. However, the value of the joint venture can be greater than the sum of the individual partners' contributions.

In some joint ventures, partner companies divide capital expenses among themselves and share the costs, depending on the market and the partners' preferences. Additionally, engaging in a joint venture requires a company to commit substantial managerial resources and might require considerably more time to enter a foreign market than to enter a domestic joint venture or acquire a subsidiary.

Perhaps the single most important aspect of forming a joint venture is choosing the right partner or partners. This choice is important because the companies share resources, managerial responsibilities, technology, and profits, among other things.

A company may choose foreign direct investment over foreign trade for a number of reasons. Barriers to trade, both those occurring naturally (for example, transportation costs and language and cultural differences) and otherwise (for example, tariffs, quotas, or political issues) contribute to a company's need to gain direct access to markets through direct investment.

Companies seeking direct foreign investment fall into three general categories:

- Resource seekers—Companies that enter a foreign market seeking that country's resources, such as oil reserves, lower-cost labor, or technology

- Market seekers—Companies that enter a foreign market to acquire new customers outside their own countries' boundaries

- Market followers—Companies that follow their customers into foreign countries, a common trend in service industries such as insurance and banking

OVERVIEW OF INTERNATIONAL INSURANCE

As American businesses expand globally, they face significant loss exposures. Developing insurance programs to cover such exposures requires familiarity with international business-related laws and regulations, as well as with the local laws, insurance systems, and cultures of other countries.

The globalization of American business is one of the strongest drivers of growth in the United States economy, as U.S.-based companies capitalize on increased opportunities to do business with both established trade partners in Europe and emerging markets such as Latin America, China, and India. According to analysts from Standard & Poor's, as of May 2012, more than 47 percent of revenue from firms listed in the S&P 500 stock index emanates from overseas sources,[4] and smaller companies are rapidly following suit.

However, businesses operating on foreign shores face unique dangers, complex risks, and significant loss exposures. Sales in a new country may be subject to corporate licensing, consumer protection, and product safety laws, creating a need for localized liability insurance. Companies opening foreign offices, plants, ventures, or subsidiaries must address common property risks, such as fire or weather-related losses, but also must be familiar with the diverse patchwork of coverages available in each country to protect people and financial assets. In some cases, companies may encounter new or unfamiliar risks. For example, a country may require minimum liability coverage for professional or medical liability; assets may be nationalized; or strikes, riots, or civil commotion may result in ancillary loss of profits.

Further, the availability of certain kinds of insurance differs widely by location, often affected by national insurance schemes or systems. Local culture, customs, and language also can significantly affect insurance transactions. Accordingly, there is no one-size-fits-all international insurance policy, and programs covering global businesses must be tailored to a company's dimensions.

General Business-Related Laws and Regulations in Foreign Countries

To prepare for determining what insurance coverages are needed for its international operations, a company should research a number of legal issues. Each jurisdiction has unique laws and regulations dictating how a foreign company can obtain a license, pay taxes, and conduct business. Even within a country, laws—particularly corporate, employee health and safety, and property-related laws such as leases—may differ from region to region and town to town. Failure to adhere to these laws can result in fines, fees, or penalties and may delay licensing approvals or even prohibit companies from doing business altogether.

From an insurance or risk assessment perspective, an even broader review of laws and regulations may be necessary to fully understand the exposures a company faces in each region in which it does business.

Laws Affecting Claims and Losses

To build an effective insurance program, a company must consider "noninsurance" laws potentially related to its products, services, or operational facilities. Wide variations may exist with respect to environmental laws, building codes, consumer protection, and worker health and safety, for example. Local laws can frequently determine the kinds of liability or contractual claims that could arise or the types of losses that could be incurred. For example, Shari'ah Law in some Middle Eastern countries does not recognize economic losses; in these countries, risk is reduced because a plaintiff has less recourse for damages.

Two major questions for companies to research are "What legal theories affect whether a third-party claimant can bring a lawsuit?" and "How can such theories affect a casualty policy?" For example, European Union (EU) and Asian directives have adopted a legal standard of strict liability for defective products in addition to providing more specific safety mandates. Examples of this standard in Asia include those imposed by the Consumer Protection Law in Taiwan and by the Toys and Children's Product Safety Ordinance in Hong Kong. Under both laws, retailers and manufacturers have similar liability—and thus similar insurance needs—to their U.S. counterparts. Businesses operating in emerging markets where no such laws exist may need different, or less, coverage.

Settlement of Claims and Disputes

A related question is how claims or disputes are resolved in specific jurisdictions. This issue is partly legal, related to how a country's administrative and court systems are set up, and partly cultural. While the U.S. and the United Kingdom (U.K.) have common-law court systems providing for trial by jury for many matters, other countries that follow a common-law system, such as Germany and India, prefer hearing civil cases before a sole judge.

Some countries avoid litigation at all costs, so companies may go to greater lengths to resolve differences by agreement or settlement. For example, the Japanese, who place personal relationships over the idea of legal protection, dislike contracts and formal written agreements. They rarely consult lawyers concerning disputes, preferring to settle disagreements privately. Courts are a last resort, and such matters as car accident coverage disputes are frequently arbitrated.

Additional considerations relate to how judgments or settlements in overseas disputes are enforced and how claims are paid. Many countries are parties to international treaties providing for the enforcement of a judgment by a foreign corporation, but such enforcement is not a universal right. The legal and practical ability to attach property or seize assets varies from country to country, and questions may arise about whether claims must be paid in local currency if a local policy is required.

Extraterritorial Laws of the United States

A U.S. company doing business internationally must also be aware of U.S. laws that not only apply to its U.S. operations but that govern its behavior in other jurisdictions. Many of these laws have foreign counterparts that can be more or less restrictive. Such laws may involve anti-bribery, anti-money-laundering, trade sanctions, and privacy and data protection. Some apply specifically to insurance company practices; others may affect any business's loss exposures.

Anti-Bribery Laws

The U.S. Foreign Corrupt Practices Act (FCPA) of 1977 is an example of an anti-bribery law. It prohibits companies "in interstate commerce" from paying bribes or giving kickbacks to foreign government officials "for the purpose of influencing any act of that foreign official in violation of the duty of that official, or to secure any improper advantage in order to obtain or retain business."[5] The law provides for both criminal and civil penalties for violations.

In the U.K., the Bribery Act of 2010 applies to acts of bribery both within the U.K. and internationally. It defines bribery as promising or giving a financial or other advantage to anyone—not just to public officials. It also expands the notion of accepting a bribe to include agreeing to accept or receive a financial or other advantage.

Directors and officers liability (D&O) policies may provide coverage for company expenses related to defense of bribery-related violations, investigations, and proceedings. However, D&O policies generally do not cover fines or penalties assessed against a company if an illegal act has been proven.

Anti-Money-Laundering Laws

Anti-money-laundering laws prohibit companies from conducting certain kinds of transactions that help obscure the true source of money generated from illegal activities, such as drug dealing, gambling, or theft. Many countries have enacted legislation, or are considering steps, to prevent, foil, and catch a growing population of money launderers, many of whom are connected to large organized-crime networks.

While many anti-money-laundering laws are targeted to banks and insurers, which are charged with monitoring customer transactions for indicators of fraud, global business may inadvertently become entangled in money-laundering schemes. For example, a casino may exchange cash for chips with an individual, only for the individual to cash in those chips for a casino's bank check and to deposit the check as "winnings." Also, real estate may be bought with illicit funds and then sold, or entire businesses can be created with illicit funds and then sold. The income from such sales appears for all purposes to be legitimate.

Trade Sanction Laws

Trade sanction laws make it illegal for companies to do business, directly or individually, with certain governments, citizens, or businesses. These laws are generally enacted by one or more countries against another country for political reasons, either as punitive measures against, or to force certain behaviors of, governments that have violated international laws.

In the U.S., sanctions programs are administered by the U.S. Treasury Department's Office of Foreign Assets Control (OFAC). OFAC regulations ban all dealings between U.S. persons and "sanctions targets"—countries such as Cuba, Iran, Burma (Myanmar), and Sudan, plus more than 5,000 individuals and entities, referred to as Specially Designated Nationals (SDN). Money earned from prohibited transactions can be seized, and civil and criminal penalties can be assessed. Similar sanctions lists are issued by Canada and the EU, and a separate list is maintained by the U.K. Each country's list is unique and may need to be reviewed.

OFAC enforcement initiatives against insurers and their clients have resulted in fines into the hundreds of millions of U.S. dollars.[6] Because of these regulations, insurers not only may be prevented from issuing policies in specific countries but may be hesitant to write policies in surrounding countries, where trade with a business in a sanctioned nation might occur.

Privacy and Data-Protection Laws

Over the past ten years, more than 100 countries have developed extensive laws protecting the privacy of individuals' information collected by companies. With the explosion of Internet communications and business dealings, information protection is a rapidly growing target of government regulation and legislation worldwide. Generally, information that companies now need to protect includes personal identifying characteristics (name, address, and government ID number), finances (bank account, credit card number, and credit rating), and protected health data and history (illnesses, disease, medications, and doctors).

Privacy laws differ from country to country and often conflict. In the U.S., they also vary by state. Application of the laws can be extraterritorial; that is, companies may be held to have violated the laws of the domicile of a policyholder, claimant, or potential customer even if the related data is sent, maintained, or released in another country without privacy laws.

Complying with the myriad privacy and data-protection laws is a challenge and a major financial investment for many international operations. Failure to comply typically results in steep fines and can subject a company to litigation by both governments and individuals, even if the noncompliance is accidental. Insurance for privacy breaches is becoming more widely available in the U.S. and Europe but may not be available in all countries. Such insurance generally covers only the cost of providing notice of breach and perhaps credit monitoring or similar incidental costs. Customer business lost because of a breach, and the resulting damage to the company's reputation, is not readily insurable.

Insurance Laws, Systems, and Market Offerings

Insurance systems and market offerings vary widely from country to country. A country may have an obligatory national insurance scheme, or insurance may be provided only through a national insurer. Companies contemplating expanding into other countries should also research issues such as prohibitions against purchasing **nonadmitted insurance**; the availability of financial assistance for personal injury or property damage through noninsurance means, including government benefits and social programs and government-sponsored insurance; and the general local market for, and availability of, certain lines of insurance.

Nonadmitted insurance
Insurance provided in a jurisdiction by an insurer that is not licensed to do business within that jurisdiction.

Nonadmitted Insurance

One of the first considerations in securing insurance for international business is whether a locally purchased policy is legally required. Many countries require insurance on local property or for the benefit of its citizens to be written by a locally licensed or locally authorized insurer. In some areas, writing nonadmitted insurance is a legal offense. Violators are subject to fines, and local claimants are prohibited from recovering under such policies. In addi-

Admitted insurance

Insurance provided in a jurisdiction by an insurer that is licensed to do business in that jurisdiction.

tion, the branch companies themselves may face legal actions or fines for failing to purchase compulsory **admitted insurance** or for dealing with an unauthorized company. Therefore, the purchase of a single global policy without any local policies for country operations is rare.

Other Financial Assistance via Government Resources

Whether insurance is required for a local risk and what level of coverage is necessary are contingent on the availability of alternative financial assistance for business and personal loss through government programs, social benefits, and local insurance systems. While there are many examples of the relationship between insurance and financial assistance, two of the more important involve schemes covering health/welfare and disaster risks.

In the U.S., private employer-sponsored health plans are supplemented by a network of state workers compensation programs. In contrast, other developed countries generally have some degree of government-sponsored national health programs. The potential for fraudulent schemes involving national social security, pensions, veterans' benefits, and disability programs should also be considered.

National schemes may also exist for covering property risks that are so unusual or extreme that private insurance coverage is difficult or impossible to get, such as war, riot, or terrorism. In the U.S., the Terrorism Risk Insurance Act (TRIA) of 2002 created a federal backstop for insurance claims related to acts of terrorism. The U.K. has had some form of terrorism insurance since the 1993 attacks by the Irish Republican Army, and after September 11, 2001, other countries, such as France, Germany, the Netherlands, and Australia, established permanent or temporary terrorism risk insurance programs that involve some degree of governmental participation. These programs aim to increase the availability of commercial insurance for terrorism-related loss.

Availability of Insurance for Specific Lines of Business

Finally, local market variances exist in the demand for and availability of certain lines of insurance. Auto lines and natural hazard lines, such as flood, are two examples of insurance coverages that are generally readily available in the U.S. but that may not be available in other countries.

Auto insurance is not compulsory in all countries. For example, South Africa allocates a percentage of the money from gasoline into a "road accident fund," which goes toward compensating accident victims. There are discrepancies in whether insurance, where available, covers the car or driver or both and whether physical damage or third-party liability is included. The price of insurance varies widely as well, depending on the relative safety of driving in a particular place.

Availability, terms, and conditions of natural disaster insurance also vary from one country to the next. Many foreign countries lack government-sponsored disaster programs, including flood and earthquake programs, or else offer them at premiums that are too high for most of the population and businesses.

Culture, Customs, and Language

The importance of researching and understanding the local language, culture, customs, traditions, politics, and business practices of each town, region, and country in which a company does business cannot be understated.

Understanding Local Ways

Up front, businesses must take into account many major, complex custom and cultural issues to run their foreign operations successfully. They must evaluate local socioeconomic conditions, religion, government or political structure and degree of stability, and general risks of physical danger, such as the potential for war, riots, and kidnapping. Also, there are practical, everyday issues to consider, such as differences in holidays, attitudes toward gender and race, and business practices (such as use of business cards, handshakes, entertaining etiquette, meeting protocol, and attire expectations).

In all business dealings, and particularly in global transactions, personal relationships are crucial. Failure to make a real effort to know the culture and people of a foreign site and to adhere to local customs and practices can lead to problems such as these:

- Business-licensing approval or legal-authorization difficulties
- Increased governmental fines and fees during operations, over time
- Disputes with partners, vendors, and/or suppliers
- Significant human resource issues
- Increased legal and financial claims against the company
- Failure to reach or connect with customers and potential employees

Use of Language and Translations

While many countries use English as a common business language, the degree and extent of fluency fluctuates, and fluency should not be presumed. Learning at least the most common spoken phrases of the local market is necessary—to show courtesy, help build business relationships, and prevent losses through simple misunderstandings.

For all written documents, including insurance policies, a professional translator should be on hand as part of the network of both the company and its insurance broker or agent. Anyone translating a contract or other legal document should be a local resident or native speaker with a solid grasp of the grammatical and definitional intricacies needed to translate detailed industry-specific concepts. Some international translators specialize in various industries.

An additional concern related to insuring international operations is inconsistency in insurance-related terms and definitions. Standard terms for insurance liability and coverage concepts in the U.S. may mean something totally different in a foreign setting. For example, it is a fundamental concept in the U.S. that a purchaser of an insurance policy must have an "insurable interest" in the contract. Insurable interest may not have the same meaning in all countries, raising an inherent risk of fraud. Further, in some countries, "excess" insurance means the policy has a deductible instead of an additional layer of coverage, and builders risk insurance is called contracts and architects risk in the U.K. or other countries that follow U.K. practices. Also, in some countries, "motor" insurance does not cover a machine's engine, but the term may be used to refer to commercial auto insurance.

As a result of language differences, a broker or agent placing insurance for an international risk may have a heightened obligation to explain coverages more clearly, by location, highlighting any known ambiguities or differences in country-specific wordings. The broker should also work closely with local market insurance partners and strong legal advisers, whenever possible, to ensure that the coverage sought and ultimately purchased is what was intended for the client.

REGULATORY COMPLIANCE

When establishing an international insurance program, the insurer, broker, and client company must comply with all insurance-related regulations in each country that the policyholder has operations. Failure to conform to local laws can lead to a spectrum of consequences—including civil penalties, such as fines and loss of license, and criminal penalties, such as imprisonment—depending on the country and the severity of the infraction.

Most international insurers have dedicated regulatory compliance departments that help them monitor and adhere to myriad international regulations and that develop positive relationships with governmental agencies. Insurance brokers should also be familiar with the legalities of transacting insurance in foreign countries, and all parties involved in insurance transactions should continually assess and monitor changes in laws, business process rules, and local regulations.

Some legal concerns that arise from global insurance require the attention of top management—for example, capitalization and surplus issues, authorization and licensing of the insurer and its agents, the types of business the insurer will write, and the forms and policies the insurer will issue in various countries. Other legal concerns may involve managing relationships with vendors and customers, including determining how claims will be covered, processed, and paid; ensuring staff compliance; training staff; and managing and storing data and records relating to compliance.

In addition, many regulatory compliance issues relate to the everyday business of insurance, including placing coverage for an insurance program and meeting customers' needs. Underwriters, agents, and brokers must be aware of all regulations regarding these issues in any country in which they transact business, as these regulations can affect their activities and decisions. Regulations relate primarily to these subjects:

- Nonadmitted insurance
- Compulsory coverages
- Mandatory participation in government insurance programs
- Permissible insurance activities
- Premium taxes

A wide range of other regulations also affect insurance transactions.

Insurance professionals can get the information they need for regulatory compliance from various sources. Some of the largest international insurers and brokers maintain databases of key compliance information for all nations of the world. Other insurers and brokers obtain information through law firms, consultants, accounting companies, and services provided by commercial legal and business research publishers. One such publisher widely used in the international insurance arena is Axco Insurance Information Services. Axco insurance market reports are set out by territory and include up-to-date information on legal, compliance, and business requirements, as well as background information on the local political and business climate.

Nonadmitted Insurance

While each nation has its own insurance rules and regulations, a set of common legal principles could be considered universal in placing international insurance:

- Insurers must adhere to local insurance and corporate regulations.
- Licenses to do business must be held by the insurer, unless a legal exemption applies to permit nonadmitted insurance.
- Certain mandatory/compulsory coverage must be purchased by the insured, as required by local law.

An insurer must typically file a license or registration to do business in each country in which it intends to write. In most cases, such filing involves significant documentation of corporate business plans and activities and maintenance of a minimum level of capital and surplus. Nonadmitted insurance, sometimes referred to as unauthorized insurance, is coverage written by a company that is neither licensed nor registered to do business in the country where the property or risk is located.

Some countries permit businesses to buy nonadmitted insurance from insurers domiciled outside the jurisdiction. Further, some countries allow unauthorized insurers to assume some risks, while other countries limit business written by unauthorized companies by increasing regulatory oversight or assessing more taxes.

Similar to individual states in the United States, other countries require insurers to be authorized to ensure their solvency and ability to pay future claims. A country may also have underlying economic or political goals to favor domestic businesses. In either case, requirements for admitted insurance are typically aggressively enforced. Argentina, Brazil, China, France, India, Italy, and Russia are examples of nations that prohibit nonadmitted insurance with few exceptions. Canada, the United Kingdom (UK), Hong Kong, and Singapore typically allow nonadmitted insurers to write multiple classes of local business.

What happens if a business secures coverage from an insurer that is not licensed or authorized in the country where its loss exposures are located? In countries that prohibit nonadmitted insurance, fines are frequently imposed on the nonadmitted carrier, and in some jurisdictions, jail time is not uncommon. According to the new (draft) insurance law in Mexico, for example, nonadmitted insurers that offer their products in Mexico are subject to fines of up to 100,000 days' minimum salary, and guilty individuals may receive prison sentences of up to fifteen years.[7]

For the purchasing company, business consequences can include these:

- The insurance contract may be voided or canceled and the premium returned.
- Coverage may be nullified or not enforced.
- Claim payments may be limited, and claim defenses based on otherwise enforceable policy terms and conditions may be disallowed.
- Cross-border court judgments and/or mediation and settlement agreements may not be enforced.

A country may require purchase of some lines of coverage from admitted insurers because of concerns about insurer solvency in the face of the high risk and volume of claims and the effect of loss on the population. For example, nearly all countries require local admitted coverage for auto liability because auto accidents have a significant impact on individuals as well as the healthcare and social services provided within the locale.

Other major exposures that require admitted coverage are those that may result in serious personal injury or severe financial loss. Examples are workers compensation, employers liability, and professional liability coverage for resident lawyers, doctors, dentists, auditing companies, and certain classes of consultants operating internationally. Special rules may also apply to directors and officers liability insurance; errors and omissions liability insurance; specialty lines that cover such exposures as clinical trials, medical products, and dangerous or high-risk products; and environmental coverage. General liability coverage is also sometimes required to be provided by an admitted insurer.

Compulsory Coverages

Compulsory insurance is coverage that individuals or businesses are required by law to purchase before engaging in specific activities. In many cases, policy rates, forms, and statutory limits may also be predetermined by the government.

Similar to admitted insurance, the main purpose of compulsory coverage is to help protect the general population and ease the burden on public resources in the face of common or catastrophic injury claims. Compulsory insurance also helps maintain insurer solvency by ensuring that enough individuals and businesses purchase insurance from the carrier to avoid **adverse selection** and allow the insurer to underwrite and price the class effectively in accordance with the **law of large numbers**.

One of the most common examples of compulsory insurance is auto insurance. As in most U.S. states, many countries require individuals to provide proof of insurance when registering a vehicle or renewing a driver's license, or upon demand by law enforcement. Failure to maintain auto insurance can result in substantial fines, revocation of driving privileges, and, in some severe cases, jail sentences—particularly if the person has been in an accident. Mexico and France are among the long list of countries in which auto insurance is mandatory in some form. Workers compensation and employers liability are also commonly compulsory coverages.

Other compulsory coverages vary widely, often changing frequently in response to local social, economic, and political concerns. In France, for example, the list of compulsory coverages shown by Axco includes these:

- Third-party liability for cable cars, railroads, river transport, aviation, oil tankers, and the public transportation of passengers and goods
- Professional liability for individuals in more than seventy professions, including accountants, architects, auditors, barristers, insurance brokers, healthcare professionals, and financial advisers
- Construction coverage for private dwellings

Further, some elements of coverage may not be compulsory as stand-alone policies but may be required as additions to other insurance contracts. In France, for example, every property damage policy issued must include coverage for natural perils under the national natural catastrophe insurance program, as well as for windstorm and terrorism. Other types of activities may require specific types of bonds or financial guarantees in addition to traditional insurance.

Adverse selection

In general, the tendency for people with the greatest probability of loss to be the ones most likely to purchase insurance.

Law of large numbers

A mathematical principle stating that as the number of similar but independent exposure units increases, the relative accuracy of predictions about future outcomes (losses) also increases.

Mandatory Participation in Government Insurance Programs

Policyholders may also be required to participate in government insurance programs, pools, and associations. Loss exposures subject to government programs are generally those that may be susceptible to catastrophic consequences and have a perceived lack of availability in the traditional insurance and reinsurance markets. Catastrophe (flood, earthquake, and windstorm) and terrorism insurance are among the most popular kinds of government-sponsored insurance.

For example, in France, property policies must include coverage for certain natural catastrophe perils, with this extended coverage provided through a national natural catastrophe insurance program. France also has a mandatory terrorism insurance program and a mandatory third-party liability insurance guarantee fund that protects insureds that have—and insurers that provide—compulsory coverages such as construction and professional liability.

Other programs have been crafted in response to unique business and niche market needs. For example, France has sought to limit the medical malpractice exposure to doctors and has developed a program to provide government stop-loss coverages for practitioners above a certain limit per year, to supplement traditional insurance. As another example, as genetically modified organisms are increasingly used in the agricultural sector, insurance to cover contamination risks to neighboring farms when such organisms are used has been hard to develop privately.

Further, in some countries, certain types of insurance must be purchased from government-owned insurers. China had monopolistic national insurance in the past, and India currently owns at least six insurers. In Mexico, an agency of the federal government, the Mexican Institute of Social Security, provides the compulsory workers compensation insurance.

Around the world, government-owned or "nationalized" insurance companies are becoming less common, as many governments have moved to privatize their once-owned industry, either to reduce their government's financial risk, cut operating costs, or foster more international trade. However, state-sponsored insurers have been a significant market force over time and should be considered in any regulation review because foreign companies that must deal with state-sponsored insurers may not be eligible to write business in the state for certain classes or may be subject to heightened standards for registration and regulation.

Permissible Insurance Activities

Many countries have rules governing specific kinds of insurance activities. For example, their laws and regulations may broadly define the terms "negotiate"

or "negotiation," "sell" or "sale," and "solicit" or "solicitation" in the context of an insurance transaction.

In many cases, insurers must be registered or admitted in a country before they can undertake any activity that could be considered an insurance transaction or sale. Some activities may fall into a gray area, including performing risk audits, hiring third-party administrators, collecting or transmitting premiums, and signing contracts, even if negotiated or executed in another jurisdiction.

Claim-related activities may also be regulated, either through specific directives relating to the claim process or more generally as part of the insurance transaction. Accordingly, even if a policy was appropriately issued in one country, insurers must be aware of any claim regulations that may apply to negotiation or payment of claims in the country where a policyholder's offices are located, where a policyholder generally does business, where a claimant lives, or where a claim or loss has occurred.

Premium Taxes

Other major legal issues that insurers and brokers should consider when establishing an international insurance program relate to what premium taxes apply and how they should be allocated among the exposures and countries involved in the transaction. Each jurisdiction has its own unique and diverse tax codes, and foreign taxes may apply to master policies that are issued in the U.S. but that cover exposures in other countries.

As a general rule, premium for all covered exposures must be separately identified and allocated to the country where specific exposures are situated. Most countries expect that premium for multinational policies will be apportioned by country where the exposure, contract, or line of business is situated. This principle is easier said than done, however, and compliance with international tax laws can be incredibly complex.

For property policies, the parties may be able to allocate premium on the policy to specific localities, branch offices, sales locations, or storage facilities. For professional liability policies, allocation of premium by country may be based either on sales volume or risk exposure units assumed. In many cases, particularly those involving master policy structure, the underwriting process may not have been specific enough to support an exact accounting; thus, tax allocation can be subject to frequent regulatory audits and disputes with and between affected regulators, who may reallocate premium and taxes if the original allocation is deemed unreasonable.

Other important questions relating to international taxes and government charges include these:

- What tax rate applies to each coverage? Rates can change frequently, and keeping abreast of the latest ones can be a challenge.

- Who is responsible for payment of taxes—the insurer, the policyholder, or the broker?

- Other than premium taxes, what levies might be made on insurers (for example, assessments to build up compensation and to guarantee funds for particular classes of business)?

Other Regulations

Once the preceding compliance issues are addressed, all parties must be aware of, and monitor changes to, a wide range of other regulations that affect insurance transactions. Notably, several categories of laws should be fully researched for their specific application to the contemplated transaction. Research should cover both any U.S. law that may apply to companies operating internationally and laws of the jurisdictions where loss exposures are located or business is being conducted. The categories that should be researched include these:

- Anti-money-laundering laws—For example, Mexico requires insurers to file an anti-money-laundering application before they can issue insurance invoices.

- "Know your customer" and antiterrorism laws—These laws require insurers and brokers to match customer information to lists of known terrorists and/or criminals published by local governments. The U.S., the UK, the European Union, and Canada all have detailed antiterrorism programs.

- Licensing regulations for insurer representatives, brokers, and agents.

- Agency laws, particularly those related to premium payment—Japan, India, and a few other countries have "cash before cover" rules that prohibit insurers from extending any coverage before they have received the premium for the coverage. Other countries allow coverage to begin when the premium payment is mailed or received by the broker.

REVERSE FLOW BUSINESS

As United States-based insurers and brokers began providing insurance services to U.S. companies in foreign countries, they discovered opportunities to help overseas businesses obtain insurance coverage in the U.S. Over time, insurance provided from the U.S. to overseas markets became known as "home/foreign" business, and insurance flowing back to the U.S. from overseas was referred to as "reverse flow" business.

International trade is a two-way street. Currently, foreign investors own more than $2 trillion in U.S. property, plant, and equipment.[8] In addition, the

U.S. imports more than $2 trillion in goods each year from overseas manufacturers.[9] Reverse flow placements for these investments and imported goods represent a sizeable portion of the U.S. insurance marketplace.

Just as U.S. multinationals seek to maintain control and obtain efficiencies of scale over their foreign insurance placements, foreign companies want the same benefits for their insurance placements in the U.S. In addition, foreign companies are well aware that the U.S. is an extremely tough marketplace and often welcome the opportunity to work with U.S. producers and insurers that are sensitive to foreign concerns.

Methods of Writing Reverse Flow Business

Foreign corporations seeking to purchase U.S. insurance policies have four basic options:

- An insurer domiciled in the U.S.
- A fronting insurer domiciled in the U.S.
- A U.S.-domiciled subsidiary of a home-country insurer
- A nonadmitted alien insurer

Insurer Domiciled in the U.S.

Many foreign companies choose to insure their U.S. plants or operations with local U.S. insurers. This may be the only option if the parent organization has no global program in place in its home country. Also, a U.S. branch of a foreign-based company that does not have close ties with its global parent may resist being part of a global program in the belief that an unaffiliated insurer can provide less costly and more individualized coverage.

U.S. insurers treat their foreign-based customers in the same manner they treat any other client. The client does not benefit from economies of scale and cannot leverage any special treatment it would otherwise receive because of its size in its home market. Rates and coverages are the same as those available to U.S.-based accounts of similar size and exposures.

Under these arrangements, the U.S. insurer expects to make a profit simply by writing an additional account that meets the insurer's underwriting standards and is anticipated to generate acceptable underwriting results. The foreign-based client receives the coverages and services it is able to negotiate on its own.

Fronting Insurer Domiciled in the U.S.

Insurers domiciled outside the U.S. are referred to as **alien insurers** in the context of U.S. insurance regulation. Some alien insurers have developed special arrangements with U.S.-domiciled insurers that agree to provide insurance to a foreign company's U.S. operations. The U.S. insurer then cedes (transfers) the entire risk to the alien insurer by way of a reinsurance

Alien insurer

An insurer domiciled in a country other than the United States.

agreement. Under this kind of arrangement (called fronting) the U.S. insurer (called the fronting insurer or fronting company) expects to make a profit by retaining a fee equal to its administrative and claim settling costs, plus a small allowance for profit.

The alien insurer expects to benefit by combining the risk portion of the U.S. premium with other premiums received from the client in the home country and generating a profit on the entire account. Additionally, by providing services to the foreign operations of a home country client, the insurer solidifies its relationship with that client and reduces the likelihood of losing the account to a competitor.

The client's U.S. operation receives coverages and services from a knowledgeable U.S. insurer and benefits from the economies of scale and business leverage that results from being part of a much larger insurance program.

U.S.-Domiciled Subsidiary of the Home-Country Insurer

A number of large alien insurers have made the business commitment and financial investment needed to establish their own insurance operations in the U.S. Although these insurers may also compete for purely U.S. accounts, one of their primary functions is to provide insurance for the U.S. operations of clients whose principal operations are based in their home country.

By placing their insurance with a U.S. subsidiary of their home-country insurer, foreign companies in the U.S. can benefit from economies of scale and business leverage. In many cases, they can also deal directly with insurance company representatives who speak their language and understand their business culture.

These U.S. insurance subsidiaries offer a high degree of control over the coverages and services provided to their foreign-based clients. However, such arrangements do pose disadvantages:

- An alien insurer must undertake significant expense to build a U.S. insurance operation that is able to offer a wide variety of coverages and a full range of services in all fifty states. In nearly all cases, some degree of compromise is necessary.
- U.S.-domiciled subsidiaries are officially U.S. corporations that must comply with all federal and state regulations and tax laws. They must also be managed in such a way that they remain viable business entities. These requirements may limit the degree to which subsidiaries can accommodate their clients' demands, no matter how profitable the insurer/client relationship may be in their home country.
- Subsidiaries are prohibited by law from passing their risks back to their home offices by way of reinsurance. They must maintain their own reinsurance treaties, the long-term profitability of which must be acceptable to the reinsurance community.

In spite of these disadvantages, working through subsidiaries is still the most preferred method for alien insurers to provide services to their important home-country clients. By providing services to the foreign operations of their home-country clients, the insurer also can solidify its relationships with these clients.

U.S. insurance subsidiaries often solicit the U.S. operations of other businesses from the same home country even if they are not currently clients of the parent company. By writing the U.S. exposures of an unrelated business, the U.S. subsidiary may open the door for the parent insurer to successfully compete for that company's business back home.

Nonadmitted Alien Insurer

In some cases, foreign businesses with U.S. exposures choose to make use of **surplus lines laws** in the U.S. and insure certain exposures with their home country insurer by placing coverage on a nonadmitted basis. Under the U.S. Nonadmitted and Reinsurance Reform Act (NRRA), with which all state surplus lines laws in the U.S. must comply, eligible surplus lines risks can be insured with any alien insurer named in the current *Quarterly Listing of Alien Insurers*, published by the National Association of Insurance Commissioners (NAIC). Because nonadmitted insurers are not subject to rate and form filing regulations in most states, the surplus lines approach allows the insurer significant flexibility in pricing and in selecting terms and conditions. However, this approach is available only when coverage for the risk is unavailable in the standard market. For example, surplus lines placement might be available for a high-value property that exceeded the standard market's capacity, but it is not usually permissible for workers compensation or primary automobile liability coverages mandated by state laws.

When placing insurance with a nonadmitted alien insurer, the client becomes responsible for the payment of premium taxes and excise taxes.

Another concern with nonadmitted insurance from an alien insurer is the manner in which claims are paid. In some cases, claim payments that are made to a U.S. operation from a nonadmitted overseas insurer have been viewed as taxable income to the U.S. operation.

Surplus lines law

A state law that permits any producer with a surplus lines license issued by that state to procure insurance from an eligible surplus lines insurer if the applicant cannot obtain the desired type of insurance in the admitted market.

Underwriting Reverse Flow Business

Foreign companies with U.S. operations want to control the cost of their insurance and to benefit from the business leverage that comes with being part of a large organization. Many of these companies pay huge premiums in their home countries and can therefore negotiate the best terms and conditions. When they open operations in the U.S., these clients want to receive the same level of consideration.

If the U.S. placements are made through a fronting arrangement, technically, the fronting company is in a "no lose" situation. If properly negotiated, fronting fees pay all of the fronting company's expenses, plus a profit factor, so the company suffers no losses even if the coverage it provides is too generous or the rates are too low. Nonetheless, a fronting company is subject to the same laws and regulations that apply to any other insurer and must demonstrate to regulators that the premiums and coverages it offers as a fronting company are the same as those it offers to other insureds.

In contrast with fronting insurers, U.S. companies that retain the risk for their own books of business. They must use the same caution in underwriting reverse flow accounts as they use for any other account.

Similarly, U.S. subsidiary operations must underwrite in a manner that allows them to remain financially viable. They must also protect their reinsurance treaties from adverse loss results. However, financial and treaty considerations can be managed on an overall basis, so underwriting and pricing exceptions can be made for one account if the potential for loss is accompanied by the potential for gain somewhere else.

In all instances, underwriters must comply with their companies' rate filings, underwriting guidelines, and state regulations. Historically, companies writing reverse flow accounts have been severely criticized for making too many concessions and, as a result, are now often put under greater scrutiny during insurance department market conduct examinations.

Producers' Role in Writing Reverse Flow Business

Several global brokers have established profit center operations to handle reverse flow accounts. These brokers often assign representatives in their affiliated offices in Europe, Asia, and elsewhere to cultivate relationships with multinational corporations in those regions that are then turned into increased business for the brokers' U.S. offices.

The brokers typically establish dedicated units in their larger offices to handle reverse flow business and staff them with people who speak the language and are familiar with the business culture of their target clients. A few U.S.-domiciled producers specialize almost entirely in writing reverse flow business. However, a large volume of reverse flow business is controlled by agents and brokers who handle a few foreign accounts but spend most of their time working with U.S. clients. To be successful in handling these accounts, the agent or broker must consider these factors:

- Communication with the client is immensely important with reverse flow accounts. In many foreign countries, the producer's role may differ significantly from that of U.S. producers, so producers should constantly explain what they are doing and why they are doing it.

- Communication with the client's home office will probably be far more detailed and take much more time than it would with a typical U.S. account. A foreign organization's U.S. risk manager or insurance buyer may have considerably less decision-making authority than his or her U.S.

counterpart. Premium payment can be delayed because of the need for multiple layers of approvals.

- Commission sharing is common with reverse flow accounts. U.S. producers must be prepared to give up a share of their income to the overseas producer, whether or not the foreign producer actually makes a contribution.

Many producers find reverse flow business frustrating and/or unprofitable. It is commonly said that servicing some reverse flow accounts requires up to two times the effort of handling a similar-size U.S. account. However, handling reverse flow business is its own specialty and is a necessary skill for some U.S. insurers.

INTERNATIONAL INSURANCE SOLUTIONS

When a business, a charity, or another organization takes its first step outside the United States, its exposure to loss may be relatively low, and finding the appropriate insurance solution can be fairly simple and inexpensive. However, as its international activities grow, an organization must be constantly aware of the types of new exposures it faces and the range of insurance solutions available.

A U.S. manufacturer that sells a few products to overseas buyers may find a nominal level of insurance protection from its standard U.S. policies. The same is true for a church that sends a small group of volunteers to help with relief efforts in a country ravaged by a natural disaster. Likewise, standard U.S. policies provide basic insurance coverage when a Chicago law firm sends a partner to Tokyo to consult with a Japanese client that is building a plant in Illinois.

Matters become more complicated, however, when the manufacturer decides to open a sales office in London, the church decides to build an orphanage in Haiti, or the law firm opens a liaison office in Japan. Fast forward even further to a time when the manufacturer has plants in a dozen countries, the church has established missions throughout Africa and Latin America, and the law firm has full-service offices staffed by American and local attorneys in several cities in Asia.

As international exposures change at each step of an organization's development, so also do the solutions available to address them. Four common methods of addressing international insurance exposures are these:

- Territorial endorsements to U.S. market policies
- International package policies
- Local placements
- Controlled master programs (CMPs)

These methods are not necessarily mutually exclusive. Rather, they should be considered a continuum along which an organization may move as its international insurance needs grow and become more complicated.

For purposes of this discussion, "local" refers to the foreign countries or locales in which a U.S. organization does business. For example, a local insurer is an insurer authorized to do business in a country or in a political subdivision of that country, such as a state within Mexico.

Territorial Endorsements to U.S. Market Policies

Although some standard insurance policies written in the U.S. provide minimal coverage for overseas exposures, an organization can significantly enhance its overseas protection by adding one or more simple endorsements to its U.S. policies. These endorsements may extend a U.S. policy's territory to cover claims arising from overseas exposures or add coverages to address overseas exposures.

Commercial Liability, Property, and Auto Coverages

Through its definition of "coverage territory," the Insurance Services Office, Inc. (ISO) Commercial General Liability (CGL) Coverage Form provides international coverage only for a limited number of exposures: persons making short foreign trips on behalf of the insured; products liability coverage (but not completed operations coverage) for goods made or originally sold in the U.S. and its territories and Canada; and personal and advertising injury claims related to the Internet. However, for the standard CGL policy to respond, the insured's liability to pay damages must be determined either by a lawsuit brought within the basic coverage territory (consisting of the U.S. and its territories or possessions, Puerto Rico, and Canada) or in a settlement that the insurer agrees to.

ISO's Amendment of Coverage Territory—Worldwide Coverage endorsement (CG 24 22) can be used to extend standard CGL coverages "anywhere in the world, with the exception of any country or jurisdiction which is subject to trade or other economic sanctions or embargoes by the United States of America."

This endorsement provides coverage for suits brought in foreign courts. However, in those countries where the insurer is prohibited from providing a defense or paying losses on behalf of the insured, the insured is required to provide its own defense (in consultation with the carrier's claim department) and pay any judgments. In these cases, the insurer will reimburse the insured for any defense and claim expenses.

Commercial umbrella liability policies can vary by insurer. Typically, these policies cover anywhere in the world with the exception of countries subject to trade or other economic sanctions or embargoes by the U.S. However, policies often require that suits must be brought in U.S. or Canadian courts. By endorsement, policies can be extended to handle overseas claims in a similar way as under the CGL.

Commercial property policies generally do not cover losses that occur outside the U.S. and its territories and possessions, Puerto Rico, and Canada. Occasionally, underwriters will add a foreign location to the list of scheduled locations, but this approach is usually used only for a small amount of goods stored in an overseas warehouse. In addition, ISO commercial property endorsements are available for providing limited international coverage for either direct property losses or business income losses occurring outside the usual coverage territory.

Under standard commercial auto policies, international coverage is limited to only short-term auto rental contracts and only if the claimant files a lawsuit in the basic coverage territory of the U.S. and Canada. In addition, some insurers will endorse a commercial auto policy to provide international liability coverage on an excess basis. However, because most foreign jurisdictions do not recognize auto insurance issued by a **nonadmitted insurer**, purchasing auto insurance from a local (admitted) insurer is nearly always necessary.

Nonadmitted insurer
An insurer not authorized by the state insurance department to do business within that state.

Workers Compensation and Employers Liability Coverages

The standard workers compensation policy provides the coverage specified in a given state's workers compensation statute. Generally, if a U.S. employee is injured overseas while working on a "temporary" basis, the employee is covered. However, most state workers compensation statutes do not define "temporary."

Employers liability coverage (usually provided in the same policy that provides workers compensation coverage) specifically excludes coverage for "bodily injury occurring outside the United States of America, its territories or possessions, and Canada." However, the exclusion does not apply to bodily injury to a U.S. or Canadian citizen or resident who is "temporarily" outside the coverage territory. Again, "temporarily" is not defined.

In the case of an occasional foreign business trip, these coverages may be sufficient. However, endorsements are available that provide coverage that is better suited for employers with even limited international exposures. Examples of such endorsements are these:

- The Voluntary Compensation Endorsement (WC 99 00 41) covers employee injuries or disease outside the U.S. and Canada, but not in countries or jurisdictions on which the U.S. has imposed trade or economic sanctions. This endorsement extends coverage for both workers compensation and employers liability and provides for "voluntary" payments equal to the benefits required in the state of hire of the employee.

- Repatriation expense coverage pays the additional expense necessary to bring severely injured employees to U.S. hospitals. If an employee dies overseas, this endorsement pays the additional expense to return the employee's remains to the U.S.

- An endemic disease endorsement amends the definition of occupational disease to include illnesses that are endemic or common to a particular country or region that an employee might not have been exposed to had he or she not been traveling on the job.

Advantages and Disadvantages of Endorsements

Territorial endorsements to existing U.S. policies offer an organization both advantages and disadvantages. Advantages are these:

- Adequate coverage for minimal overseas exposures—Territorial endorsements are most useful for organizations that have no physical presence (no "bricks and mortar") in foreign countries but that do engage in occasional foreign business travel.
- Low premiums and convenience—Premiums are relatively low for territorial endorsements, and the endorsements can usually be obtained through the organization's current agent and insurers.

Disadvantages of territorial endorsements include these:

- Nonadmitted coverage issues—Local courts and governments do not recognize the coverage provided by these endorsements. In fact, in many countries it is illegal to purchase nonadmitted policies. If the existence of nonadmitted insurance is discovered, authorities may ask why a premium tax was not paid.
- Coverage differences—Local policy forms are designed for the needs of the local marketplace. Simply adding endorsements to U.S. policies may not address local needs. For example, in France, automobile liability is written without a monetary limit of insurance. No endorsements to U.S. policies are available to provide that coverage.
- Deficient claim services—Even though many U.S. insurers add these endorsements, most lack expertise dealing with international claims. They may also be legally barred from handling claims locally because the coverage provided by endorsements is nonadmitted. As a result, insureds can be left with little or no assistance when dealing with claims, unless they are dealing with one of the few carriers with local, in-country claim networks.

International Package Policies

International package policies

A policy that bundles the property and casualty coverages commonly needed by businesses with international loss exposures.

Several insurers with the ability to provide worldwide services offer policies that are specifically designed for the needs of organizations with growing foreign exposures. These policies, variously called **international package policies**, foreign package policies, global insurance policies, or exporters package policies, are separate from the client's domestic policies and cover only the insured's overseas exposures.

For example, a single international package policy could include commercial property, general liability, commercial auto, commercial crime, and voluntary workers compensation coverages, as well as specialty coverages such as political risk, kidnap and ransom, and ocean cargo. Some insurers also include travel accident insurance to cover employees and their families while they are outside the U.S.

International package policies sold to companies headquartered in the U.S. are typically issued by insurers that are domiciled in the U.S. Consequently, these policies are nonadmitted insurance in other countries. For that reason, any auto coverages included in such policies are provided as excess coverages only because primary auto liability coverage cannot be offered on a nonadmitted basis.

International package policies offer several advantages:

- Broad coverages at low prices—In some cases, international package policies can save money by allowing certain organizations to separate their export sales from their domestic sales. For example, by writing an international package policy, an organization with $20 million in sales, of which 20 percent are exports, can show $16 million in sales on the U.S. policy and $4 million on the international package policy. Because products liability rates for export sales are substantially lower than those for domestic sales, this approach can result in substantially lower premiums than if the entire $20 million in sales were covered under a worldwide endorsement.

- Flexibility—International package policies use familiar forms and conditions, so insurance buyers can easily compare coverages; yet, because these policies offer so many options, they can be easily modified to cover only those exposures for which the buyer needs coverage. The insurers that write international package policies typically have the capacity to cover high property values.

- International expertise—Insurers that sell international package policies usually have many years of international underwriting and claims experience.

Because international package policies are nonadmitted insurance, they present the same disadvantages as those resulting from territorial endorsements. However, because many insureds use these policies to insure larger operations and higher property values, the problems resulting from using nonadmitted coverage can be aggravated.

Coverage From Nonaffiliated Local Insurers

When a new "bricks and mortar" operation is formed in a foreign country, often the quickest way to deal with insurance needs is to buy coverage locally. Similarly, when an organization expands overseas by acquiring an indigenous organization, that organization's existing insurance program is commonly left in place and its administration is left to the local staff.

Local insurance policies are most often purchased from insurers based in the host country. They typically offer only those coverages that are customary in that insurance market, including property, employee dishonesty, third-party liability, and automobile. Some coverages may differ from what is considered normal in the U.S.

For example, property coverage may be written on a named perils basis instead of an open perils basis; auto and general liability limits may be much lower; and property and auto physical damage deductibles may be close to zero. Also, in many countries, workers compensation is provided through government programs or as part of national health plans. Even if the local insurance markets offer their own versions of employers liability or supplemental workers compensation, they have little resemblance to their U.S. counterparts.

There are several advantages to buying insurance in local markets:

- Compliance with local laws—Coverage is on an admitted basis, and there are no issues with local tax regulations.
- Coverage match—Policies are designed to specifically match local coverage requirements.
- Claim services—Local insurers can provide knowledgeable in-country claims support.
- Image—Working with local insurers helps foreign entities maintain a "good citizen" image.
- Familiarity with coverages—Local managers understand the coverages and are comfortable working within a familiar framework.

From the perspective of an organization's home office, buying local policies from local insurers has several disadvantages:

- Solvency issues—It may be difficult to judge the solvency of local insurers.
- Home office unfamiliarity—Local policies with unfamiliar conditions written in a foreign language make it difficult for home office managers to determine the adequacy of the protection they provide.
- Lack of economies-of-scale—Stand-alone policies in individual markets do not offer economies of scale and provide no leverage in times of disputes.
- Lack of control—Local policies complicate efforts to maintain central control and overall continuity of protection.

Controlled Master Program

Controlled master program

An insurance arrangement that provides comprehensive coverage for organizations operating internationally by linking one or more master policies written in the organization's home country to local policies in countries in which the organization does business.

A **controlled master program (CMP)** allows home office managers to create, implement, and control a global insurance strategy. By working with a global broker and a global insurance provider, managers can ensure that their strategy is implemented as uniformly as possible in each country where the entity has exposure.

Technically, a CMP fully covers all of the insured's international exposures. However, the master policies (the policies written in the organization's home country) state that wherever possible, claims will be adjusted in the countries where they occur and any claim payments made in foreign countries under the terms of any local policy will reduce the amount collectible under the master policies. It is also agreed that any premium paid overseas to purchase admitted policies reduces the premium due under the master policies.

If a property loss occurs at an overseas location caused by a peril that is not covered under the local policy, the claim will be paid in the U.S. under the terms of the master property policy. If a serious liability claim exceeds the limits of the local policy, the policy limits will be paid locally and the excess amounts will be paid in the U.S. through the master liability policy. In this way, the master policies provide "difference in conditions" (DIC) (sometimes referred to as "difference *of* conditions") and "difference in limits" (DIL) coverages and ensure that all the assets and activities of the international entity are protected to the same degree.

Finally, master policies usually contain additional coverages that cannot be included in local policies. These additional coverages can include political risk coverage, business interruption coverage relating to interdependencies between operations in different countries, and workers compensation coverage for U.S. employees and third-country nationals working outside their home countries.

Setting up a CMP involves four basic stages:

1. Local managers in each country are instructed to appoint the local office of the global broker as their agents. Together, the local managers and local brokers assess the exposures and insurance needs in their country and report their findings to the home office.

2. Home office managers and the global broker develop a global strategy relating to risk tolerance, insurance purchasing philosophy, and management accountability; present it to various global insurers for bids; and then select a global insurer. Managers in the organization, the global broker, and the global insurer finalize the terms of the comprehensive master program, including coverages, limits, deductibles, and total premiums to be charged on a global basis.

3. The organization's local managers coordinate with and purchase their insurance policies from the local offices of the global brokers, working to make sure local coverages and premiums come as close as possible to the terms, conditions, and rates of the master program.

4. In the U.S., master policies are written that provide all agreed-upon coverages on a nonadmitted basis.

Advantages of writing a CMP include these:

*   Economies of scale—By working with one broker and one insurance provider, the organization is able to negotiate much better prices and far

broader coverages than would be possible if policies were purchased on a piecemeal basis.

- Admitted coverage—By purchasing as much local coverage as possible, the organization avoids most of the compliance and tax complications that can arise from nonadmitted coverage.

- Claim services—The organization has access to a combination of extensive local claim networks under the supervision of the global insurer's claim managers.

- Centralized control—Home office managers can closely monitor and manage their organization's coverages, costs, and compliance issues on a global basis.

- Seamless coverages—The organization receives the combined benefits of local coverages tailored to its exposures in each separate country and the assurance that potential coverage gaps will be picked up by the DIC/DIL features of the master program.

- DIC/DIL tax coordination—A CMP offers the best vehicle to address tax issues related to where and how DIC and DIL claims payments are handled.

Creating and managing a CMP are not without difficulties, including these:

- Need for expertise—A CMP is not easy to set up and manage. To be successful, the home office insurance manager must possess an understanding of international insurance and of the inner workings of the organization.

- Need for communication and cooperation—Creating and effectively managing a CMP requires extraordinary cooperation and communication. It is often difficult to obtain timely information regarding local exposures and insurance requirements from foreign managers. This is complicated by language problems, conflicting priorities, and cultural differences. Regular, open communication must continue after a CMP is implemented, and close cooperation is required between local managers, local agents, and local insurers in every country.

- Need for control—The organization's top management must recognize the importance of the CMP and grant the insurance manager sufficient authority to establish a CMP and keep it running efficiently. It is not unusual for local managers to resist relinquishing control over local insurance programs. As a result, some CMP programs take several years to fully implement.

- Difficulty in finding partners—There are only a limited number of global brokers and global insurers. An organization may find it challenging to find partners in the right countries that have the expertise and service capabilities to meet its needs.

SELECTING INTERNATIONAL INSURANCE SOLUTIONS

Tracking the phases in a company's expansion of its international business is a good way to see how international insurance solutions can be selected to meet a company's changing international loss exposures.

Cook Ware Inc. (CWI), which manufactures a variety of cookware products, has its headquarters, warehouse, and factory in Houston, Texas. CWI has been in business for thirty years, manufacturing in its own factory and selling mainly to United States customers. CWI is now expanding its operations to include manufacturing in Mexico and exporting sales to France. Here is a summary of the three phases in CWI's expansion of its international business:

- In Phase 1, CWI contracts with Mexican companies to manufacture certain products for CWI. CWI also retains the services of a French company to distribute CWI's products exported to France.
- In Phase 2, CWI's Mexican operations remain essentially the same. However, French sales increase and CWI forms a French subsidiary to distribute CWI's products in France.
- In Phase 3, CWI forms a Mexican subsidiary to operate a factory in Mexico and transfers to this factory all manufacturing operations for all the products formerly made by CWI's Mexican contractors and CWI's factory in Texas. In Europe, CWI establishes branch sales offices in several other European Union member countries.

A different mix of insurance solutions can be selected to provide appropriate coverage for CWI's loss exposures in each phase of its international business expansion. See the exhibit "Coverage Parts Included in CWI's Insurance Program."

Phase 1 Loss Exposures

CWI's Mexican loss exposures result primarily from CWI executives' travel to Mexico to meet with managers of the Mexican companies that are manufacturing products under contract with CWI. These exposures include the possibility of these types of events:

- CWI employees becoming sick or injured while in Mexico
- CWI employees becoming legally liable for bodily injury or property damage resulting from their use of short-term auto rentals
- CWI experiencing loss by theft or other perils of transported laptops and other property
- CWI employees being kidnapped and held for ransom or extorted

In addition, CWI's Commercial General Liability (CGL) Coverage Form does not cover liability arising out of products unless they are made or sold by

---

Coverage Parts Included in CWI's Insurance Program

- Commercial property (including business income/extra expense)
- Commercial general liability
- Commercial auto
- Workers compensation and employers liability
- Commercial crime
- Equipment breakdown
- Commercial inland marine, including annual transit
- Umbrella/excess liability
- Directors and officers liability
- Employment practices liability
- Fiduciary liability
- Pollution liability

[DA08960]

CWI in the U.S. or its territories or possessions or Canada. Because some of the Mexican-made products are shipped directly from Mexico to the French distributor, they are neither made nor sold in the restricted coverage territory, and therefore any liability arising out of such products would not be covered under the CGL form.

Finally, CWI is exposed to loss by theft or other perils of finished products while in transit from the manufacturer's premises to either CWI's warehouse in Texas or the distributor's warehouse in France. Shipments to CWI's warehouse are carried exclusively by truck. Shipments to France (packed in intermodal containers) are carried from the Mexican factories by truck to a port city, where they are loaded onto containerships and carried across the Atlantic Ocean. Once they reach France, they are carried by truck to the French distributor's warehouse. CWI is the party at risk from the time the containers leave the Mexican factories until they reach their final destinations.

CWI's French loss exposures result primarily from CWI employees' travel to France to meet with the French distributor that is acting as CWI's selling agent in France. The agency agreement does not give CWI any ownership stake in the French company, nor does it obligate CWI to provide insurance for any operations performed by the agent.

Thus, CWI is exposed to essentially the same types of travel-related loss exposures in France as it is in Mexico, although frequency, severity, and probability of loss could differ significantly. For example, the probability of a kidnap loss is higher in Mexico, and the potential severity of an auto liability loss is higher in France.

Phase 1 International Insurance Solutions

CWI's international insurance solutions for Phase 1 will consist of territorial endorsements to its U.S. policies, an international package policy, and (to a limited extent) local insurance. Although the international package policy CWI has selected is nonadmitted insurance, the insurer providing this policy is experienced in covering international loss exposures and has claim networks and language resources in Mexico, France, and most other countries. Moreover, the coverages that can be provided in the international package policy are more comprehensive than most of the coverages that can be added by endorsement to CWI's existing policies.

Workers Compensation and Employers Liability

Sickness or injury to CWI's employees while traveling in Mexico or France might be covered under CWI's existing workers compensation and employers liability policy because of the extraterritorial provisions in the applicable state workers compensation statute, which vary widely by state. To be more certain that coverage will apply for a visit considered longer than temporary, CWI purchases voluntary compensation coverage, along with coverage for repatriation expense and endemic disease, under its international package policy, the insurer of which has the international resources to facilitate claim services and provide guidance in the event of a medical emergency.

Short-Term Auto Rentals

Regarding CWI's short-term auto rentals in Mexico or France, the Insurance Services Office, Inc. (ISO) commercial auto forms cover auto accidents involving short-term rental cars anywhere in the world, subject to the usual provision that the insured's responsibility to pay damages must be determined either in a suit made in the U.S. or its territories or possessions or Canada or in a settlement that the insurer agrees to.

However, this extension of the coverage territory is not recognized as valid auto insurance in many countries, including both Mexico and France, because it is nonadmitted insurance. CWI's international package policy also provides contingent liability and physical damage coverage for rental autos, but these coverages, too, are nonadmitted insurance.

Therefore, to comply with the laws of these countries, a practical solution is for CWI's employees to purchase the liability, physical damage, and any other required coverages offered through the rental car company and underwritten by authorized local insurers. CWI's international package policy and commercial auto policy would then be available, subject to their own terms and conditions, as excess indemnification for CWI, if needed. However, France is one of many countries that has unlimited motor liability laws, so local French coverage has no policy limit for bodily injury liability. CWI could also recommend that its employees decline physical damage coverage under local rental car contracts because the international package can provide primary coverage for physical damage, subject to deductibles.

Commercial Property and Business Income

Coverage for loss of laptops and other items carried by CWI employees could be covered by endorsement to CWI's commercial property coverage part. For example, an ISO endorsement that could be used for this purpose is Business Personal Property—Limited International Coverage (CP 04 32). Another ISO endorsement, Property in Process of Manufacture by Others—Limited International Coverage (CP 04 33) could be used if CWI wanted to insure property in the process of being manufactured by the Mexican companies with whom CWI has contracted.

Despite the availability of these and similar endorsements, CWI obtains the desired property coverage under its international package policy, which provides broader coverage at an affordable price.

If a suspension of operations because of fire or other covered perils at any of its Mexican partners' factories could result in a significant business income or extra expense loss for CWI, then CWI should consider purchasing contingent business income and extra expense insurance for those Mexican locations. A similar exposure could exist for CWI because of a suspension of operations at CWI's French distributor's premises. The ISO endorsements for providing these coverages are Business Income From Dependent Properties Limited International Coverage (CP 15 01) and Extra Expense From Dependent Properties Limited International Coverage (CP 15 02). However, CWI can obtain broader contingent business income coverage as a component of its international package policy and therefore chooses that solution.

Kidnap/Ransom/Extortion

To cover its kidnap and extortion exposures in Mexico and France, CWI would need to purchase kidnap/ransom insurance with a coverage territory that included, at the very least, those two countries. A better alternative would be to obtain a worldwide coverage territory (subject to some exceptions of nations subject to trade sanctions) because of the high likelihood that CWI employees will travel to other countries. CWI may purchase this level of kidnap/ransom insurance as a component of its international package policy or may, instead, purchase a separate kidnap/ransom policy.

Products Liability

Regarding its liability exposure for products made in Mexico and sold outside the U.S., CWI could ask its insurer to add the ISO Amendment of Coverage Territory—Worldwide Coverage endorsement (CG 24 22) to CWI's CGL policy. This would broaden the coverage territory for products liability coverage and all other coverages provided by the policy. CWI's international package policy also includes international general liability insurance that covers products liability as well as premises and operations liability. CWI's umbrella liability policy, which covers anywhere in the world, provides excess coverage for products liability. CWI's insurance broker should make sure that CWI's CGL policy and international package policy are both listed in the schedule of underlying coverages in CWI's umbrella liability policy.

Property in Transit

To cover truck shipments from the Mexican factories to CWI's warehouse, CWI can purchase an endorsement to its annual transit policy that broadens the existing coverage territory (U.S. and Canada) to include Mexico. CWI has also purchased an ocean/international cargo policy to cover all ocean shipments made during the policy period, including connecting land segments, in which CWI has an insurable interest. This policy will cover shipments from the Mexican factories to the French distributor, as well as any overseas shipments to or from CWI's premises. If the ocean/international cargo policy also covers truck shipments from Mexico, CWI could eliminate that coverage from the inland transit policy.

In summary, CWI has selected a mix of endorsements to its existing policies and the purchase of an international package policy to cover most of its international loss exposures. The only exposure for which CWI will obtain local insurance is short-term auto rentals; to cover this exposure, it will purchase auto liability (and maybe physical damage) coverage at the rental company's sales counter. See the exhibit "Summary of CWI's Phase 1 International Insurance Solutions."

Phase 2 Loss Exposures

After a year of marketing its products through its selling agent in France, CWI is encouraged by the sales levels reached. However, CWI believes that it could increase its local presence in France and multiply its profits from French sales by replacing the agent's services with a CWI subsidiary staffed with French employees. CWI also believes that having a French subsidiary could provide a base of operations for expanding its business into other European countries, one of CWI's eventual goals. Therefore, CWI forms a French company, *Outils de Cuisine International* (OCI), which hires employees and leases a combined office and warehouse building. CWI's Mexican operations will not change during Phase 2.

Summary of CWI's Phase 1 International Insurance Solutions

Exposure	Solution	Coverage
Workers compensation	Workers compensation and employers liability policy	Extraterritorial provisions vary by state.
	International package policy	Voluntary compensation coverage for repatriation expense and endemic disease.
Auto (short-term rental)	Local rental car insurance	Liability, physical damage, and any other coverages offered.
	International package policy	Excess over rental policies.
Commercial property	International package policy	Broader than coverage provided by endorsements.
Business income	International package policy	Broader than coverage provided by endorsements.
Kidnap/ransom/extortion	International package policy (or separate policy)	Worldwide kidnap/ransom coverage.
Products liability	International package policy	International general liability insurance.
	Umbrella liability	Worldwide excess coverage.
Property in transit	Endorsement to annual transit policy	Broadens existing coverage territory to include Mexico.
	Ocean/international cargo policy	Covers all ocean shipments and connecting land transit.

[DA08961]

In addition to CWI's Phase 1 loss exposures, which will continue into Phase 2, CWI now has additional loss exposures, including these:

- The building lease contains mutual waivers of rights of recourse between OCI and the building owner, thus eliminating any subrogation rights of their insurers against OCI and the building owner. Moreover, OCI agrees to insure the building for the account of the landlord.
- OCI employs French citizens.
- OCI has provided its managers and sales executives with company cars.

- OCI's board of directors consists of individuals from both the U.S. and France.
- OCI sends shipments from its warehouse to distributors throughout France. Previously, the selling agent was responsible for insuring shipments from the agent's warehouse.

Phase 2 International Insurance Solutions

Now that CWI has a physical presence in France, local insurance will be needed for several of CWI's loss exposures. France prohibits nonadmitted insurance, subject to only a few exceptions, such as marine and aviation insurance and coverages that are not available locally. Because it would be illegal to insure OCI's loss exposures with nonadmitted insurers, the international insurance solutions for Phase 2 will consist of the Phase 1 solutions (to cover loss exposures that have not changed from Phase 1) plus several policies issued by local insurers to cover loss exposures of the new OCI entity.

Property and General Liability

The building lease requires OCI to insure the building against fire and other causes of property loss for the owner's account. This insurance, as well as insurance on OCI's business personal property and business income coverage, will be purchased from an insurer authorized to do business in France.

Moreover, this insurance must include coverage for several causes of loss (such as hurricane, flood, earthquake, landslide, tidal wave, and avalanche) in accordance with France's natural catastrophe insurance system, known as *Catastrophes Naturelles* (CAT NAT). Property insurance issued in France must also include terrorism as a covered cause of loss in accordance with another national insurance plan.

The same insurer that writes OCI's property coverages will provide general third-party liability (GTPL) insurance covering liability arising out of OCI's premises, operations, and products. The European Union has no uniform model for GTPL coverage as compared with U.S. CGL coverage. It is difficult to compare GTPL and CGL because of the diverse wording of various European GTPL coverages. For example, GTPL coverage includes loss of use for pure financial loss without requiring a property damage or bodily injury trigger.

Workers Compensation and Employers Liability

In France, workers compensation coverage is provided as part of France's Social Security system, financed by employers' payroll contributions. Private insurers cannot write workers compensation coverage in competition with the French government, as is the case in the few U.S. states that have monopolistic state workers compensation funds.

The French workers compensation system, as with its U.S. counterpart, eliminates employees' rights to sue for occupational injury or disease in most instances. However, French employers, as with their U.S. counterparts, have a residual employers liability exposure arising out of circumstances in which employees are able to sue their employers. In France, injured employees can sue their employers under the doctrine of *Faute Inexcusable* (inexcusable fault). In recent years, French courts have been more likely than in the past to find inexcusable fault when an employee suffers serious injury or death.

Employers liability coverage has traditionally been provided in French GTPL policies. Although such policies exclude bodily injury to any employee of the insured, insurers have been willing to add employers liability coverage as a buy back, subject to a specified sublimit. Recently, however, as the exposure has become more severe, it is often written in a separate policy. If OCI cannot obtain this coverage as an extension of its GTPL policy, it will buy a separate employers liability policy. In either case, the policy will need to be issued by an authorized insurer.

Other Coverages

OCI intends to provide complete auto insurance (including liability and physical damage) on the company cars provided to some OCI employees. Auto liability insurance is compulsory in France and must be written by an authorized insurer.

OCI will also purchase directors and officers (D&O) liability coverage from a French insurer that specializes in this line of business and uses a policy form that is appropriate for covering D&O loss exposures under French law. This policy can be placed in conjunction with a global D&O program.

Because there is no requirement that property in transit in France be insured locally, CWI has opted to cover shipments from the OCI warehouse by an inland transit extension to CWI's existing ocean cargo policy, which covers international shipments from Mexico and the U.S. to the OCI warehouse. OCI has also been added as an additional named insured under CWI's ocean cargo policy. See the exhibit "Summary of CWI's Phase 2 International Insurance Solutions."

Phase 3 Loss Exposures

Phase 3 of CWI's international expansion will involve operations in Mexico, France, and other countries in the European Union.

To consolidate and streamline its manufacturing operations, CWI forms a subsidiary, named CWI Mexico (CWIM), that will begin making all the products formerly made by CWI's Mexican contractors and CWI's factory in Texas. CWI will continue to operate its office and warehouse in Texas. CWIM's

Summary of CWI's Phase 2 International Insurance Solutions

Exposure	Solution	Coverage
Property	Local policy	Coverages (including fire) required by OCI's building lease, business personal property, and business income coverages; coverage under France's natural catastrophe insurance system; and terrorism coverage
General liability	Local policy	Premises, operations, and products
Employers liability	Local policy (either extension of OCI's local general liability policy or separate employers liability policy)	Residual employers liability coverage for employee suits based on doctrine of inexcusable fault
Auto (for OCI company autos)	Local policy	Complete auto coverage, including liability and physical damage
Directors and officers (D&O) liability	Local policy	Coverage for OCI's directors and officers for D&O loss exposures under French law
Property in transit	Inland transit extension to CWI's ocean cargo policy	French domestic shipments from OCI warehouse

[DA08962]

principal property loss exposures and the causes of loss that give rise to them include these:

- Buildings—fire and allied
- Business personal property, including raw materials, stocks in process, and finished stock—fire, allied, and theft
- Money and securities—theft, burglary, robbery, and kidnap/ransom
- Production equipment—breakdown
- Property in transit—transportation, theft, fire, and allied
- Automobiles—collision, comprehensive

In addition, CWIM is exposed to net income loss resulting from business interruption caused by accidental damage to CWIM's buildings, business personal property, or production equipment.

CWIM's principal liability exposures include these:

- Premises and operations liability
- Products liability
- Auto liability
- Pollution liability
- Directors and officers liability

CWIM will hire over 100 Mexican employees, an action that will require careful negotiation with the prevailing labor unions. In addition to complying with all other relevant provisions of Mexico's Federal Labor Law, CWIM must register with the Mexican Institute of Social Security (IMSS), the governmental entity that serves as the exclusive workers compensation insurer in Mexico. IMSS will determine the workers compensation premium that CWIM will pay as a percentage of its payroll.

In France, CWI executives will use OCI's location as a base for expanding its sales operations into several additional countries in the European Union, including (initially) Spain, Italy, Switzerland, and Germany. In each of these countries, OCI will establish branch offices by leasing space, hiring sales representatives, and leasing autos for the sales representatives.

Phase 3 International Insurance Solutions

CWI has hired a new insurance broker that specializes in international accounts. After reviewing CWI's Phase 3 loss exposures, the broker recommends a controlled master program (CMP) that combines master policies (one for property coverages and another for casualty coverages) written in the U.S. with local policies in Mexico, France, and the other countries into which CWI is expanding. The broker has selected an insurer that has extensive experience in writing CMPs, as well as the international networks that will facilitate procurement and coordination of all the coverages that CWI needs for itself and its subsidiaries.

The recommended CMP will replace CWI's previous international package policy and eliminate the need for international endorsements to CWI's U.S. insurance policies, although CWI might choose to keep some or all of the endorsements in effect as additional coverage.

The master policy for property insurance will include these coverages:

- Commercial property (buildings and business personal property)
- Business income and extra expense

- Contingent business income and extra expense
- Equipment breakdown

The master policy for casualty insurance will include these coverages:

- CGL
- Commercial auto
- Workers compensation and employers liability
- Voluntary compensation, repatriation expense, and endemic disease for employees outside their home countries

Separate global insurance programs will be placed for these coverages:

- Kidnap/ransom
- Annual transit and ocean cargo
- Political risk
- Crime
- Directors and officers liability
- Environmental impairment liability

Through the CMP approach, the insurer will be able to accommodate further expansion of CWI's international business by combining local policies with master policies that provide difference in conditions (DIC) and difference in limits (DIL) coverages to ensure that all of CWI's assets and activities are protected.

In Europe, "freedom of services" (FOS) insurance legislation allows an insurer to issue a single policy that will be recognized as valid insurance in most European countries. An FOS policy is in effect considered to be admitted insurance across the European Economic Area (EEA), lessening the risk of noncompliance if losses occur in countries that prohibit nonadmitted insurance. The EEA includes the twenty-seven member countries of the European Union plus Iceland, Norway, and Liechtenstein. An insurer domiciled in any EEA member country can issue policies in any other EEA member country without having a subsidiary there, as long as the insurer complies with local legislative and tax requirements.

For example, the French insurer that provides local coverage for OCI's loss exposures in France could legally insure OCI's new operations in any EEA member country without having a subsidiary insurer in that country. Notably, however, Switzerland is not a member of the EU or the EEA. Therefore, any local coverage that OCI must have for its new Swiss operations would need to be purchased from an insurer authorized to do business in Switzerland.

An FOS policy, although it facilitates the placement of international insurance in the EEA member countries, is not always the best solution. For example, assume that when OCI begins operations in an EEA member country, OCI leases an office there, and the property owners require OCI to insure the office building on the owners' behalf. Although this insurance could legally be written by OCI's French insurer, the property owners might object to a French-language insurance policy because of their inability to read French. See the exhibit "Summary of CWI's International Operations and Insurance Solutions."

Summary of CWI's International Operations and Insurance Solutions

	International Operations	Insurance Solutions
Phase 1	Outsources some manufacturing operations to Mexico Uses a French company to distribute CWI's products in France	Endorsements to EWI's U.S. insurance policies International package policy Local insurance (for rental autos)
Phase 2	Continues to outsource some manufacturing operations to Mexico Forms a French subsidiary to distribute CWI's products in France	Same as Phase 1 except that local insurance is added to cover the French subsidiary's property-casualty loss exposures
Phase 3	Forms Mexican subsidiary to perform all CWI's manufacturing Continues to operate French subsidiary Establishes branch sales offices in several other EU member countries	A controlled master program (CMP) replaces the previous insurance program. The CMP provides an integrated package of all the international coverages that CWI and its subsidiaries need.

[DA08963]

STRUCTURING AN INTERNATIONAL INSURANCE PROGRAM

Businesses cannot ignore the opportunities in the global market and typically must expand internationally to achieve their highest growth potential. Yet as a company expands internationally, so does its risk. In response, its risk management professional must know how to best structure its international insurance program to address that risk.

When structuring an international insurance program, an insured's risk management professional must decide whether to buy admitted insurance (for a decentralized structure) or nonadmitted insurance (for a centralized structure). This decision should be based on the advantages and disadvantages of both types of insurance. It is also possible that the best structure is a package policy, such as for exporters who have no foreign, permanent place of business to insure. For those multinational companies with permanent foreign locations, the preferred structure often includes a collection of admitted and nonadmitted insurance called a controlled master program. Such a program has advantages and disadvantages to consider before selecting it as a structure.

Admitted Versus Nonadmitted Insurance

An **admitted insurer** is authorized to do business in the country in which it sells polices. If a multinational company relies heavily on admitted insurance for its coverage, then it is likely following a decentralized approach to cover its international exposures. Relying on locally written coverage has several consequences, such as the policy being written in the language of the country in which it was sold and in compliance with local laws.

Purchasing admitted coverage locally offers several advantages:

- The policy will be serviced locally, and local management is more likely accustomed to local practices.
- Premiums paid to admitted insurers are tax-deductible as a business expense, while those paid to an insurer that is not admitted may not be tax-deductible.
- Premiums and claims are paid in the local currency, which eliminates foreign exchange rate risks unless purchases must be on imported equipment or materials.
- Local agents and brokers may be able to understand local coverage nuances and advise coverage better.
- Complying with local laws and doing business locally helps integrate the company into the local economy and community.

Purchasing admitted coverage locally has several disadvantages as well:

- The risk manager for a multinational company may have difficulty interpreting a policy written in a foreign language, which could lead to multiple problems, such as nonuniform conditions, coverage gaps, and underinsurance.
- If competition among insurers locally is not robust or if tariffs are high, the local policy may be more expensive. It can be more difficult to assess the financial strength of the local insurer as well.

Admitted insurer

An insurer to which a state insurance department has granted a license to do business within that state.

- Effective solvency regulation, financial statements, and rating agencies of insurers may be lacking locally.
- Purchasing locally also lessens a company's purchasing power and decentralizes risk management strategy, which can weaken the implementation of **enterprise risk management (ERM)**.

Enterprise risk management
An approach to managing all of an organization's key business risks and opportunities with the intent of maximizing shareholder value. Also known as enterprise-wide risk management.

A nonadmitted insurer is unauthorized to do business in the country in which it sells policies. For example, when an insurer in the country of a parent company sells insurance to the parent company's subsidiary in a foreign country (where the insurer is not an authorized insurer by the foreign country's government), it has sold nonadmitted insurance.

Purchasing nonadmitted coverage locally offers several advantages:

- Administrative control can be centralized, which can be more efficient.
- The financial strength of the insurer is more easily determined.
- The policy is written in the language of the country where the parent company is domiciled, making it easier to understand and administer.
- The insurance coverage may also be cheaper because of lower tariffs, rate regulation, or consolidation of purchasing power.
- The premium and claim payments will be made in the domestic country's currency, thereby eliminating foreign exchange rate risk if only a single currency is used.

Purchasing nonadmitted coverage locally has these disadvantages as well:

- Claim adjusting can be substantially more complicated without local coverage and local insurer representatives; this can be especially prominent with liability claims.
- Local management may not have confidence in the nonadmitted coverage provided by the parent company's insurer and may decide to buy its own coverage locally.

Exporters Package Policy

Exporters package policy
Nonadmitted package policy tailored to organizations with incidental exposures in countries other than their home country.

The **exporters package policy** is intended for those insureds without a permanent office or place of business in the foreign country where they operate. Insureds that are expanding their business on a global basis often find themselves in this situation and discover they have several new loss exposures that can be covered by this package policy. The policy covers foreign general liability, nonowned and hired automobile insurance, and foreign voluntary workers compensation. The policy also offers coverage for personal property (such as laptops, projector equipment, and sales samples), kidnap and ransom, and travel accident losses. For an insured with a permanent place of operations in a foreign country, its coverage needs may be better addressed by a controlled master program.

Controlled Master Program

A **controlled master program** is a collection of admitted and nonadmitted insurance policies. The admitted policies cover the foreign subsidiaries of a multinational business and are purchased in the local insurance market of the foreign countries. The nonadmitted policy covers all of the insured's international operations on a blanket basis and is often purchased in the country where the parent company is domiciled. The nonadmitted policy is a master policy that can include difference-in-conditions or difference-in-limits coverage that would prevent a gap in protection if the admitted policies purchased locally provide lower limits or less coverage than the parent company requires.

United States multinational companies usually have separate policies for their U.S. domestic exposures. These policies help prevent potential difficulties in foreign or domestic insurance from affecting each other. Non-U.S. multinational companies also often purchase separate policies for their U.S. exposures. This can prevent their global program from being exposed to an unfavorable U.S. liability environment.

The exhibit illustrates an insurer providing admitted insurance to a multinational company's subsidiaries located in foreign countries. The local subsidiaries purchase property and liability insurance that provides local compulsory coverage as well as other coverage placed locally. Risks that are not covered locally because of limit of coverage or restriction on perils covered may be covered under the master policy. The master policy insurer also covers the company's domestic exposures in the country where it is domiciled with separate property and liability policies. Toward the top of the exhibit, two excess polices are shown. One is the umbrella policy, which protects the company from excess liability losses in selected lines of coverage. The other is the whole account insurance, which protects the company from excess losses in the entire portfolio of coverage. See the exhibit "Illustration of an Integrated Controlled Master Program."

All policies are coordinated from one central location. This collection of policies has several advantages and disadvantages.

Advantages of Controlled Master Programs

Controlled master programs provide numerous advantages, including a uniformly consistent insurance program that is centralized yet captures the benefits of local policies. The benefits of local policies include compliance with individual countries' regulations on contracts, nonadmitted insurance, premium allocation, and tariffs.[10]

By combining the policies under one program, the company's purchasing power is consolidated, and duplicate coverage is eliminated. Both of these factors reduce premiums and other costs. Further, the global nature of the program allows a company to negotiate worldwide rates, terms, and condi-

Controlled master program

Nonadmitted master policy issued in the country in which the insured is domiciled paired with locally admitted policies issued in the foreign countries in which the insured operates.

Illustration of an Integrated Controlled Master Program

Coverage for excess losses in the entire portfolio

Umbrella liability policy

Primary property and liability policies for domestic exposures

Master policy

Local property and liability policies for subsidiaries' exposures

Based on: Harold D. Skipper and W. Jean Kwon, Risk Management and Insurance: Perspectives in a Global Economy (Malden, Mass.: Blackwell Publishers, 2007), p. 366. [DA08697]

tions that reflect its global size and experience. So the company gains greater **economy of scale** and scope in external risk financing through insurance.[11]

The centralized global approach of the program makes a company's risk management goals more likely to be realized and gives a risk manager more opportunities to implement a consistent global ERM strategy.

The multinational reach of the program also reduces the accumulation of risk and diversifies the risk across a company's subsidiaries. The program generates a large volume of useful risk management information from countries around the world. This allows risk managers to determine best practices and form an intra-company risk management community.

The primary advantage is the prevention of gaps in coverage. What the local policy doesn't cover, the master policy may cover. In addition to difference-in-conditions or difference-in-limits coverage, master policies can also cover currency devaluation, coinsurance deficiency, tax liability, or neighbors and tenants liability. These coverages are usually not available in U.S. policies but are frequently needed by multinational companies.

Disadvantages of Controlled Master Programs

Controlled master programs create disadvantages as well. The program generates a large amount of information that must be reviewed and analyzed. This consumes considerable resources to stay current.

Another disadvantage is that local risk managers may resist relinquishing their responsibility of purchasing all the coverage for a foreign subsidiary. It may be

Economy of scale

A reduction in the average cost of a product or a process as the size of a company increases.

difficult for the local risk manager to instead focus on coordinating coverage with a master policy.

Also, if the same insurer and its foreign local subsidiaries are used to provide the master policy and the local policies to further aid in coordinating coverage between policies, a **counterparty risk** may be a concern.

Counterparty risk
The risk that the other party to an agreement will default.

Apply Your Knowledge

Julie exports leather goods in a dozen foreign countries. She sells her goods exclusively through vendors and has no stores or warehouse storage facilities in any foreign country. However, she frequently goes to vendors' offices to make sales presentations to convince them to sell her goods. She brings her laptop and samples of her goods on the sales calls. She also rents a car to travel to and from the sales calls. She has heard that some of the countries to which she goes on sales calls have problems with kidnapping and ransom. What coverage should she consider?

Feedback: Julie should consider an exporters package policy. It covers foreign general liability, nonowned and hired automobile insurance, and foreign voluntary workers compensation. She particularly needs the nonowned and hired automobile insurance coverage as she drives to and from the sales calls. Optional coverage is available for her personal property, which would include her laptop and sales samples. Another optional coverage she may want to consider is for her kidnap and ransom exposure.

CAPTIVES AND MULTINATIONAL INSURANCE PROGRAMS

A multinational organization faces many challenges in establishing, coordinating, and operating an insurance program within its domicile country and the countries in which it has subsidiary operations. A multinational organization can use a captive insurer to facilitate the numerous transactions involved in a multinational insurance program.

A multinational organization will often use a captive insurance company and a fronting company to construct a global insurance program to address these country-specific issues and challenges:

- Restrictions on purchasing foreign currency in countries such as Argentina and Venezuela.
- Laws requiring a minimum reinsurance cession to the local market before ceding to companies domiciled outside the jurisdiction. For example, Brazil requires a minimum cession to its local market.

- Taxes levied on reinsurance placements and, in some jurisdictions, the imposition of value-added tax (VAT).

- Local laws requiring specific contract wording that adheres to normal market practice or the pre-approval of manuscript wording.

- Local currency volatility and its potential effect on local policy valuation and claims adjustment.

- Local laws requiring the use of an admitted insurance company.

Multinational Insurance Program Options

These are the three main options for a multinational organization to secure coverage for its foreign exposures:

- Secure a policy issued by an insurer licensed in the local jurisdiction

- Obtain global policies from insurers that are licensed to transact business in the organization's home country

- Develop a controlled master program that includes both local policies and a global policy providing worldwide coverage

A multinational organization that owns a captive insurer will most likely reinsure a significant portion of its worldwide risks back to its captive. See the exhibit "Retaining Multinational Risk in a Captive Insurer."

It is important for the multinational organization to understand which countries within which it has insurable exposures have foreign exchange restrictions and/or require a local insurer to issue a policy, collect premiums, and ultimately pay claims. The local insurer or fronting insurer will issue the locally admitted policy and reinsure the premiums and losses to the captive, less any mandatory local cessions. The captive owner may purchase a master **difference in conditions (DIC) policy** and/or a **difference in limits (DIL) policy** for any risks that may not be covered by the local policy or require limits in excess of what the local policy provides.

Difference in conditions (DIC) policy, or DIC insurance

Policy that covers on an "all-risks" basis to fill gaps in the insured's commercial property coverage, especially gaps in flood and earthquake coverage.

Difference in limits (DIL) policy

A policy that provides coverage for gaps resulting from different limits in a commercial insurance program.

Retaining Multinational Risk in a Captive Insurer

The diagram shows a typical example of how a multinational organization uses a captive. Each operating subsidiary purchases its local coverages from a fronting company licensed to operate in the local jurisdiction. The fronting company, in turn, reinsures the operating subsidiary exposures with the captive owned by the multinational organization. The captive then reinsures those exposures in excess of its retention with the panel of retrocessionaires (reinsurers of reinsurers) writing the controlled master program.

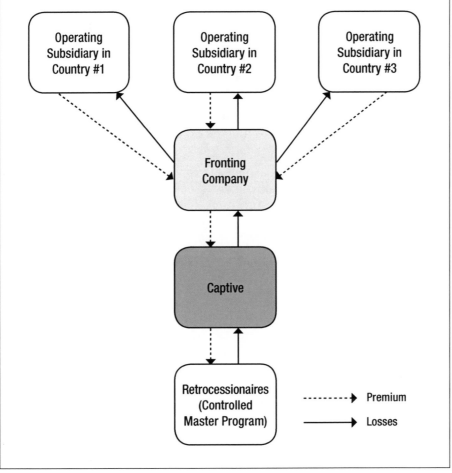

[DA11463]

Advantages of Using a Captive Insurer in a Multinational Insurance Program

A number of benefits may be realized by a multinational organization captive owner that assumes the reinsurance of the locally issued policies covering the exposures of its foreign subsidiaries:

- The limits, types of coverage, and risk transfer terms for the organization's worldwide exposures are likely to be consistent, without the possibility of gaps that could be created by differences in these items among the local and global policies.

- The breadth of coverage afforded at the local level can be controlled through the use of a manuscript reinsurance policy, resulting in consistent terms throughout the program.

- The overall pricing on the program may be more favorable, generating savings for the captive owner.

- The reinsurance transaction and a consolidated panel of outside reinsurers enable the captive insurer to limit its exposure to high hazard risks it does not want to directly insure.

- Any premium tax or local income tax can be managed with appropriate transfer pricing arrangements.

Review Questions

1. Describe the three key strategic reasons why insurers pursue global expansion.

2. Describe the three key areas for an insurer to evaluate in making a strategic decision about expansion into a global market.

3. Compare the approaches of strategic alliance, merger, and a wholly owned subsidiary for an insurer planning to expand into a global market.

4. Describe the key issues related to regulatory compliance and sales contracts for organizations involved in foreign trade.

5. Explain how insurers participating in worldwide insurance markets can insure global risks without violating United States sanctions laws.

6. Explain how licensing is used to regulate goods imported into the U.S.

7. Explain how the United Nations Convention of Contracts for the International Sale of Goods (CISG) facilitates international trade.

8. Distinguish between the open account and letter of credit methods of payment.

9. Explain how a domestic firm considering granting a product license to a foreign firm can protect its assets.

10. Identify an important aspect of franchising as a method of conducting international business.

11. For an organization planning to establish operations in a foreign country, list the two major questions the organization should research in relation to how that country's laws affect claims and losses.

12. Describe in general terms the application of directors and officers (D&O) liability coverage to violations of anti-bribery laws.

13. Describe in general terms the information an organization must protect under privacy and data-protection laws in the various countries in which it does business.

14. Describe the issues related to insurance laws, systems, and market offerings that an organization should research when contemplating expansion into another country.

15. Describe the business consequences that could result from a company's purchase of nonadmitted insurance coverage for its exposures in a country that prohibits nonadmitted insurance.

16. Describe how compulsory coverage requirements and government-owned insurance programs in some countries can affect international insurers.

17. Describe the regulatory issues related to premium taxes that insurers and brokers should consider when establishing an international insurance program.

18. Describe each of these options of a foreign corporation seeking to purchase United States insurance coverage:

    a. An insurer domiciled in the U.S.

    b. A fronting insurer domiciled in the U.S.

    c. A U.S.-domiciled subsidiary of a home-country insurer

    d. A nonadmitted alien insurer

19. Describe an advantage fronting arrangements have over U.S. insurers in underwriting U.S. insurance for foreign accounts.

20. Identify the factors an agent or broker must consider to be successful in handling foreign accounts.

21. Describe how an organization can use territorial endorsements to its United States insurance policies enhance its overseas protection.

22. Describe the advantages and disadvantages of using territorial endorsements to U.S. insurance policies.

23. Describe the advantages of using international package policies to cover overseas exposures.

24. Describe how an organization can use coverage from nonaffiliated local insurers to insure its overseas exposures.

25. Describe the advantages of using a controlled master program (CMP) to cover international exposures.

26. Describe the advantages of purchasing admitted coverage locally.

27. Describe who the exporters package policy is intended for.

28. Describe who the admitted policies of a controlled master program cover.

29. Identify the primary advantage of a controlled master program.

30. Explain the country-specific issues a multinational organization addresses by using a captive and a fronting company to construct its global insurance program.

31. Explain the three main options a multinational organization has to secure coverage for its foreign exposures.

32. Explain why a captive owner might purchase a difference in conditions (DIC) policy.

33. Explain why a captive owner might purchase a difference in limits (DIL) policy.

34. Describe the benefits a multinational organization captive owner that assumes the reinsurance of locally issued polices covering the exposures of its foreign subsidiaries might realize.

Application Questions

1. Innovative Components Inc. (ICI), a United States company, has manufacturing plants in several countries, including Indonesia. ICI international exposures are covered under a controlled master program (CMP).

An Indonesian court recently found the ICI Indonesia plant liable for polluting a village's water supply and imposed damages that exceed the limits of its local liability policy. Describe how the CMP would handle this claim.

2. The Fashion Handbags Corporation (FHC), headquartered in New Jersey, has a small plant where handbags are assembled. The handbags are sold in upscale boutiques in the northeast United States. Internet sales have grown exponentially, and the handbags are in great demand in Europe and Southeast Asia. Management of FHC has decided to open plants to manufacture handbags in Hong Kong and Berlin. Each plant will also include a sales office that will employ local representatives who will travel in their own countries and to neighboring countries to market the handbags to shops and boutiques.

   FHC will begin by sending employees to the two cities to locate facilities to lease for the plants and sales offices and to hire and train local employees. Once operations are established, several U.S. employees will remain in both cities to manage assembly and sales.

   FHC management now must determine its insurance needs and solutions in relation to its expansion. Among its current coverages are a Commercial General Liability (CGL) policy, commercial auto coverage, commercial inland marine (including annual transit) coverage, and workers compensation coverage.

   a. Identify the exposures FHC will take on as it expands into both Hong Kong and Berlin.

   b. Identify the international insurance solutions that involve endorsements to FHC's existing insurance policies, an international package policy, or local policies that FHC could use to address the exposures identified in a. (Answers may vary.)

   c. Describe how FHC could use a controlled master program to cover its international exposures rather than an international package policy and/or endorsements to current policies.

3. Joan is a risk management professional working for the parent company of a multinational corporation. She is trying to decide whether she should buy admitted or nonadmitted insurance to cover her employer's foreign subsidiary. Last year she purchased coverage from an admitted insurer. In that year, major claims went unpaid because of the insolvency of the insurer. The insurer also disputed the validity of the claims, saying Joan had misinterpreted the policy, which was written in the language of the country where the foreign subsidiary was domiciled. How will last year's lack of coverage likely influence Joan's decision to buy coverage from an admitted versus a nonadmitted insurer?

4. A captive owner of a multinational organization has purchased a number of locally issued policies for its subsidiaries in those countries. The local insurer has agreed to reinsure the exposures under the policies it has issued back to the captive insurer. The captive owner has also requested

that the local insurer provide a much larger limit and "all-risks" perils under its local policy. The local insurer has refused the captive owner's request. What options are available to the captive owner to secure the additional limits and the broadened coverage?

SUMMARY

The strategic reasons for global expansion include revenue growth and financial stability along with global competitiveness. However, there are significant risks associated with expanding into global markets, and insurers need to perform a market analysis and evaluate economic considerations along with political risks before deciding to expand into a global market. Insurers can enter a foreign market by forming a strategic alliance, joint venture, or merger with an insurer operating in that country. Alternatively, insurers can form a new company or acquire an existing one to establish a subsidiary in a new global market.

Companies can engage in international business through foreign trade, foreign contractual relationships, or foreign direct investment. Foreign trade involves the import and/or export of goods. Foreign contractual relationships include product licensing and franchising. Direct foreign investment can occur through the use of subsidiaries or joint ventures.

Companies operating in foreign countries face unique challenges, complex risks, and significant loss exposures. Insurance programs covering global businesses must be tailored to a company's individual needs. In all countries in which they conduct business, companies must be familiar with diverse laws, regulations, and insurance schemes and systems, as well as with local cultures, customs, and languages.

When establishing an international insurance program, the insurer, the broker, and the client company must comply with all insurance-related regulations in each country where the policyholder has operations. Many of these regulations relate to the everyday business of insurance, including nonadmitted insurance, compulsory coverages, mandatory participation in government insurance programs, permissible insurance activities, and premium taxes. Most international insurers have regulatory compliance departments that help them monitor and adhere to applicable regulations and work with governmental agencies on compliance issues. Insurance brokers should also be familiar with the legalities of transacting insurance in foreign countries and with the insurance-related laws and regulations of the countries in which they do business.

Foreign organizations operating in the U.S. require insurance for their U.S. operations. This insurance is called "reverse flow business." Foreign corporations seeking to purchase U.S. insurance policies have four basic options for insurance placement:

- An insurer domiciled in the U.S.
- A fronting insurer domiciled in the U.S.
- A U.S.-domiciled subsidiary of a home-country insurer
- A nonadmitted alien insurer (as permitted by surplus lines laws in the U.S.)

As business and not-for-profit organizations expand into foreign countries, they must be aware of their changing exposures to loss and of the insurance solutions available to address these exposures. Four common methods of addressing international insurance exposures are territorial endorsements to U.S. insurance policies, international package policies, local placements, and controlled master programs.

A variety of insurance solutions can be selected to meet a company's international loss exposures. In the initial phases of international business, adequate solutions may include endorsements to the company's existing U.S. policies, an international package policy, and local placements. As the company's international exposures become more complex, the best solution is a CMP that combines local placements with master policies that provide coverage on a DIC and DIL basis.

When structuring an international insurance program, an insured's risk management professional should consider whether to buy admitted insurance (for a decentralized structure) or nonadmitted insurance (for a centralized structure). This decision should be based on the advantages and disadvantages of both types of insurance. The best structure may be a package policy, such as for exporters who have no foreign, permanent place of business to insure. However, for many established multinational companies with permanent foreign locations, the preferred structure includes a collection of admitted and nonadmitted insurance called a controlled master program. That program has advantages and disadvantages to consider as well.

A multinational organization will often use its captive insurer as a reinsurer within its global insurance program, primarily because of individual countries' requirements for locally admitted insurance policies.

ASSIGNMENT NOTES

1. U.S. Department of Commerce, *Survey of Current Business*, October 2007, pp. 114-115 and 132.

2. U.S. Department of Commerce, *Survey of Current Business*, pp. 114–115 and 132.

3. Additional information can be found at www.ustreas.gov/offices/enforcement/ofac/faq/answer.shtml#global1.

4. Lu Wang and Michael Patterson, "Birinyi Bullish as Bears With Deja Vu Can't Wait to Sell," Business Week, businessweek.com/news/2012-05-03/birinyi-

bullish-as-bears-with-deja-vu-can-t-wait-to-sell-in-may#p2, (accessed May 4, 2012).

5. 15 U.S.C. § 78dd-1, et seq.

6. Wendy Wysong and Peter Chaffetz, "OFAC Gets Tough: Recent Cases Involving Penalties Against Insurance Carriers by the Office of Foreign Assets Control Underscore the Need for a Formal Policy," Axon Group, March 1, 2009, http://findarticles.com/p/articles/mi_m0BJK/is_3_20/ai_n31444757/pg_2/?tag=content;col1 (accessed June 7, 2012).

7. This and other information in this module about insurance-related regulations in Mexico and France is summarized from Axco's Insurance Market Reports, Non-Life (Property & Casualty), with Axco's permission.

8. U.S. Department of Commerce, Table 1291, "Foreign Direct Investment Position in the United States on a Historical-Cost Basis by Selected Country, 2000 to 2010," www.census.gov/compendia/statab/2012/tables/12s1292.pdf (accessed August 1, 2012).

9. U.S. Department of Commerce, Table 1300, "U.S. International Trade in Goods and Services: 2000 to 2010," www.census.gov/compendia/statab/2012/tables/12s1300.pdf (accessed August 1, 2012).

10. Zack Phillips, "Master Program Packs Advantages, Risk Manager Says," Business Insurance, April 4, 2010, www.businessinsurance.com/article/20100404/ISSUE03/304049993 (accessed February 1, 2012).

11. Harold D. Skipper and W. Jean Kwon, Risk Management and Insurance: Perspectives in a Global Economy (Malden, Mass.: Blackwell Publishers, 2007), p. 367.

Climate Change Risk, Cyber Risk and Terrorism Risk

Educational Objectives

After learning the content of this assignment, you should be able to:

▷ Explain how climate change can increase risk for organizations.

▷ Explain how an organization can have cyber risk loss exposures in each of the following categories:

- Property
- Net income
- Liability

▷ Explain how organizations can control or finance their cyber risk exposures.

▷ Describe cyber risk insurance policies in terms of the following key elements:

- Insuring agreements
- Coverage triggers
- Exclusions
- Limits of insurance
- Coverage territory

▷ Describe the Terrorism Risk Insurance Act (TRIA) in terms of the following:

- Purpose and duration of TRIA
- Definition of certified acts of terrorism
- Lines of business to which TRIA applies
- Make-available provision and disclosure requirements

Outline

Climate
Change Risk

Cyber Risk Loss
Exposures

Controlling
and Financing
Cyber Risk Loss
Exposures

Cyber Risk
Insurance Policies

The Terrorism Risk
Insurance Act

The Terrorism Risk
Insurance Program
Reauthorization
Act of 2015
(TRIPRA 2015)

Terrorism
Endorsements
for Commercial
Property and
Liability Forms

Summary

5

- Federal participation trigger
- Loss-sharing provisions and program cap

▶ Describe the purpose and application of the Terrorism Risk Insurance Program Reauthorization Act of 2015 (TRIPRA 2015).

▶ Summarize the purpose and provisions of the terrorism endorsements developed by Insurance Services Office, Inc., and the National Council on Compensation Insurance, Inc.

Climate Change Risk, Cyber Risk and Terrorism Risk

5

CLIMATE CHANGE RISK

Risk managers and insurers must address the potential effects of global warming and climate change on their organizations.

A growing body of scientific evidence has documented a gradual warming of the earth's atmosphere over the past century-and-a-half. Many scientists have attributed this phenomenon to human-caused emissions of greenhouse gases; however, global warming and its causes are subjects of continuing debate in both scientific and political circles. Controversy also surrounds the extent and nature of climate change; its implications for countries, businesses, and individuals; and appropriate responses.

As the debate continues, many governments, business organizations, and insurers are beginning to consider the potential for a wide variety of climate-change risks, including property, business, liability, environmental, regulatory, and reputational risk. Identifying, predicting, and treating these risks will become increasingly important to risk management professionals and others over coming decades.

Climate Change Debate

Although some scientists contend that global warming is the result of natural climatic variations, a consensus of scientific bodies has attributed global warming to human emissions of the byproducts of fossil fuels and other substances, such as ozone, methane, and nitrous oxide, into the earth's atmosphere.

Various scientific scenarios of global warming's effect on the earth's climate, populations, countries, ecosystems, and economies have been presented. Shrinking sea ice, receding glaciers, and thawing of permafrost in and near polar areas have been cited as evidence of the effects of global warming. Among predicted results of continued warming are rising sea levels and sea temperatures, fundamental changes to ecosystems, and more frequent and severe weather events.

Indeed, the late twentieth and early twenty-first centuries have seen many severe weather events of record intensity. Hurricanes, river flooding, ice storms, hailstorms, windstorms, prairie and forest fires, heat waves, droughts, and tornadoes have caused record losses across the globe. Some experts suggest that these events and corresponding losses result from global warming;

others attribute them to natural weather variations, which cause ever-increasing losses because of growing populations and development in vulnerable areas.

Types of Climate Change Risks

Many organizations are considering the effects of climate change on future losses in these areas of risk:[1]

- Physical risks—Increasing frequency and severity of major storm events, such as hurricanes, in areas of significant population growth may dramatically increase losses by damaging property and interrupting transportation, power supplies, and distribution chains and by causing injury or death to employees. Coastal erosion and property damage from rising sea levels could increase property losses by billions of dollars. Water shortages resulting from decreased snowpack could significantly affect manufacturing operations. Medical facilities and organizations' employee health coverages could become inadequate to deal with increased health risks caused by heat and insect-borne diseases.

- Litigation risks—Organizations may face litigation for contributing to climate change. Such claims may arise from individual shareholder suits, class action suits, and regulatory agency actions. Stockholder lawsuits could focus on whether a company's officers and directors rendered a company unprofitable by failing to plan for climate change. Climate change mismanagement could become a more common type of litigation in class action lawsuits. Organizations may also face action by government agencies for failure to comply with environmental regulations.

- Stockholder risks—Stockholders and investors are demanding more "transparency" from corporate leaders relating to their fiduciary responsibility to take action in relation to climate change. Corporate investors may petition the Securities and Exchange Commission (SEC) to require companies to disclose climate change risks. An organization that ignores climate change risk can lose investors, who may prefer, instead, to invest in organizations perceived to be environmentally responsible.

- Regulatory risks—Many governmental agencies are strengthening disclosure requirements and performance standards for energy utilization and consumption and establishing greenhouse gas emission controls. For example, European Union (EU) countries have imposed mandatory emissions reduction targets with significant noncompliance penalties. The Kyoto Protocol of the United Nations Framework Convention on Climate Change, ratified by the EU and its member states in 2002, contains legally binding emissions targets for developed countries. As of 2012, the United States had not adopted the Kyoto Protocol. However, many U.S. states and regions are enacting regulations aimed at global warming and greenhouse emissions. Other regulatory risks can include carbon taxes; energy efficiency regulations; and mandated uses of greener technologies, building materials, and building design. Risk managers of companies with international operations or exposures should be aware of differences in regulations from country to country.

- Reputational risks—Publicity about poor environmental policies or high greenhouse gas emissions can damage an organization's reputation. Repercussions of reputational damage can influence jurors in lawsuits involving the organization, local government bodies that grant zoning or construction permits, business news reporters, potential customers, environmental activists, and investors.

- Competition risks—An organization's ability to compete may be compromised by its failure to address climate change risks. Organizations that establish effective policies to deal with climate change exposures will have the competitive advantage among customers and interest groups who are concerned about environmental issues.

Climate Change Risk Treatment

Climate change risk can be addressed through risk control, risk finance, and risk transfer techniques.

Risk Control

Organizations can adopt a variety of risk control measures in relation to climate change, including these:

- Appointment of team or individual to be responsible for climate change risk management—A person or team with a working knowledge of climate change should be appointed to address the climate change exposure.

- Risk avoidance—An organization may choose to withdraw from business areas that present climate change risk. An analysis of environmental costs and risks for various products or processes could reveal new market and product opportunities that may reduce climate change risk.

- Disclosure of financial risks—A detailed disclosure of an organization's climate change risks indicates a company's good-faith effort to measure, mitigate, and control climate change loss exposures. Such a disclosure may help encourage and retain investors.

- Disaster planning—Organizations must develop disaster planning for catastrophic events such as hurricanes, which may increase in frequency and intensity. These plans may include evacuation procedures, arrangements for alternative facilities, stockpiling of emergency supplies, and more frequent computer data backup.

- Reduction of greenhouse gases—Companies that emit greenhouse gases should assess their internal emissions reduction opportunities in comparison with externally available approaches.

- Energy conservation and alternate energy usage—Energy conservation can include actions such as installing energy-efficient windows, using energy efficient lightbulbs, and adopting alternate energy approaches such as wind power and solar power.

- Adoption of "green" building measures and approaches—Structures can be built to promote energy conservation and use environmentally friendly construction products and processes such as geothermal heat pumps, rainwater collection, and radiant ceilings.

- Support for stricter building codes—Organizations should support and use stricter building codes that seek to prevent or reduce hurricane and other climate-related losses.

- Integration of climate change with overall business strategies—Climate change risk management decisions should be aligned with an organization's business strategies.

Risk Finance

The key risk finance technique for climate change loss exposures is insurance, particularly coverages for property, general liability/environmental, and directors and officers (D&O) liability.

If climate change causes more frequent and severe events, such as floods, fires, and hurricanes, property losses will increase. Property insurance costs could rise, and some insurance coverages may be unavailable. Organizations should work closely with their insurance agents and brokers to determine the effects of climate change on their property loss exposures and take steps to mitigate and control the losses.

Whether climate change liability is covered under commercial general liability policies is uncertain; in some cases, coverage may depend on how the pollution exclusion is applied. Insurers could conceivably use the pollution exclusion to deny claims of loss resulting from greenhouse gas emissions. Even if a causal connection is established among an insured's emissions, specific climate change, and the loss, an insured could theoretically argue that the loss was proximately caused by an effect of climate change, such as flooding, and only secondarily caused by greenhouse gas emissions. For example, if an organization's emissions were proved to have contributed to warming the atmosphere sufficiently to cause sea levels to rise and flooding to occur, the proximate cause of loss would be flooding, thereby avoiding the pollution exclusion.

Because of this uncertainty, risk managers should consider special environmental liability coverage. However, these policies may apply only when a causal connection is established between the insured's action and measurable harm. Insurers could cite the continuing scientific debate about the cause of global warming and the difficulties of measuring effects in denying coverage under environmental liability policies.

Risk managers should also consider climate change risk as it relates to D&O liability insurance. Shareholders may sue directors and officers for failure to disclose liabilities, loss of revenues or market share, and reputational damage resulting from climate change exposures. However, some D&O policies specifically exclude coverage for liability relating to climate change or global warming. Risk managers should also review D&O policy provisions that exclude or limit coverage for bodily injury or property damage, personal injury torts, or intentional misconduct to determine how such provisions might apply to climate change risk. To mitigate risk under D&O policies, organizations should take measures to fully disclose their financial risks and should use alternate energy sources.

Risk Transfer

Organizations may be able to transfer some climate change risk with techniques other than insurance. Two such techniques include weather derivatives and carbon trading.

Organizations can use weather derivatives to reduce financial risk associated with adverse weather conditions. A weather derivative is a financial contract whose value is based on the level of a weather-related index derived from variables such as average temperatures, snowfall, precipitation, or wind velocity during a designated period.

For example, a ski resort could purchase a weather derivative to mitigate the financial risk arising from insufficient snowfall or from higher-than-normal temperatures. Such a derivative could be designed to pay an agreed-upon amount for each inch the cumulative snowfall falls short of the base amount needed by the end of December to ensure the resort a profitable season.

Similarly, a power plant could use a derivative based on temperature to mitigate losses resulting from reduced energy use during a warmer-than-normal winter. Such a derivative could be designed to pay an agreed-upon amount per "heating degree days" (HDDs) within a designated period. The HDD measures the difference between average daily temperature and the base temperatures in a particular location. Financial organizations and experts continue to develop innovative indexes on which to base weather derivatives and innovative ways to gather data for such indexes. For example, derivatives based on indexes of soil moisture content could help farmers and agricultural businesses reduce the financial risk of drought; and soil moisture content can be derived from satellite images.

Carbon or emissions trading is used to control the overall amount of pollution in a given geographical area or country. Typically, a governing body establishes a cap on the amount of a pollutant that can be emitted. Companies are issued emission permits with credits or allowances that allow them to emit specific amounts of pollutants. The total amount of credits cannot exceed the cap. Organizations that need to exceed their emissions allowance limit can buy credits from organizations that pollute less. The transfer of these credits is called a trade.

In effect, the buyer of emissions credits pays for its emissions beyond its allowed allotment, and the seller is rewarded for reducing its emissions below its allotment. As a result, organizations that can easily reduce greenhouse emissions most inexpensively will do so, and the overall cost of reducing pollution is, in theory, reduced. Two of the largest carbon-emissions trading markets are the European Union Emissions Trading Scheme and the voluntary Chicago Climate Exchange program.

Critics of carbon trading suggest that the approach does not effectively reduce emissions. For example, caps that are set too high can result in surplus credits. Organizations are likely to purchase these readily available credits rather than reduce emissions. Furthermore, because credit allotments are based on past emission levels, an organization that successfully reduces its emissions may receive fewer credits in the future, reducing its incentive to reduce emissions even further. See the exhibit "Climate Change Litigation."

Climate Change Litigation

In 2011, the United States Supreme Court ruled that federal regulation of emissions of carbon dioxide and other greenhouse gases preempts a plaintiff's right to sue under common law to stop a defendant's actions alleged to contribute to global warming.

Eight states and several conservation groups filed suit against the operators of five fossil-fuel fired power plants, demanding that they be required to reduce their emissions of carbon dioxide on the grounds that such emissions contribute to global warming. The district court dismissed the case, ruling that the environmental issues involved were within the purview of the legislative and executive branches rather than the courts.

The appeals court reversed the ruling on the basis that the executive branch's Environmental Protection Agency (EPA) did not at that time regulate carbon greenhouse gas emissions under the Clean Air Act; therefore, the plaintiffs could seek recourse in their common-law nuisance complaint. Although the EPA subsequently promulgated emission regulations, the Supreme Court ruled that even if the EPA were to decline to regulate emissions, the fact that Congress had delegated that authority to the EPA was sufficient to preempt common law actions.

State of Connecticut, et al., v. American Electric Power Company, Inc., et. al., 131 S.Ct. 2527 (2011). [DA08687]

CYBER RISK LOSS EXPOSURES

Organizations that use the Internet—for example, web-based sales and services—as part of their daily operations may have more value residing in their databases than in their warehouses. Therefore, they must consider the risks presented to their electronic systems and electronic data as well as to those of their customers and suppliers.

A typical organization may rely on a computer network, electronic data, digital devices (for example, cell phones and personal digital assistants [PDAs]), and a website to conduct its business operations. Such technology-based systems can be damaged and their security unintentionally or intentionally compromised by the organization's employees or by customers and suppliers. Therefore, the use of such systems increases an organization's exposure to property, net income, and liability loss.

The high-tech risk posed to organizations that conduct their operations electronically and/or digitally is commonly known as "cyber risk." Additional terms for this type of risk and related loss exposures include e-commerce, cyber liability, Internet liability, cyber coverage (or insurance), and cyber security. The term cyber risk is a generic term that is generally accepted as the insurance industry standard. Cyber risk includes property, net income, and liability loss exposures.

Property

All organizations, not just those who routinely conduct online business transactions, should consider whether they have cyber risk property loss exposures. For example, a plumbing contracting business that is not involved in online sales or that does not have a website may believe it has no cyber risk property loss exposures. However, this may not be the case if the plumbing contractor has a computer network that supports its accounting, finance, and customer database. The data in such a network are exposed to multiple cyber risks, including computer viruses and corruption, which could severely impair the contractor's operations.

Property exposed to loss due to cyber risk typically falls into one or both of the two categories of personal property: **tangible property** and **intangible property**. The distinction between tangible property and intangible property is important because many commercial liability coverage forms define property damage to mean damage to tangible property and state that electronic data are not tangible property for coverage purposes. Although commercial property forms typically do not distinguish between tangible and intangible property, they usually limit coverage for loss of electronic data to an amount that is insufficient for most insureds. Consequently, a number of specific cyber risk loss exposures are not adequately covered, or not covered at all, by basic commercial property and liability insurance policies.

Tangible property
Property that has a physical form.

Intangible property
Property that has no physical form.

Human resources?
└ prop.

Loss of or Damage to Tangible Property

In the context of cyber risk, tangible property exposed to loss or damage can include computer equipment and related media, such as software and computer hardware. Additionally, other types of tangible property, such as money and securities, may be exposed to theft resulting from cyber attack. Organizations should identify loss exposures from both viruses originating externally (for example, via incoming email or by employees accessing an external website) and viruses originating internally (for example, by employee sabotage).

An organization's computer network and the software installed on it can be particularly vulnerable to cyber risk loss exposures such as network server damage and theft, as well as software damage or corruption. Additional tangible property cyber risk loss exposures include destruction of or damage to hardware (such as laptop computers or PDAs) because of security breaches and unauthorized use. Such exposures can significantly add to an organization's costs.

Loss of or Damage to Intangible Property

Although intangible property has no physical form, it can often be of substantial value to an organization. In the context of cyber risk, intangible property exposed to loss or damage can include electronic data (for example, confidential information such as Social Security and credit card numbers) and goodwill. Electronic data are particularly vulnerable to cyber loss exposures, such as corruption or virus contamination. For instance, consider a telemarketing organization that installs a software upgrade to its computer network. If the upgraded software contaminates the organization's data, the organization may be unable to perform its daily business operations because of the loss of its intangible property (the data).

Intellectual property

The product of human intelligence that has economic value.

Intangible property exposed to loss also can include **intellectual property**. For example, a trade secret is a practice, process, or other information used confidentially by an organization to maintain a competitive advantage in the marketplace. An unknown third party could obtain unauthorized access to an advertising firm's computer network and threaten to divulge the firm's trade secrets, a form of "cyber extortion."

Additional intangible cyber risk loss exposures include those resulting from trademark infringement, copyright infringement, or malicious code attack (software that, when installed on a computer system, produces harmful consequences such as "Trojan horses" or computer viruses). Intangible property loss exposures can significantly increase an organization's costs and harm its reputation.

Net Income

An organization can assess the potential extent of its cyber risk net income loss exposures by considering how it might be affected by a reduction in or cessation of its normal business operations as a consequence of a cyber loss. Such reductions in or cessations of normal business operations are commonly known as "business interruptions." Any possible business interruption that decreases revenues, increases expenses, or both should be considered by an organization when reviewing its cyber risk loss exposures.

Cyber risk net income loss exposures that result in business interruption can relate not only to the organization itself, but also to its key customers and suppliers. For example, an online toy retailer has a net income cyber loss exposure if it derives significant revenue from Internet sales. It may also lose income if a cyber loss (such as corrupted software that interrupts the toy manufacturing process) affects one of its key toy suppliers, thus reducing its inventory during its peak sales season.

Net income exposed to cyber risk loss can be discussed in terms of loss of business income (including contingent business income) and extra expenses. Both of these amounts can be affected should a cyber loss strike an organization.

Loss of Business Income (Including Contingent Business Income)

Loss of business income occurs when an organization's net income and normal operating expenses change as a result of a loss. In terms of cyber risk loss exposures, organizations typically examine potential losses that can occur to computer networks (hardware, software, data, and related media). For example, a denial-of-service attack can slow or block users' access to a website, an email address, or a network by flooding an organization's network with requests for website pages or with numerous email messages. For an organization that generates business income via its website, a denial-of-service attack can be very costly, directly affecting sales revenue.

An additional example of a cyber risk business income loss exposure is one in which a virus infects an organization's network, corrupting data and destroying software. An organization should routinely create a duplicate copy (backup) of its data. Although software can be replaced, at a cost, the organization will sustain a business income loss if it cannot conduct its normal operations during the period of restoration.

Cyber risk contingent business income loss exposures relate to an organization's income that is contingent (or dependent) on a location that is not owned or operated by the primary organization. For example, a key customer of an electronics components manufacturer typically places its orders to the components manufacturer through the Internet. If the key customer's computer network is attacked (for example, through a virus, a denial-of-service attack, or sabotage) and cannot be used to place orders, the resulting loss in revenue, if it cannot be replaced, is a contingent business income loss. Additionally, an organization that uses a web-hosting company to manage its business website could suffer a contingent business income loss if the web-hosting company's server is rendered inoperable for an extended time.

Similar cyber risk contingent business income exposures can apply to an organization's suppliers, utilities, and third-party outsourcers, including exposures related to the consequences of business interruption resulting from a utility's off-site power failure; failure of a third party to properly manage and secure data (possibly resulting in identity theft); website defacement; and abuse of wireless networks. All of these loss exposures can result in contingent business income losses.

Extra Expense

In addition to normal operating expenses, including payroll, that an organization has during a time of suspended or impaired business operations, it may also need to incur extra expenses (in excess of its normal expenses) to minimize the effects of the business interruption or continue its operations.

An organization may have cyber risk extra expense loss exposures if, as a consequence of a cyber loss, it has to purchase items such as software, hardware, or other electronic media or hire labor to recreate lost or stolen electronic data. For example, if a database is infected with a virus, the data may need to be restored or cleansed by technology specialists at an additional expense.

Liability

Organizations that maintain a presence in cyber space face increased cyber risk liability loss exposures. These exposures arise from activities such as using e-mail, maintaining websites, developing software, and conducting daily business operations (for example, sales and service) on the Internet.

The Federal Bureau of Investigation (FBI) reported that online crime complaints increased 22.3 percent from 2008 to 2009. The total loss linked to online fraud was $559.7 million in 2009, double the loss in 2008.[2] Because not all cyber crimes are reported and liability can result from noncriminal activity, actual liability losses are likely to be significantly higher. The categories of cyber risk liability loss exposures are bodily injury and property damage liability, personal and advertising injury liability, intellectual property liability, and errors and omissions (E&O) liability.

Bodily Injury and Property Damage Liability

Organizations engaging in technology-related activities, such as transmitting electronic data, maintaining information on or conducting business through websites, or designing and supporting software, must be on guard against the bodily injury and property damage loss exposures generated by these activities.

Cyber risk bodily injury liability loss exposures can occur because of an organization's software development. For example, a software developer develops a program for physicians and pharmacists regarding the potential adverse interactions of different prescription medications. Because of a formulary error in the program, physicians and pharmacists conclude that a particular combination of prescription drugs is safe when the combination actually produces a serious or fatal reaction in a number of patients. The patients and their families sue because of the bodily injury that resulted from the software error.

Another example of a cyber risk bodily injury loss exposure entails misinformation obtained from an organization's website. Some organizations do not exercise the same degree of care in monitoring information published on their online sites as they do with information published using traditional methods.

For example, if an individual obtains information from a superstore retailer's website regarding common home health care treatment tips, but the information excludes or incorrectly states an important step, causing injury, the individual could sue the superstore for the resulting bodily injury.

Cyber risk property damage loss exposures can occur because of an organization's overall technology operations, including those related to software, hardware, electronic data, and other media. For example, an insurance industry software provider issues an updated version of its software to an insurance brokerage. However, because of a security failure that occurred when the software upgrade was developed and transmitted to the brokerage, upon installation, the upgrade renders the brokerage's computer network inoperable, causing significant property damage to the system. The insurance brokerage then sues the software provider for the property damage to the network.

Personal and Advertising Injury Liability

Organizations assess personal and advertising injury liability loss exposures as part of their general liability loss exposure analysis. Typical loss exposures include liability resulting from offenses such as malicious prosecution, slander, libel, defamation, disparagement, or false advertising. However, coverage for a number of personal and advertising injury liability loss exposures related to cyber risk is either limited or excluded by basic general liability coverage. These exposures should be addressed.

For example, consider an online stock market trading company that also offers discussion forums for its users. A user posing as an "insider" posts false information about the valuation of Company A and its stock, which eventually damages Company A's reputation as well as its market position. Company A sues the trading company for defamation. Additionally, in an attempt to gain a competitive edge, the same trading company might disparage other online trading companies on its own website by making such statements as "Why use Company B if their website is always down?" or "You may think Company C costs less than us, but ask them about their service fees!" Company A's competition can sue for disparagement.

Organizations that conduct business on websites should be concerned about any personal and advertising injury liability arising from the consequences of advertisements of products for which the insured has assumed liability under contract or agreement. The organization is responsible for any loss exposures and related liability that is assumed by contract. Consider an online tire retailer that contracts to advertise and sell a particular manufacturer's tires. The online retailer advertises "Tires last for 50,000 miles!" However, in reality, the manufacturer's tires wear out after only 15,000 miles. Customers sue the online tire retailer for false advertising relating to the representations made about the manufacturer's tires.

Intellectual Property Liability

Cyber risk intellectual property liability loss exposures can affect an organization's copyrights, trademarks, patents, or trade secrets. For example, a copyright infringement loss exposure can occur when a major political blog site's owner posts on the blog copyrighted articles, in their entirety, from a well-known newspaper. If the site owner refuses to accede to the newspaper's demand that the blog stop posting the articles, the newspaper can sue the blog for copyright infringement.

Another example of a cyber risk intellectual property liability loss exposure relates to trademark infringement. A new social networking website could have as its logo a distinctive design that soon becomes very popular. However, if the logo is identical to one that belongs to a long-established real estate firm, that also does business on the Internet, the firm could sue the website owners for trademark infringement.

Errors and Omissions Liability

As organizations continue to expand their business operations into cyber space, whether they are manufacturing traditional products for sale online, developing software for retail sale, or maintaining computer networks, they should be aware of cyber risk E&O liability. E&O liability presents the possibility of considerable damage to the organization, not only financially but also to its reputation, market standing, and goodwill.

Organizations should consider the scope of their daily business operations and how their actions or failure to act could result in errors and omissions liability. For example, cyber risk E&O liability loss exposures can include design errors, manufacturing errors, or service errors. To illustrate, consider a high-tech company that specializes in software design and sells a software program to an Internet-based company that offers music and video downloads for purchase. Because of a design error in the software company's program, thousands of customers were unable to complete the download process over a long holiday weekend, causing them to pay for music and video downloads they did not receive. The Internet music and video company holds the software design company liable for the design error in the software program and for the resulting damages caused by lost revenue.

Additional cyber risk E&O liability loss exposures can include loss resulting from errors relating to a company's product or the work it produces. For example, if a programmer creates a website for a retail client and neglects to include security safeguards to protect the site, the client could incur significant damages because of a business interruption if the website is hacked.

CONTROLLING AND FINANCING CYBER RISK LOSS EXPOSURES

Internet-related technology has created new opportunities for growth for all types of organizations; however, these opportunities increase organizations' vulnerability to cyber risk loss exposures from many sources, both internal and external. Theft of information and electronic data has now surpassed physical theft at global companies.[3]

Because cyber risk loss exposures have the potential to damage an organization's assets, reputation, market standing, and customer and supplier relationships, risk control measures for these exposures are essential for any organization.

Many organizations will also need risk financing for their cyber risk loss exposures. Typical commercial insurance policies often exclude or restrict coverage for cyber risk loss exposures.

It is important for risk management and insurance professionals to be aware that cyber risk is rapidly evolving. As technology becomes more widely used and more complex, cyber risk loss exposures increase in both frequency and severity. In response, new companies and products enter the insurance market to provide coverage.

Risk Control Measures for Cyber Risk

Specialized risk control measures are usually necessary for an organization to control cyber risk loss exposures involving property, net income, and liability. These risk control measures begin with an organization's determining the scope of its cyber risk loss exposures, often with assistance from a risk management or security specialist. A cyber risk security strategy should incorporate the organization's business objectives and available budget and should include an assessment of the appropriateness of the risk control measures for the loss exposures that are being addressed. Properly structured, a cyber risk security strategy can preserve an organization's resources, reduce the severity of losses that do occur, and hasten the organization's recovery from a cyber loss.

Specific risk control measures to prevent, deter, or mitigate cyber risk include these:

- Physical controls
- Procedural controls
- Personnel controls
- Managerial controls
- Investigation and prosecution of cyber crimes
- Post-cyber incident rapid recovery program

Physical Controls

Physical controls place barriers between cyber criminals and their targets. Organizations should provide basic physical protection, such as guards, locked doors, central security alarms, and automatic devices to detect intruders. Additionally, organizations can physically limit access to computer equipment and programs and can implement other administrative and managerial safeguards that control physical access to systems or to the computer network environment.

Cyber criminals may use tactics to which computer hardware and software are particularly vulnerable, such as damaging them through the magnetic disruption and interruption of electrical power. Therefore, surveillance should be used for highly sensitive areas where data are stored. Access to such areas should be controlled by requiring personnel to identify themselves with badges or through **biometrics**.

Biometrics

Biological identification of an individual using anatomy or physiology.

Procedural Controls

Procedural controls specify that tasks be performed in secure ways that prevent or reduce losses. In terms of cyber risk, procedural controls apply to how a computer system and all of its associated data are protected. Security policies should clearly state system authorization requirements for use of the system, levels of system access, and system response measures to unauthorized access.

Protection from hackers is a critical reason for organizations to create, implement, and regularly update procedural controls. Hackers have many motives for their attacks, including identity theft, extortion, destruction of competitive advantage, surveillance and reconnaissance, terrorism, political protest, and the satisfaction of defeating an organization's computer security system. If appropriate safeguards are not in place, organizations may never notice clandestine hacker intrusions that are designed to steal information. Other intrusions that use malicious software or codes (malware) are designed to deliberately and noticeably disrupt operations. Procedural controls that organizations use to thwart hackers include passwords, antivirus software, data encryption for stored data and data in transit, and firewalls.

Additionally, an organization can specify monitoring procedures in its procedural controls to prevent inappropriate access or use of its computers. For example, monitoring procedures may prohibit employees from using the organization's computers to access pornographic or other inappropriate Web sites, thereby eliminating activities that might expose the organization to a malware attack. Procedural controls may also be designed for network updates to ensure that new programs are tested before they are used to process actual data, possibly preventing an errors and omissions liability claim.

Other procedures can include establishment of a privacy policy and procedures for how, when, and under what terms an organization will allow material from other Web sites (such as hyperlinks or content) to appear on its own

Web site. These policies and procedures could prevent claims for violation of privacy laws and for trademark or copyright infringement.

Personnel Controls

The attitudes, performance, and behavior of employees can leave an organization exposed to a cyber attack, regardless of whether the resulting loss or damage was intended. Some employees are inadvertently the source of cyber losses—for example, employees who download software from the Internet and unknowingly introduce a virus to the system. Others deliberately commit cyber crimes such as stealing intellectual property or committing identity theft. Disgruntled former employees with knowledge of or access to proprietary information are also potential sources of cyber losses.

Organizations can institute sound personnel controls to mitigate the cyber risk loss exposures presented by their employees. Personnel controls include such measures as preemployment screening, training, outlining unacceptable cyber behavior with associated consequences, and termination procedures that include revoking access and passwords.

Personnel controls can also extend to how the organization deals with its customers, suppliers, and neighbors. For example, a frustrated customer could become hostile and launch an electronic attack against the business by posting inflammatory information on public message boards and/or infecting the business's computer network with a virus or a **denial-of-service attack**. Consequently, the organization and its employees should try to maintain positive relationships with customers and other stakeholders and report any threat or suspicion of a cyber attack.

Denial-of-service attack
An attempt to overwhelm a computer system or network with excessive communications in order to deny users access.

Managerial Controls

Managerial controls reduce cyber loss exposures by establishing an environment that prevents cyber losses or assists in their detection. Managerial controls include centralizing responsibility for cyber security. Many organizations have a chief information officer (CIO) or a chief risk officer (CRO) whose responsibilities include overseeing all technological aspects of the organization's operations. Managerial controls also involve ensuring that systems and procedures that have been adopted are monitored and followed to control cyber loss exposures. This effort can include monitoring the cyber risk security plan and ensuring compliance with risk control measures such as the creation and storage of backup files and the segregation of responsibilities to prevent any individual from having control of the entire system or inappropriate system access.

Additionally, an organization should continually evaluate and revise its risk control measures. As quickly as risk control measures are instituted to combat cyber risk, the technology that cyber criminals use to overcome them evolves. Therefore, organizations must be prepared to update their techniques accordingly.

Investigation and Prosecution of Cyber Crimes

Often, organizations do not report cyber crimes to authorities because they fear negative publicity, worry that competitors could take advantage of an incident, or believe authorities cannot assist them in prosecuting cyber crimes. Although some initial negative publicity may result when an organization reveals that it has been attacked by a cyber criminal, the organization also may experience a public relations benefit by voluntarily releasing the news regarding a cyber crime, particularly if it is an innocent victim. The organization can describe the measures it is taking to prevent such an incident from recurring, thereby restoring consumer confidence and neutralizing any advantage competitors might gain from initial negative publicity. Additionally, many law enforcement agencies possess expertise in cyber crime and can help organizations control their loss exposures. Furthermore, organizations that vigilantly investigate and prosecute cyber criminals are less likely to be viewed as an "easy target" by cyber criminals.

Reporting certain types of cyber crimes may not be optional for some organizations. Most states now require organizations to disclose to authorities and affected individuals instances when data security breaches occur that expose personal information to identity theft or other types of cyber crime.

Post-Cyber Incident Rapid Recovery Program

A post-cyber incident rapid recovery program aids in reducing the severity of an organization's cyber losses and in restoring operational functionality as soon as possible. Implementing a rapid recovery program focuses on the organization's ability to preserve and sustain its net income in the event of a cyber loss.

Risk control measures the organization can use as part of a post-cyber incident rapid recovery program include maintaining full backups of the computer system—complete with an operational Web site, e-mail, and Internet links— at an alternate location. Additionally, all vital legal and technical documents, as well as copies of computer storage media, should be secured in a fire-resistive, off-site repository, such as those operated by specialized data storage companies.

Contingency measures should be established to provide equipment, software, or any additional personnel that may be necessary to analyze, repair, cleanse, and restore lost or damaged data. Also, plans should be developed to address the effects on suppliers and customers.

A rapid recovery program should also include a public relations component so that, if necessary, the organization's public image, as well as customer and supplier relationships, can be preserved in the aftermath of a cyber loss. See the exhibit "Top Ten Most Effective Technologies To Use Against Cyber Criminals."

Top Ten Most Effective Technologies To Use Against Cyber Criminals

2007 Rank	Technology (2007 Percentage)
1	Stateful firewalls (firewalls that identify and monitor the state of network connections or communications crossing them) (82%)
2	Access controls (79%)
3	Electronic access controls (78%)
4	Application layer firewalls (72%)
5	Host-based anti-virus programs (70%)
6	Password complexity (70%)
7	Encryption (69%)
8	Heuristics-based spam filtering (filters with header or content sensitivity) (69%)
9	Network-based policy enforcement (68%)
10	Network-based anti-virus programs (65%)

Adapted from 2007 eCrime Watch Survey CSO Magazine, U.S. Secret Service, CERT®Program, Microsoft Corp.
[DA05048]

Risk Financing Measures for Cyber Risk

Organizations exposed to cyber risk must consider the financial consequences of a property, net income, or liability loss and whether they wish to transfer or retain those losses. Sources of risk financing can be arranged before (pre-loss financing) or after (post-loss financing) a loss occurs. Although an organization may have risk financing measures in place to address basic property, net income, and liability loss exposures, additional risk financing measures may be necessary to address cyber risk loss exposures. Risk financing measures include insurance, noninsurance risk transfer, and retention.

Insurance

Because the field of cyber risk is an emerging and dynamic one, many organizations are uncertain of the value of cyber risk insurance or even of its availability as a technique for dealing with cyber risk. Cyber risk insurance coverage forms are still evolving. However, insurance is an important technique for organizations to use to manage their property, net income, or liability losses and the costs of compliance (for example, notification of customers after a theft of computer data) as a consequence of cyber risk loss exposures.

The cost of cyber risk can be significant. Hackers increasingly focus on attaining "back door" access to organizations and obtaining proprietary information that they can use for quick financial gain. A survey of computer security professionals reports that the average loss from cyber crime was $350,424 in 2007.[4]

 **Reality Check**

Cost of Data Breach

The cost of a data breach at an organization, whether or not the breach results in theft or damage, can be significant because of compliance with requirements to notify customers of the breach and other regulatory requirements. Even if no customer business is lost as a result of the notifications, the cost of the notifications and assistance to customers, such as monitoring their credit reports, can pose a risk to the bottom line of an organization.

For example, in one case, a January 2007 data breach at TJX Companies, the company paid, in addition to other large losses, $9.75 million to settle claims from forty-one state attorneys general relating to TJX's failure to adequately safeguard customers' financial information.

"Attorney General Martha Coakley Announces Multi-State Settlement with the TJX Companies, Inc., Over Massive Data Breach," Office of the Attorney General, Commonwealth of Massachusetts, June 23, 2009, www.mass.gov/?pageID=cagopressrelease&L=1&L0=Home&sid=Cago&b=pressrelease&f=2009_06_23_tjx_settlement&csid=Cago (accessed November 15, 2010). [DA06671]

One serious cyber loss could threaten any organization's financial position. Therefore, it is important for organizations to carefully consider insurance coverage as part of their cyber risk management programs.

Noninsurance Risk Transfer

Organizations can use noninsurance risk transfer as one means of risk financing. When entering into contracts or online agreements, organizations must ensure that the contractual language properly protects them from cyber risk loss exposures. A **hold-harmless agreement, or indemnity agreement**, is a type of noninsurance measure that organizations can use to receive reimbursement for cyber risk losses or to transfer their cyber risk loss exposures. For example, a Web site hosting company could sign a hold-harmless agreement promising to indemnify a customer, such as a retailer, for lost online sales if its server malfunctions. Another example is for an organization, through an indemnity agreement, to request to be named an additional insured under the indemnitor's insurance policy.

In addition to using hold-harmless agreements, many software firms also use liability disclaimers. While disclaimers do not transfer risk or act as risk financing, they can be used to limit the scope of liability. For example, organizations that collect their customers' personal information can post liability

Hold-harmless agreement (or indemnity agreement)
A contractual provision that obligates one of the parties to assume the legal liability of another party.

disclaimers and disclosure statements on their Web sites to fully inform customers of how their personal information may be used and the extent of the organization's liability should the information be illegally disclosed. They can also require electronic signatures from the customers to indicate consent.

Retention

An organization may use **retention** to finance its cyber risk loss exposures. One advantage of retention is that it encourages risk control. For example, when an organization pays the cost of its own losses, it may have a greater incentive to prevent and reduce them. A disadvantage associated with retention is that when an organization decides to retain its cyber risk loss exposures, the associated uncertainty of loss outcomes can negatively affect its financial position.

Should an organization decide to finance its losses by retaining rather than transferring them, it faces the possibility that retained losses will be more frequent or severe than expected. Because of this uncertainty, an organization should limit its retention for each individual loss to a severity level at which it can tolerate the potential variability in the sum of its retained losses. For example, a social networking Web site could purchase insurance for its third-party liability cyber risk loss exposures and decide to retain its first-party cyber risk loss exposures. Another organization could opt for both first-party and third-party coverage and strategically use deductibles when placing its coverage.

> **Retention**
> A risk financing technique by which losses are retained by generating funds within the organization to pay for the losses.

CYBER RISK INSURANCE POLICIES

Cyber risk insurance emerged as a specialized product category to meet the need for coverage that was not provided by traditional policies. Specialized cyber insurers, as well as traditional insurers, offer a variety of cyber risk insurance policies that can be customized to meet an organization's specific cyber risk loss exposures. Cyber risk insurance is one of the fastest growing lines of business. Written premiums for 2010 are estimated at $600 million, double the premiums written in 2006.[5]

Traditional commercial property and liability policies either exclude cyber risk loss exposures or provide limited coverage that is inadequate for most organizations. Meanwhile, the use of technology and related loss exposures continue to increase and create demand for insurance coverage. In 2009, e-commerce grew at a rate of 11 percent, compared to overall retail growth of 2.5 percent. Before the economic downturn in 2008, e-commerce was growing at an annual rate of 20 percent.[6] As technology continues to evolve with advances such as cloud computing, the loss exposures also evolve.

The lack of traditional insurance coverage and the expansion of the Internet provided an opportunity for new insurance products to meet the growing demand. An increasing number of insurers are entering the market. In addition to offering specialized cyber risk insurance policies, some insurers now offer Internet liability coverage in their management liability policies.[7]

The specific provisions of cyber risk insurance policies differ by insurer. Insurers typically offer policies containing first-party-only coverage (property and theft), third-party-only coverage (liability), or both in a combination policy format. Because first-party cyber risk losses can be difficult to assess and quantify, policies that offer first-party coverages have not been as widely available as those that include third-party coverages. Some insurers offer combination property and liability policies. Combination policies in particular allow insurers and organizations to match coverage with cyber risk loss exposures. Insurance and risk management professionals should understand the general aspects of cyber risk policies, including insuring agreements, coverage triggers, exclusions, limits of insurance, and coverage territory.

Insuring Agreements

The cyber risk coverage needs of organizations are as variable as the available coverage options. Therefore, some insurers allow their customers to supplement a basic product with the insuring agreements that are appropriate for them, while others allow for full policy customization using insuring agreements. Other insurers offer a standard package of insuring agreements or "modular policies" that include a particular range of coverage options.

Insuring agreements apply to various coverage areas. Their names can vary slightly from insurer to insurer. For example, "digital asset" coverage with one insurer may be known as "electronic data" coverage with another insurer. Insuring agreements that are commonly found in cyber risk insurance policies fall into these categories:

- Electronic data protection
- Cyber extortion
- Cyber crime
- Notification or remediation
- Business interruption
- Network security liability
- Privacy liability
- Electronic media liability
- Technology errors and omissions liability
- Intellectual property liability
- Terrorism coverage

The insuring agreements discussed do not represent any single insurer's insuring agreements, either with regard to policy language or coverage. Rather, the discussion focuses on the types of coverage available. Careful review of an actual policy is required to determine the coverage provided by that particular policy.

Electronic Data Protection

An electronic data protection insuring agreement typically provides coverage for costs to recover or restore electronic data that have been altered, destroyed, deleted, or damaged. For instance, a computer virus attack can damage an insured's software and corrupt its associated data, requiring the insured to purchase and install replacement software and restore corrupted data.

— 1st party

Cyber Extortion

A cyber extortion insuring agreement provides coverage for expenses related to computer network kidnap and/or ransom events. For example, a hacker may covertly penetrate an organization's computer network and threaten to reveal specific details regarding the attack's execution unless the organization capitulates to his or her demands.

— 1st party

Cyber Crime

A cyber crime insuring agreement covers theft of money and securities and, depending on the insurer's form, intangible property. Cyber crime losses typically result from computer attack or computer fraud. For example, a cyber criminal could gain unauthorized access to an insured's computer network and, through fraudulent billing, divert funds from the insured's cash accounts.

— 1st party

Notification or Remediation

A notification or remediation insuring agreement provides coverage for expenses related to crisis management during and after a cyber risk loss (typically related to a security breach). Coverage can include crisis management-related expenses such as costs to notify customers of a security breach and costs to develop and execute a public relations campaign to manage any negative publicity surrounding the breach and to maintain the insured's reputation.

— 3rd party?

Business Interruption

A business interruption insuring agreement provides coverage for loss of business income, loss of contingent business income, and payment of extra expenses incurred as a consequence of a business interruption or suspension of the insured's computer system (or dependent system) due to cyber risk loss. Depending on the insuring agreement offered by the insurer, in some cases only business income coverage (without extra expense coverage) is provided. For example, if an online retailer's website is forced offline for several days during a peak sales period because of a denial-of-service attack, the business

— 1st or 3rd party

interruption insuring agreement can compensate the retailer for loss of business income.

Network Security Liability

A network security liability insuring agreement provides coverage for liability arising from security breaches to an insured's computer network. Examples of sources of network security liability losses include a situation in which a cyber criminal attempts to gain access to the insured's network for personal financial gain, a random **malware** transmission, and a denial-of-service attack. The resulting liability losses include, for example, damage to customers' data, customers' loss of use of services, or misappropriation of funds from customer accounts.

Malware
Malicious software, such as a virus, that is transmitted from one computer to another to exploit system vulnerabilities in the targeted computer.

Privacy Liability

A privacy liability insuring agreement provides coverage for liability arising from unauthorized disclosure or use of the private information of others or, depending on the insuring agreement, liability arising out of an insured's failure to comply with privacy provisions contained in laws such as the Health Insurance Portability and Accountability Act (HIPAA), the Gramm-Leach-Bliley Act (GLBA), or any anti-identity theft legislation. Actions typically are generated by a network security breach or unauthorized access to or use of information. For example, a bank employee could gain unauthorized access to the bank's customer database and obtain customers' Social Security numbers, generating a privacy liability. The employee could also reveal the Social Security numbers and other personal customer information to an accomplice, who could use the information to commit identity theft.

Electronic Media Liability

An electronic media liability insuring agreement provides coverage for liability arising from the insured's electronic content. Depending on the insuring agreement, the coverage can include e-mail communications; website content; and message board or discussion forum content that results in actual or alleged acts of defamation, disparagement, libel, slander, or false advertising. Electronic media liability also can be categorized as errors and omissions in the written or spoken word resulting in claims alleging financial loss or damage. For example, a company may post advertising on its website that makes certain claims about its product that are subsequently proved to be greatly exaggerated or simply untrue. In such a case, a competitor or customer can sue the company for false advertising under its electronic media liability coverage.

Technology Errors and Omissions Liability

A technology errors and omissions liability insuring agreement provides coverage for liability arising from any negligent act, error, or omission relating to an insured's products or services provided to others. For example, an information technology (IT) consultant may recommend that a customer test its network after performing a software update. The customer runs the test and the computer network crashes, causing the customer's business operations to be interrupted for a week. If the customer sued the consultant for loss of business income and recovery costs, the consultant could be protected against this suit by technology errors and omissions liability coverage. Depending on the insuring agreement, the coverage can also apply to the employees of the insured's independent contractors.

Intellectual Property Liability

An intellectual property liability insuring agreement provides an insured with coverage for any copyright, trade secrets, trademark, or patent infringement claims arising out of the use of the insured's protected ideas or works (or infringing on the protected ideas or works of another). For example, a website offers copyright-protected films available for viewing and downloading, for a fee. If some of the videos are not yet authorized for release by the film studios who own their distribution rights, the website owner may be sued for copyright infringement.

Terrorism Coverage

Cyber risk policies, like most other commercial insurance policies, are subject to the Terrorism Risk Insurance Act (TRIA) of 2002, as amended in 2005 and 2007. Therefore, an insurer writing cyber risk coverage must include coverage against "certified acts of terrorism" as defined in TRIA, unless the insured declines the coverage. TRIA does not prohibit the insurer from excluding terroristic acts other than "certified acts of terrorism."

Coverage Triggers

Cyber risk insurance policies are usually subject to a claims-made coverage trigger. A claim is typically made when the insured first becomes aware of facts that could cause a reasonable person to assume that a loss of a type covered by the policy has occurred. Because insuring agreements vary, so, too, can the claim-triggering events, which can include a denial-of-service attack, loss of data, or a computer virus attack.

As is typical with claims-made policies, coverage is usually available for prior acts, subject to a retroactive date found either in the base form or added by endorsement.

Some insurers that provide policies focusing more on media liability, intellectual property liability, and technology-related coverages may offer forms with an occurrence coverage trigger. Occurrence coverage triggers are also specified in the insuring agreements and can include any covered event that occurs during the policy period, such as liability arising out of website content errors and omissions or trademark infringement liability. Because there is typically a provision in these policies that the trigger for coverage is the date of publication of the content that allegedly violates a trademark, patent, or copyright, an occurrence coverage form usually is more appropriate than a claims-made policy.

Exclusions

Exclusions restrict and clarify the coverage available under cyber risk policies and can vary by specific insuring agreements, a group of insuring agreements, or by overall policies. Just as the types of cyber risk policies offered vary, so do the types of policy exclusions.

Some cyber risk policies contain exclusions that are commonly found in standard property-casualty insurance coverage forms. These standard exclusions, which can include exclusions for pollution, strikes, war and insurrection, civil commotion, and nuclear energy, are not specific to cyber risk loss exposures. Additional standard exclusions typically relate to perils such as fire, explosion, lightning, wind, earthquake, or flood; these perils relate to loss exposures that are otherwise insured under other property and liability policies.

As with the various cyber risk insuring agreements, the particular exclusions found in cyber risk coverage differ. Exclusions contained in cyber risk coverage forms should be examined closely and considered together with other policy provisions to determine how coverage is applied as well as to make accurate comparisons among insurers. Insurance and risk management professionals should note that the described exclusions are commonly found in cyber risk policies but are not standard exclusions; some insurers may not include them (thereby providing the otherwise-excluded coverage), while other insurers may add exclusions less commonly used. Additionally, the language of each insurer's exclusion provisions varies. Therefore, all or part of the coverage excluded by the provision may also vary. Cyber risk policy exclusions can be grouped for this discussion into these categories:[8]

- General insurance exclusions
- Product-related exclusions
- Service-related and security-related exclusions
- Cyber risk-related exclusions

General Insurance Exclusions

General insurance exclusions are those exclusions found in cyber risk policies that may also be found in other types of policies that provide professional insurance coverage or related errors and omissions-type coverage, such as management liability insurance or professional liability insurance. Examples of general exclusions include those applying to losses due to dishonest, fraudulent, criminal, or malicious acts; intentional acts; Securities and Exchange Commission (SEC) violations; unfair competition; and punitive damages.

Product-Related Exclusions

Product-related exclusions are found in cyber risk policies that apply to products produced by the insured and/or serviced and supported by the insured. Examples of product-related exclusions include those applying to losses due to product recall, defects in design, bodily injury and property damage, and breach of warranty.

For example, an insured organization could be an information technology consultant that designs computer networks. The insured designs and installs a network for a particular customer, and the network design is executed according to specifications. However, if a flaw in the design itself causes the network to malfunction after installation, any claim the customer presents for damages arising from the network design defect may be excluded under cyber risk policies.

Service-Related and Security-Related Exclusions

Service- and security-related exclusions are found in cyber risk policies that are typically purchased by technology services and support providers. Examples of service- and security-related exclusions are those relating to losses due to contractual liability, performance delay, security breach, failure to prevent a computer virus from spreading, and theft of data.

For example, many technology-based companies funded by venture capital firms are required to carry cyber risk insurance that includes computer network security coverage. However, some cyber risk policies may exclude claims for losses relating to unauthorized access to the network, electronic data theft, denial-of-service attacks, transmission of computer viruses, or unauthorized e-commerce transactions.

Cyber Risk-Related Exclusions

Cyber risk-related exclusions are found in the cyber risk policies typically purchased by technology-oriented organizations that have website ownership and/or operations as a primary focus of their business operations. Examples of cyber risk-related exclusions are those pertaining to losses related to personal injury, advertising injury, intellectual property (including patent and copyright infringement), and adverse effect on **goodwill.**

For instance, an insured software distributor acquires another software distribution company and sells software licensed to the acquired company. The developer of the software could sue the insured for copyright infringement, claiming that the insured's continued sale of its software violates the original license agreement. However, some cyber risk policies exclude losses arising from copyright infringement.

Goodwill

The value an organization has attained beyond the value of its tangible assets because of its favorable reputation.

Limits of Insurance

Several types of limits of insurance are available for cyber risk policies. The structure and application of the types of limits offered typically depend on whether the policy has an annual aggregate limit of insurance (also referred to as a policy aggregate limit or simply an annual aggregate). If a cyber risk policy does not have a policy annual aggregate, as in most package or modular policies, the insuring agreements work independently, each with its own limit of insurance.

For example, in the case of a modular policy without an annual aggregate, a $1 million limit of insurance applies to a cyber extortion insuring agreement (less any applicable deductible). A separate $3 million limit of insurance applies to electronic data protection. A total of $4 million in coverage is available between the two insuring agreements.

A policy aggregate limit of insurance is the maximum amount an insurer will pay during the policy period for the sum of all losses that occur. If a cyber risk policy is written with an annual aggregate, each of the policy's accompanying insuring agreements will have an insuring agreement aggregate limit of insurance. An insuring agreement aggregate limit of insurance is the maximum amount an insurer will pay for the sum of all losses that occur during the policy period relating to that specific insuring agreement. Insuring agreement aggregates are subject to the policy aggregate and as such reduce the policy aggregate in the event of loss.

Policy retentions and/or deductibles apply to each insuring agreement, per loss, and are often packaged with specific limits, particularly if the cyber risk policy is modular. Defense expenses are payable within the policy limits, thereby reducing the limit of insurance. Some insurers offer a blanket limit applicable to separate insuring agreements, which is helpful to an insured organization that is uncertain about where its maximum possible cyber risk loss exposure may exist. See the exhibit "Cyber Risk Policy Sample Limits of Insurance."

Coverage Territory

Cyber risk insurance policies usually differ from standard property-casualty coverage forms in terms of the scope of coverage territory stipulated in the policy provisions. Virtually all cyber risk insurers provide worldwide coverage. Some variations apply, contingent on whether a loss is a first-party loss or a third-party loss and in what geographic location a suit for damages is brought.

For example, some insurers provide worldwide coverage only if a suit is brought in the United States, its territories, Puerto Rico, or Canada. Others provide worldwide coverage if a suit is brought anywhere in the world, subject to certain conditions or restrictions, such as settlement provisions for first-party losses that are applicable only if a suit is brought in the U.S.

Cyber Risk Policy Sample Limits of Insurance

	Coverage Applies Y/N	Limit	Retention
Policy aggregate limit of insurance	Y	$3,000,000	
Electronic data protection	Y	$3,000,000	$25,000
Cyber extortion	Y	$3,000,000	$25,000
Network security liability	Y	$3,000,000	$25,000
Business interruption	Y	$5,000/hour	8 hours with $500,000 aggregate

[DA05049]

THE TERRORISM RISK INSURANCE ACT

The aftermath of the terrorist attacks of September 11, 2001, awoke the United States insurance industry to the catastrophic loss exposure posed by terrorist acts. Insurers responded by excluding terrorism losses from commercial property policies, especially for risks in central business districts. Most reinsurers subsequently announced that they would exclude terrorism coverage in their contracts.

The Terrorism Risk Insurance Act (TRIA) of 2002 was enacted to help alleviate the urban economic instability, lack of growth, and job loss that occurred after the September 11, 2001, terrorist attacks. TRIA created a backstop intended to satisfy market concerns over future terrorist acts by providing federal reinsurance for terrorism losses. This enabled insurers and reinsurers to offer coverage for acts of terrorism, allowing property owners to secure financing to resume construction projects that had been halted in the absence of such coverage.

Intended to expire at the end of 2005, TRIA was modified and extended two years by the Terrorism Risk Insurance Extension Act (TRIEA) of 2005. Before TRIEA expired, the Terrorism Risk Insurance Program Reauthorization Extension Act (TRIPRA) of 2007 further modified and extended TRIA. TRIPRA extended the program for seven additional years with certain changes. References to TRIA in the remainder of this material include the cumulative modifications of TRIEA and TRIPRA.

A review of TRIA provisions includes these general topics:

- Purpose and duration of TRIA
- Definition of certified acts of terrorism
- Lines of business to which TRIA applies

- Make-available provision and disclosure requirements
- Federal participation trigger
- Loss-sharing provisions and program cap

Purpose and Duration of TRIA

The potential costs of a terrorist attack are too unpredictable for insurers to properly price the exposure, and the continuing threat deters insurers from offering terrorism coverage, especially for policyholders that are perceived to be particularly at risk. Before the passage of TRIA, insurers generally would not accept the terrorism exposure or would do so only at a price that discouraged property owners from purchasing coverage in central business districts. The federal government postulated that private insurance market forces would eventually be able to manage the terrorism exposure. TRIA, with the modification provided by TRIEA, provided temporary relief for insurers through a federal reinsurance program. However, the period that the legislation allotted for insurers to find long-term solutions for the terrorism exposure ultimately proved insufficient.

The passage of TRIPRA extended the TRIA provisions for seven more years to allow time for the insurance industry and the government to develop alternate means to manage the terrorism exposure. TRIPRA is scheduled to expire on December 31, 2014.

Definition of Certified Acts of Terrorism

To qualify for reinsurance coverage under TRIA, an act of terrorism must be certified by the Secretary of the Treasury, in concurrence with the Secretary of State and the U.S. Attorney General. The Treasury Secretary cannot delegate this responsibility to any other party.

To be a "certified act of terrorism," an act must meet these requirements:

- It must be a violent act or an act that is dangerous to human life, property, or infrastructure.
- It must result in damage within the U.S. (including its territories and possessions and Puerto Rico; certain air carriers or vessels; or the premises of a U.S. mission).
- It must be committed by individual(s) in an effort to coerce the U.S. civilian population, to influence U.S. policy, or to affect U.S. government conduct by coercion.
- It must result in aggregate property-casualty insurance losses that meet or exceed $5 million.

An important change to the law in the 2007 extension expanded the program to include domestic terrorism as well as foreign acts of terrorism in the U.S. For example, a domestic terrorist attack such as the 1995 bombing of the Alfred P. Murrah Federal Building in Oklahoma City would currently be covered under TRIA.

Except for workers compensation coverage, an act may not be certified as an act of terrorism if it is committed in connection with a war that Congress has declared. Additionally, TRIA does not require that insurers offer coverage for nuclear, biological, chemical, or radiological (NBCR) acts of terrorism if the policy would not cover such losses if caused by a non-terrorism event (for example, because of a nuclear or pollution exclusion). Insurers cannot accurately estimate losses and price coverage for such attacks because of the unpredictability of their long-term effects. The TRIPRA modifications contain a requirement for further study of NBCR terrorism.

Lines of Business to Which TRIA Applies

TRIA applies to all commercial lines of business other than these, which it specifically excludes:

- Commercial auto
- Professional liability (other than directors and officers)
- Burglary and theft
- Farmowners multi-peril
- Crop
- Private mortgage
- Medical malpractice
- Financial guarantee
- Life and health
- Flood coverage provided under the National Flood Insurance Program (NFIP)
- Reinsurance
- Surety

Make-Available Provision and Disclosure Requirements

TRIA contains what is called a "make-available provision." This provision requires insurers to offer coverage for certified acts of terrorism on the same terms that the insurer offers non-terrorism coverage. In most instances, this means that the insurer is required to offer a policy without a terrorism-specific exclusion or limitation. Insurers must offer the coverage at the time of the initial offer, purchase, and renewal of insurance.

In conjunction with this make-available provision, insurers must provide clear and conspicuous disclosure to their policyholders of the premium for coverage for certified acts of terrorism. They must also clearly state that the aggregate liability of insurers and the federal government for damages from certified acts of terrorism will not exceed a $100 billion mandated annual cap. Insurers must advise their policyholders that if the aggregate cap is met, insurance coverage for acts of terrorism may be reduced.

Federal Participation Trigger

Under TRIA, the federal government will not make any payment for certified acts of terrorism until the aggregate industry insured losses in a single calendar year resulting from the certified act meet or exceed $100 million (the federal participation trigger). For example, although an event causing aggregate losses between $5 million and $100 million could be certified as an act of terrorism, insurers would not receive any federal reinsurance for losses from that event because its associated aggregate losses did not meet the $100 million trigger level.

Loss-Sharing Provisions and Program Cap

TRIA specifies loss-sharing provisions that define the responsibilities of insurers and the government. These provisions require insurers to meet a deductible before any federal reimbursement will occur. After the deductible is met, remaining losses up to an annual aggregate program cap are shared between the insurer and the federal government on a quota share (proportional) basis. The provisions include these:

- An insurer's deductible is 20 percent of its prior year's direct earned premiums.
- The insurer pays 15 percent of losses that exceed its deductible.
- The federal government pays 85 percent of losses that exceed the insurer's deductible.
- The annual aggregate program cap of $100 billion applies for insurer and government liability for payments under the program.
- The Treasury Secretary must develop a process for determining the allocation of pro rata shares of insured losses (below the cap) when the $100 billion program cap is exceeded.
- The insurance marketplace aggregate retention is $27.5 billion.

The 2007 passage of TRIPRA strengthened the $100 billion cap by eliminating wording in the original act stating that the aggregate applied until Congress acted otherwise regarding such losses. Furthermore, the Treasury Secretary must now notify Congress within fifteen days of an act of terrorism if insured losses are expected to exceed $100 billion.

An insurance marketplace aggregate retention amount combines all insurers' deductibles and quota share loss amounts. If the federal payments made for losses incurred in a calendar year ultimately are less than the insurance marketplace aggregate retention, insurers must begin mandatory recoupment of at least some part of the federal share of losses through policyholders' surcharges according to the time schedule described in TRIA. See the exhibit "TRIA Loss-Sharing Summary."

TRIA Loss-Sharing Summary

$100 Billion Program Cap	
Insurer's Share of Losses: 15%	Government's Share of Losses: 85%
Insurer Deductible: 20% of prior year's direct earned premium	
$100 Million Federal Participation Trigger	

[DA05050]

– indeed & cite

THE TERRORISM RISK INSURANCE PROGRAM REAUTHORIZATION ACT OF 2015 (TRIPRA 2015)

The insurance industry experienced substantial losses following the terrorist attacks of September 11, 2001. Reinsurers and primary insurers reduced exposure to future terrorism-related losses by excluding coverage from their policies, which made terrorism coverage for businesses either unavailable or unaffordable. Congress enacted the Terrorism Risk Insurance Act of 2002 (TRIA) as a temporary solution to this issue. The Terrorism Risk Insurance Program Reauthorization Act of 2015 (TRIPRA 2015) reauthorized TRIA through 2020.

TRIA established a cost-sharing program that allowed the insurance industry and the federal government to jointly pay claims resulting from certain acts of terrorism. Congress enacted TRIA with the expectation that the insurance industry would develop a permanent, affordable solution to the lack of coverage for terrorism-related acts before the legislation was scheduled to expire. However, because a viable, permanent solution to the availability and affordability issues did not, in fact, arise prior to its expiration, Congress amended and reauthorized the program three times (2005, 2007, and 2015).

TRIPRA 2015 is the most recent reauthorization of the TRIA program and is designed to provide continued stability in the insurance market regarding terrorism coverage, gradually increasing the insurance industry's participation while reducing the federal government's participation in the payment of future terrorism-related losses. The program applies to all commercial lines of insurance with the exception of those specifically excluded under the act.

Losses to Which TRIPRA 2015 Applies

The threat of terrorism in the United States remained significant following the events of September 11, 2001. As reinsurers and primary insurers reduced their exposure to losses resulting from future terrorist acts, businesses were unable to secure adequate coverage for terrorism-related losses. TRIA and its amendments provided a governmental backstop program, which helped stabilize the insurance market by guaranteeing the availability and affordability of private coverage for terrorism-related losses. The federal government assumed a large percentage of the payment of such losses.

TRIPRA 2015 retains many of the provisions of TRIA and its amendments. However, it also makes several significant changes to the original law, many of which are designed to reduce the federal government's future participation in the program and transfer a larger percentage of the risk for payment of terrorism-related losses to the insurance industry.

TRIPRA 2015 requires all commercial property-casualty insurers to make coverage available for losses resulting from acts of terrorism as defined in the act. The term "act of terrorism" means any act that is certified by the U.S. secretary of the Treasury, in consultation with the secretary of Homeland Security, and the U.S. attorney general to meet all these criteria:

- It is an act of terrorism.
- It is a violent act or an act that is dangerous to human life, property, or infrastructure.
- It resulted in damage within the U.S. (except under specific instances).
- It was committed by an individual or individuals as part of an effort to coerce the civilian population of the U.S. or influence U.S. government policy or conduct through coercion.

Any act committed as part of the course of a war declared by Congress or any act that does not result in aggregate insured losses exceeding $5 million cannot be certified as an act of terrorism.

Although an act may meet all the criteria for certification as an act of terrorism, it is still not eligible for federal participation in the payment of losses unless the act results in aggregate insured losses in excess of the program trigger. TRIA originally established a program trigger of $5 million. The $100 million program trigger under TRIPRA 2015 increases each calendar year in increments of $20 million, ultimately reaching $200 million in 2020.

Most commercial lines of insurance are eligible for TRIPRA 2015's loss-sharing program except federal crop, private mortgage, financial guaranty issued by monoline financial guaranty insurance companies, medical malpractice, health or life (including group life), flood, burglary and theft, professional liability (other than directors and officers liability), commercial auto, farm owners, multiperil, surety, and reinsurance. Personal lines of insurance are not eligible.

TRIPRA 2015's Effect on Insurers

TRIPRA 2015, like its predecessors, requires property-casualty insurers to offer terrorism coverage without terrorism-specific exclusions or limitations at the initial offer and at the renewal of an insurance policy. The coverage offered may not differ materially from the terms, amounts, and other limitations applicable to losses arising from nonterrrorist acts.

Each individual insurer is responsible for 100 percent of all terrorism-related losses up to a deductible of 20 percent of the insurer's direct earned premium for the previous calendar year. Once the insurer has met its deductible, the federal government and the insurer share the cost of losses in excess of the deductible. TRIPRA 2015 is designed to increase the insurance industry's participation in the payment of losses over time while reducing the federal government's participation.

TRIPRA 2015 limits the ultimate exposure of insurers and the federal government to losses from certified acts of terrorism. The total annual aggregate for government and insurer liability is capped at $100 billion—this means that no federal or private payments will be made to insureds for any certified terrorism losses after the aggregate insured losses under TRIPRA 2015 reach $100 billion.

Insurers are required to provide disclosures to insureds regarding certain aspects of TRIPRA 2015, including the premium amount for the terrorism coverage, the federal government's share of compensation for insured losses, the annual aggregate federal and insurer liability cap, and the fact that the cap may reduce coverage under their policies. All disclosures must be specifically and prominently included in notices to insureds.

TRIPRA 2015 mandates that insurers retain, through their deductibles and co-pays, an industry retention threshold of $27.5 billion, gradually increasing to $37.5 billion. Beginning in 2020, the industry retention threshold will be the lesser of $37.5 billion or the annual average of the sum of insurer deductibles for all commercial insurers for the prior three calendar years. (That sum will be determined by the secretary of the Treasury through regulation.)

If insured losses exceed the industry retention threshold, the federal government is required to recoup its share of payments made to insurers. The amount of the mandatory recoupment is calculated as the difference between the total industry insured losses—up to the annual industry retention amount—and the total amount paid by the insurance industry through its deductibles and co-payments. The recoupment amount is collected through a surcharge on all commercial property-casualty policies in the years following a certified terrorist attack. The total amount of the federal loss share recouped is 140 percent of any mandatory recoupment amount.

Additional TRIPRA 2015 Mandates

The secretary of the Treasury is required to conduct studies, such as these, to monitor the effectiveness of TRIPRA 2015:

- Evaluate data collected from property-casualty insurers on terrorism insurance coverage, including the lines of insurance with terrorism exposures, premiums earned from terrorism coverage, location of the exposures, pricing of coverage, take-up rates for coverage (that is, the percentage of eligible insureds who purchase terrorism coverage), the amount of private reinsurance purchased for acts of terrorism, and any other relevant information. The secretary of the Treasury is then required to provide Congress with an annual report on the data collected.

- Complete a study on the certification process and establish time frames in which the secretary of the Treasury will determine whether an act of terrorism meets the criteria for certification.

- Complete an annual study to identify competitive challenges small insurers face in the terrorism risk insurance marketplace.

- Appoint the Advisory Committee on Risk-Sharing Mechanisms to provide advice, recommendations, and encouragement with respect to the creation and development of nongovernmental risk-sharing mechanisms. The participants must be directors, officers, or other employees of insurers, reinsurers, or capital market participants.

- The U.S. comptroller general is required to complete a study on the viability and consequences of the federal government's assessing insurers and using those funds to create a capital reserve fund for losses resulting from future acts of terrorism.

TERRORISM ENDORSEMENTS FOR COMMERCIAL PROPERTY AND LIABILITY FORMS

Insurance advisory organizations have developed various endorsements to help insurers provide coverage for terrorism-related losses in accordance with federal law.

Under the Terrorism Risk Insurance Act (TRIA), the federal government shares the financial responsibility for terrorism losses with the insurance industry (through federal reinsurance). Insurers that write the lines of business subject to TRIA are required to make coverage available for certified acts of terrorism on the same terms and conditions as coverages that apply to nonterrorism events.

To help insurers comply with TRIA, Insurance Services Office, Inc. (ISO) has developed multiple versions of specific types of terrorism endorsements to complement various commercial coverage forms. The National Council on Compensation Insurance (NCCI) offers endorsements that address TRIA-related issues in workers compensation policies. ISO and NCCI also have developed endorsements specifically for states that have special provisions that affect terrorism coverages.

Disclosure Endorsements

When insurers extend an offer to purchase insurance or to renew a policy, and at the time of purchase, TRIA requires them to inform policyholders about the costs and limitations of terrorism coverage through these three required disclosures:

- The portion of the policy premium that is attributed to certified acts of terrorism—Additionally, insurers must list (in an endorsement or in the policy declarations) the coverages to which that premium applies.
- The federal share of compensation for certified acts of terrorism under the program—After the insurer's deductible is met, the federal share is 85 percent of losses attributed to certified acts up to the program cap.
- The amount of the program cap ($100 billion)—This disclosure must explain that if the program cap is exceeded, the amount of coverage for certified losses may be reduced at the discretion of the Secretary of the Treasury.

ISO has developed disclosure endorsements applicable to the ISO lines of business to which TRIA coverage applies, and NCCI has developed disclosure endorsements for workers compensation. For the ISO lines of business, policyholders can decline certified acts of terrorism coverage, in which case other options may be offered by endorsement at the insurer's discretion.

Cap Endorsements

TRIA places a $100 billion program cap on annual aggregate insured losses paid by the federal government and all insurers for certified acts of terrorism. When a policyholder accepts certified acts of terrorism coverage, the ISO *Commercial Lines Manual* requires the insurer to attach a cap endorsement developed for the specific line of business and coverage provided.

This endorsement clearly describes certified acts of terrorism as defined in TRIA (as do most of the other terrorism endorsements) and informs the policyholder that the insurer's responsibility to pay losses for certified acts of terrorism will end if the program cap is reached. Additionally, the endorsement states that if the cap is exceeded, the Secretary of the Treasury will mandate calculation of pro rata shares of insured losses below the cap, which could reduce the policyholder's coverage. The program cap does not apply to any acts of terrorism that are not certified acts of terrorism.

Certified Acts Exclusion Endorsements

ISO's certified acts exclusion endorsements exclude coverage for certified acts of terrorism when the insured has declined the insurer's offer of TRIA coverage. These endorsements may be attached for each line of business and coverage to which TRIA applies. Acts of terrorism that are not certified under the federal program are not excluded by this endorsement; however, coverage of such acts would be subject to other exclusions or limitations in the policy.

Some states require that any policy insuring property loss caused by fire provide coverage that is at least equal to the coverage provided under a Standard Fire Policy (SFP). In these states, fire losses caused by terrorist action cannot be excluded. Certified acts exclusion endorsements contain an exception for these "SFP" states indicating that coverage is not excluded for direct loss or damage by fire to covered property when the fire results from a certified act of terrorism. The exception further states that these fire losses are limited by the program cap.

This SFP exception and its related schedule are for property coverages and are not included in certified acts exclusion endorsements developed for liability (only) policies.

NBCR Exclusion Endorsements

TRIA does not mandate coverage for losses from terrorist attacks that use nuclear, biological, chemical, or radiological materials (NBCR acts of terrorism) when such coverage is not provided in the base policy. Therefore, ISO has developed endorsements for excluding losses caused directly or indirectly by NBCR acts. These endorsements may be offered, at the insurer's option, only when the insured initially rejects certified acts of terrorism coverage.

Limitations Endorsements

If a policyholder initially declines certified acts of terrorism coverage, the insurer may offer more limited terrorism coverage amounts in return for a reduced premium. An insurer may accomplish this by writing the coverage for a sublimit that is lower than the limit applicable to other exposures. Such a sublimit could apply to a subsequent certified act of terrorism that occurs within an annual policy period if the limits are not exhausted by the prior act of terrorism. ISO has developed limitations endorsements for certified acts of terrorism that include a schedule of sublimits that apply to each coverage form, coverage part, or policy to which the endorsement is attached.

Aggregate Limit Endorsements

Aggregate limit TRIA endorsements are available for use with certain commercial liability coverage forms. These endorsements limit the insurer's exposure and provide limited liability coverage for certified acts for a reduced premium. The insurer may offer the aggregate limit endorsements only when the insured initially rejects certified acts of terrorism coverage.

When used with commercial general liability and farm liability coverage forms, the Certified Acts of Terrorism Aggregate Limit applies to bodily injury, property damage, personal and advertising injury, and medical payments arising out of certified acts of terrorism. When used with the Products/Completed Operations Liability Coverage Form, the limit applies to bodily injury and property damage only.

When applicable to a particular policy, the Certified Acts of Terrorism Aggregate Limit is subject to the policy's general aggregate and products/completed operations aggregate limit. Other policy limits, such as the each occurrence limit, continue to apply (to damages arising out of a certified act of terrorism) if and to the extent that the Certified Acts of Terrorism Aggregate Limit specified in the endorsement is not exhausted.

Punitive Damages Exclusion Endorsements

Insurers providing liability coverage for certified acts of terrorism may wish to exclude payment for terrorism-related punitive damages that result from civil actions. ISO has developed punitive damages exclusion endorsements for liability coverages when state laws permit such exclusions. These endorsements exclude coverage for punitive damages awarded against a policyholder that arise directly or indirectly out of certified acts of terrorism as defined by TRIA.

Other Acts Exclusion Endorsements

ISO also makes endorsements available for excluding acts of terrorism other than TRIA-certified acts of terrorism. These endorsements allow insurers to exclude noncertified acts of terrorism occurring outside the United States (including its territories and possessions and Puerto Rico). These endorsements are available only for use with commercial liability coverages, because those coverages insure some exposures outside the jurisdictional boundaries of TRIA.

These endorsements exclude other acts of terrorism committed outside the U.S. only when one or more of these situations exist:

- The total of all damages (including business interruption) to all types of property from terrorism exceeds $25 million (in U.S. dollars).
- Fifty or more people sustain serious physical injury or death.

- The act of terrorism involves the use, release, or escape of nuclear materials or results in nuclear reaction, radiation, or radioactive contamination.
- The act of terrorism is carried out by means of the dispersal or application of pathogenic or poisonous biological or chemical materials.
- Pathogenic or poisonous biological or chemical materials are released when one purpose of the terrorist act appears to be the release of such materials.

Auto Coverage Endorsements

TRIA does not apply to auto insurance, regardless of whether coverage is provided in a primary auto liability coverage form (such as the Business Auto Coverage Form) or included along with other liability coverages in a commercial umbrella or excess liability policy. (ISO has made terrorism exclusions available for use with primary commercial auto coverage forms, although these exclusions are not specifically related to TRIA.)

With respect to the ISO Commercial Liability Umbrella Coverage Part or Commercial Excess Liability Coverage Part, ISO has developed terrorism-related endorsements that address auto liability coverage. The basic purpose of these endorsements is to either cover or exclude acts of terrorism with respect to auto liability exposures, regardless of whether coverage for terrorism is provided or excluded for exposures other than auto.

Workers Compensation Endorsements

Workers compensation insurance is subject to TRIA. Therefore, insurers must include coverage for certified acts of terrorism in any workers compensation policies they write. Moreover, state workers compensation statutes prohibit insurers from excluding or limiting coverage for acts of terrorism (whether certified or not). Therefore, few terrorism-related endorsements are needed for workers compensation policies.

NCCI has developed endorsements to help insurers comply with the TRIA disclosure requirements and to inform policyholders about premiums related to acts of terrorism. The Terrorism Risk Insurance Program Reauthorization Act Endorsement defines certified acts of terrorism and discloses the portion of workers compensation premium that is attributed to certified acts, the federal share of compensation for certified acts under the program, and the amount of the program cap ($100 billion). In contrast to the ISO disclosure endorsements, this workers compensation endorsement states that an insured loss means any loss resulting from an act of terrorism, including an act of war, for purposes of workers compensation. This endorsement also describes the insurer's deductible under the program (20 percent of direct premium earned during the prior year).

Review Questions

1. Describe the litigation risks organizations may face in relation to climate change.

2. Describe six risk control measures an organization may take in relation to climate change.

3. Describe three types of insurance that risk managers should consider in relation to climate change.

4. Identify two risk transfer techniques that may be applied to climate change risk.

5. Describe a cyber risk loss exposure.

6. Explain why, when cyber risk property loss exposures and standard coverage forms are considered, the distinction between tangible property and intangible property is important.

7. Explain how an organization with business income might be exposed to loss of contingent business income as a consequence of cyber risk.

8. Discuss how organizations may be exposed to cyber risk liability loss exposures.

9. Describe the categories of cyber risk liability loss exposures.

    a. Discuss how cyber risk bodily injury liability loss exposures occur.

    b. Discuss how cyber risk property damage liability loss exposures occur.

    c. Discuss how cyber risk personal and advertising injury liability loss exposures occur.

    d. Discuss how cyber risk intellectual property liability loss exposures occur.

    e. Discuss how cyber risk errors and omissions liability loss exposures occur.

10. Describe the benefits of a properly structured cyber risk security strategy.

11. Compare physical controls with procedural controls for cyber risk loss exposures.

12. Describe the personnel controls an organization can use to mitigate the cyber risk loss exposures presented by their employees.

13. Explain why organizations should continually evaluate and revise cyber risk control measures.

14. Discuss the reasons why an organization should report cyber crimes to authorities.

15. Identify the three methods of risk financing for cyber risk.

16. Describe the coverage provided by an electronic data protection insuring agreement in a cyber risk insurance policy.

17. Describe the coverage provided by a business interruption insuring agreement in a cyber risk insurance policy.

18. Describe the coverage provided by a privacy liability insuring agreement in a cyber risk insurance policy.
    a. Describe the coverage that could be provided in a privacy liability insuring agreement related to privacy provisions in various laws.
    b. Describe the actions that would typically trigger coverage under a cyber risk policy's privacy liability insuring agreement.

19. Describe the coverage provided by an intellectual property insuring agreement in a cyber risk insurance policy.

20. List the four general categories of exclusions in cyber risk insurance policies.

21. Discuss the different types of limits that are available for cyber risk policies.

22. What is the coverage territory for most cyber risk insurance policies?

23. Explain why the Terrorism Risk Insurance Act (TRIA) was created.

24. When will TRIA, as modified by the Terrorism Risk Insurance Program Reauthorization Extension Act (TRIPRA), expire?

25. Describe the clear and conspicuous disclosure insurers must provide to policyholders as part of the make-available provision under TRIA.

26. Describe the operation and amount of the federal participation trigger under TRIA.

27. Under TRIA loss-sharing provisions, what determines the insurer's deductible and what percentage of losses that exceed the insurer's deductible does the federal government pay?

28. What three disclosures does the Terrorism Risk Insurance Act (TRIA) require insurers to make?

29. When should an insurer offer ISO-certified acts exclusion endorsements to an insured?

30. Must an insurer offer an ISO NBCR (nuclear, biological, chemical, or radiological) exclusion endorsement to all insureds? Explain your answer.

31. What is the purpose of an ISO aggregate limit endorsement?

32. What is the purpose of the terrorism endorsements developed by the National Council on Compensation Insurance (NCCI)?

Application Questions

1. Wind Sales, Inc. (WSI) has erected dozens of windmills on a hillside to generate electricity, which it sells to business and residential customers. WSI's risk manager is concerned that changing weather patterns will reduce the amount of wind needed to generate sufficient electricity. Describe a risk transfer method that might help treat this risk.

2. Jim's Country Furniture and Crafts is a small, one-person business. Jim builds his own designs of country-styled furniture and crafts and sells them in his shop. Most of Jim's business is generated through referrals and repeat customers. Jim's wife performs the business's accounting tasks

and other business-related record keeping. The business does not have a website. Jim believes that he does not have any cyber risk loss exposures. For each of the following scenarios, explain whether Jim has a cyber risk loss exposure:

a. Jim also designs architectural elements for homes, such as fireplace mantles, wall panels, and molding. To help in the design and assembly of large elements, Jim orders partially completed pieces from a supplier, who designs the pieces according to his specifications using computer aided design (CAD) technology.

b. Jim's wife relies on a home business software program that requires periodic Internet updates to manage Jim's accounts, billings, and other record keeping.

3. Aaron, Becky, and Chuck have just formed an accounting partnership. They have a website to advertise the company and a computer system to prepare and maintain clients' financial records. When they meet with their insurance agent to set up their commercial package policy, including cyber risk insurance, they also discuss what they should do in the event of a cyber loss. Describe a post-cyber incident rapid recovery program for this company.

SUMMARY

Risk managers and insurers must address the potential effects of global warming and climate change on their organizations. Climate change risks include property, business, liability, environmental, regulatory, and reputational risk. Risk transfer, risk control, and risk finance techniques should be considered to address climate change risks.

An organization's cyber risk loss exposures affect its property, net income, and liability. Property that can be affected by cyber risk loss exposures includes tangible property and intangible property. An organization's net income that can be affected by cyber risk loss exposures includes business income, contingent business income, and extra expenses. Liability that can be affected by cyber risk loss exposures includes bodily injury and property damage liability, personal and advertising injury liability, intellectual property liability, and E&O liability.

Organizations control their cyber risk loss exposures through the use of a variety of risk control and risk financing techniques. Risk control measures include physical controls, procedural controls, personnel controls, managerial controls, investigation and prosecution of cyber crimes, and a post-cyber incident rapid recovery program. Risk financing measures include insurance, noninsurance risk transfers, and retention. By using these risk control and risk financing measures, organizations can control cyber risk loss exposures involving property, net income, and liability.

Insurers offer a wide variety of cyber risk-related policies, and their insuring agreements apply to various coverage areas. Additionally, cyber risk policies contain coverage triggers, exclusions, limits of insurance, and coverage territory provisions that often vary. Risk management and insurance professionals should thoroughly review cyber risk policies to facilitate accurately interpreting and comparing cyber risk coverage.

TRIA provides federal financial backing for insurers to help cover the exposure from certified acts of terrorism. Unless extended by Congress, TRIA will expire on December 31, 2014. Various provisions of TRIA define certified acts of terrorism and describe the lines of business to which TRIA applies; make-available provisions and disclosure requirements; the federal participation trigger; and the loss-sharing provisions and program cap.

TRIPRA 2015 extends TRIA, thus providing continued stability in the insurance market regarding terrorism coverage by ensuring the availability and affordability of coverage for terrorism-related losses. TRIPRA 2015 retains many of the provisions of TRIA and its amendments, but it also includes several significant changes intended to reduce governmental participation while increasing insurer participation in terrorism-related losses.

ISO and NCCI have developed numerous versions of terrorism endorsements to complement the various coverage forms filed by these organizations. General categories include disclosure, cap, certified acts exclusion, NBCR exclusion, limitations, aggregate limit, punitive damages exclusion, other acts exclusion, auto coverage, and workers compensation endorsements. These endorsements help insurers comply with TRIA and effectively serve their policyholders' needs.

ASSIGNMENT NOTES

1. This section and the next are based on "Climate Change Risk Management Issues," an article written for the CPCU Society eJournal by Robin Olson (copyright 2008, International Risk Management Institute, Inc.), and a more general article of the same title in Practical Risk Management, Ed., Millie Workman, International Risk Management Institute (IRMI), Risk Management Notes #222, December 2007,www.irmi.come/online/pracrisk/ch0notes/prmn0222. aspx (accessed February 29, 2012). Used with permission.

2. Internet Crime Complaint Center, (IC3), a partnership between the FBI and the National White Collar Crime Center, "IC3 2009 Annual Report on Internet Crime,"www.ic3.gov/media/2010/100312.aspx (accessed November 3, 2010).

3. "Information Theft at Global Companies Surpasses All Other Forms of Fraud for First Time," Kroll Inc. news release, October 18, 2010,www.kroll.com/news/ releases (accessed October 25, 2010).

4. Insurance Information Institute, "Cybercrimes Increase as Economy Falters," February 23, 2009,www.iii.org/press_releases/222564.html (accessed November 15, 2010).

5. Richard S. Betterley, "Cyber Risk and Privacy Insurance Market Survey 2010,"http://thebetterleyreport.wordpress.com/2010/06/21/cyber-risk-insurance-market-survey-2010-snips-from-our-latest-report/ (accessed November 18, 2010).

6. Geoffrey A. Fowler, "E-Commerce Growth Slows, But Still Outpaces Retail," Wall Street Journal, March 8, 2010, http://blogs.wsj.com/digits/2010/03/08/e-commerce-growth-slows-but-still-out-paces-retail (accessed November 18, 2010).

7. Betterley, "Cyber Risk and Privacy Insurance Market Survey 2010."

8. Categories for exclusions adapted from Richard S. Betterley, "Technology Errors & Omissions Market Survey—2008: Privacy Concerns Drive Product Enhancements and the Market," The Betterley Report, April 2008, p. 8.

Index

Page numbers in boldface refer to pages where the word or phrase is defined.

A

Additional TRIPRA 2015 Mandates, 5.36
Admitted insurance, **4.22**
Admitted insurer, **4.55**
Admitted Versus Nonadmitted Insurance, 4.55–4.56
Advantages and Disadvantages of Endorsements, 4.38
Advantages of Controlled Master Programs, 4.57–4.58
Advantages of Using a Captive Insurer in a Multinational
    Insurance Program, 4.62–4.68
Adverse selection, **4.27**
Aggregate Limit Endorsements, 5.39
Alien insurer, **4.31**
Align and Integrate, 1.12, 1.32
Aligning Business Continuity Management With Risk
    Management, 2.4
Allocate Resources, 1.12, 1.32–1.33
Alternate Marketing Stage, 2.11
Analysis of Exposures, 2.25
Analyze Risks, 1.35
Anti-Bribery Laws, 4.19
Anti-Money-Laundering Laws, 4.20
Applying the Enterprise Risk Management Framework
    and Process, 1.30
Applying the Risk Management Framework, 1.31
Applying the Risk Management Process, 1.33,
    1.33–1.34
Approaches to Global Expansion, 4.8
Assessing and Treating Legal and Regulatory Risk,
    3.30–3.31
Assumption of risk, **3.15**
Auto Coverage Endorsements, 5.40
Auto No-Fault Laws, 3.28
Automobile Liability Loss Exposure, 3.27
Availability of Insurance for Specific Lines of Business,
    4.22

B

Background, 1.21, 1.26
Balance Between Efficiency and Vulnerability to
    Disruptions, 2.15
Basis for Legal and Regulatory Risk, 3.3
Benefits of Crisis Communication, 2.20
Biometrics, **5.16**
Bodily Injury and Property Damage Liability, 5.12
Building a BCM/BCP Culture, 2.9
Business Continuity Certifications and Standards, 2.5
Business Continuity Planning, 2.6–2.7
Business Interruption, 5.23
Business risk, **4.9**

C

Cap Endorsements, 5.37
Captives and Multinational Insurance Programs,
    4.59–4.65
Case Analysis Tools, 2.22
Case Facts, 1.30, 2.21, 3.30
Certified Acts Exclusion Endorsements, 5.38
Civil law, **3.3**, 3.17
Climate Change Debate, 5.3, 5.3–5.4
Climate Change Risk, 5.3
Climate Change Risk Treatment, 5.5
Commercial Liability Loss Exposures, 3.24–3.26
Commercial Liability, Property, and Auto Coverages,
    4.36
Commercial Property and Business Income, 4.46
Commitment of Resources, 1.18
Common Law, 3.19
Communicate and Report, 1.12, 1.33
Communication, 1.19
Communication and Reporting, 1.18
Communication Stage, 2.12
Comparative negligence, **3.14**
Compensatory damages, **3.8**
Completed Operations Liability, 3.26
Components of a Risk Management Framework, 1.10
Compulsory Coverages, 4.27
Conditions for Success, 2.13
Conducting a Business Impact Analysis, 2.7
Contingency Production Stage, 2.12
Contracts, 3.5
Control Activities, 1.29
Controlled master program, **4.40**, 4.40–4.41,
    4.40–4.41, **4.57**, 4.57–4.59, 4.57–4.59
Controlling and Financing Cyber Risk Loss Exposures,
    5.15
COSO Enterprise Risk Management—Integrated
    Framework, 1.25–1.27
Counterparty risk, **4.59**
Coverage From Nonaffiliated Local Insurers, 4.39–4.40
Coverage Territory, 5.28
Coverage Triggers, 5.25
Credit risk, **1.4**
Criminal and Civil Law, 3.3
Criminal law, **3.3**
Crisis Communication, 2.17
Culture, Customs, and Language, 4.23
Cyber Crime, 5.23
Cyber Extortion, 5.23
Cyber Risk Insurance Policies, 5.21
Cyber Risk Loss Exposures, 5.8–5.9
Cyber Risk-Related Exclusions, 5.27

D

Defense Costs, 3.9
Definition of Certified Acts of Terrorism, 5.30
Denial-of-service attack, **5.17**
Designing and Implementing an Enterprise Risk
    Management Framework and Process,
    1.15–1.17, 1.15–1.18
Determination of Co-Dependencies, 2.24
Developing the Continuity Plan, 2.8
Difference in conditions (DIC) policy, or DIC insurance,
    4.60
Difference in limits (DIL) policy, **4.60**
Disadvantages of Controlled Master Programs,
    4.58–4.59
Disclosure Endorsements, 5.37
Diversifiable and Nondiversifiable Risk, 1.6, 1.6–1.7
Diversifiable risk, **1.6**

E

East Asian Law, 3.19–3.20
Economic Considerations, 4.6
Economy of scale, **4.58**
Electronic Data Protection, 5.23
Electronic Media Liability, 5.24
Emergency Stage, 2.11
Employees' Tort Suits Against Employers, 3.29
Enterprise risk management, **4.56**
Enterprise Risk Management Framework and Process
    Model, 1.9
Errors and Omissions Liability, 5.14
Evaluation of Internal and External Environments, 1.16
Evolution of BCM, 2.3
Exclusions, 5.26
Export Controls, 4.9
Exporters package policy, **4.56**
Exposure Identification, 2.22
Express contract, **3.6**
External Environment, 1.17
External Stakeholders, 2.19
Extra Expense, 5.12
Extraterritorial Laws of the United States, 4.19

F

Federal Participation Trigger, 5.32
Foreign Contractual Relationships, 4.14–4.15
Foreign Direct Investment, 4.15
Foreign Trade, 4.9
Framework, 1.23, 1.27
Franchising, 4.15
Fronting Insurer Domiciled in the U.S., 4.31

G

Gap Analysis, 1.15
General Business-Related Laws and Regulations in
    Foreign Countries, 4.18
General damages, **3.8**
General Insurance Exclusions, 5.26
German Law, 3.18

Global Competitiveness, 4.5
Global Market Considerations, 4.6
Goodwill, **5.27**

H

Hazard, **3.12**
Hindu Law, 3.20
Hold-Harmless Agreements, 3.29, **5.20**

I

Identify Risks, 1.34
Immunity, **3.14**
Implementing the Continuity Plan, 2.9
Implied contract, **3.6**
Import Controls, 4.10
Indirect Losses, 3.9
Inherent risk, **1.27**
Injunction, **3.9**
Insurance, 5.19
Insurance Laws, Systems, and Market Offerings, 4.21
Insurer Domiciled in the U.S., 4.31
Insurers' Global Expansion, 4.3
Insuring Agreements, 5.22
Intangible property, **5.9**
Integration Into Existing Processes, 1.17
Intellectual property, **5.10**
Intellectual Property Liability, 5.14, 5.25
Intentional torts, **3.5**
Internal Environment, 1.16
Internal Stakeholders, 2.19
International Insurance Solutions, 4.35–4.41
International Law, 3.22–3.24
International package policies, **4.38**, 4.38–4.39,
    4.38–4.39
International Sales Contracts, 4.11
Introduction to Business Continuity Management, 2.3
Investigation and Prosecution of Cyber Crimes, 5.18
Islamic Law, 3.20–3.21
ISO 31000 Risk Management—Principles and
    Guidelines, 1.21

J

Joint Ventures, **4.8**, 4.16

K

Key performance indicator (KPI), **1.11**
Key risk indicator (KRI), **1.11**
Kidnap/Ransom/Extortion, 4.46

L

Last clear chance doctrine, **3.14**
Law of large numbers, **4.27**
Laws Affecting Claims and Losses, 4.18
Lead and Establish Accountability, 1.10, 1.31
Legal and Regulatory Risk Consequences, 3.8
Legal Systems, 3.16–3.18
Liability, 5.12

Liability for Operation by Others, 3.27
Limitations Endorsements, 5.38
Limits of Insurance, 5.28
Lines of Business to Which TRIA Applies, 5.31
Liquidity risk, **1.7**
Loss of Business Income (Including Contingent
    Business Income), 5.11
Loss of or Damage to Intangible Property, 5.10
Loss of or Damage to Tangible Property, 5.9
Loss prevention, **3.11**
Loss reduction, **3.14**
Losses to Which TRIPRA 2015 Applies, 5.34, 5.34–5.35
Loss-Sharing Provisions and Program Cap, 5.32

M

Maintaining and Updating the Plan, 2.10
Make-Available Provision and Disclosure Requirements,
    5.31
Malware, **5.24**
Managerial Controls, 5.17
Mandatory Participation in Government Insurance
    Programs, 4.28
Market Analysis, 4.6
Market risk, **1.7**
Merger, **4.8**
Methods of Engaging in International Business, 4.9
Methods of Payment, 4.13
Methods of Writing Reverse Flow Business, 4.31
Mitigating Risk Through Crisis Communication, 2.18
Mitigating Supply Chain Risk, 2.20–2.21
Modeling an Enterprise Risk Management Framework
    and Process, 1.9–1.10
Modifying Legal and Regulatory Risk, 3.10–3.11
Modifying the Consequences of an Event, 3.14
Modifying the Consequences of Contractual Liability,
    3.15
Modifying the Consequences of Statutory Liability, 3.16
Modifying the Consequences of Tort Liability, 3.14
Modifying the Likelihood of an Event, 3.11
Modifying the Likelihood of Contractual Liability, 3.12
Modifying the Likelihood of Statutory Liability, 3.13
Modifying the Likelihood of Tort Liability, 3.11
Monetary Damages, 3.8
Monitor and Assure, 1.38–1.39
Monitoring and Improvement, 1.20
Multinational Insurance Program Options, 4.60

N

NBCR Exclusion Endorsements, 5.38
Negligence, **3.4**, 3.4–3.5
Net Income, 5.10
Network Security Liability, 5.24
Nonadmitted Alien Insurer, 4.33
Nonadmitted insurance, **4.21**, 4.25–4.26
Nonadmitted insurer, **4.37**
Nondiversifiable risk, **1.6**
Noninsurance Risk Transfer, 5.20
Notification or Remediation, 5.23

O

Objective risk, **1.5**
Other Acts Exclusion Endorsements, 5.39–5.40
Other Coverages, 4.50
Other Financial Assistance via Government Resources,
    4.22
Other Regulations, 4.30
Overview of Analysis, 2.22
Overview of International Insurance, 4.17–4.18
Overview of Steps, 1.31, 3.30
Overview of the Procedure, 3.10

P

P-D-C-A Cycle, **1.20**
Performing a Risk Assessment, 2.7
Permissible Insurance Activities, 4.28
Personal and Advertising Injury Liability, 5.13
Personnel Controls, 5.17
Phase 1 International Insurance Solutions, 4.45–4.47
Phase 1 Loss Exposures, 4.43–4.44
Phase 2 International Insurance Solutions, 4.49–4.50
Phase 2 Loss Exposures, 4.47–4.49
Phase 3 International Insurance Solutions, 4.52–4.53,
    4.52–4.54
Phase 3 Loss Exposures, 4.50–4.52
Physical Controls, 5.16
Political Risks, 4.7
Post-Cyber Incident Rapid Recovery Program, 5.18
Premises and Operations Liability Loss Exposure, 3.25
Premium Taxes, 4.29
Principles, 1.21, 1.21–1.23
Privacy and Data-Protection Laws, 4.21
Privacy Liability, 5.24
Private international law, **3.23**, 3.23–3.24, 3.23–3.24
Privilege, **3.14**
Procedural Controls, 5.16
Process, 1.23, 1.23–1.24
Producers' Role in Writing Reverse Flow Business, 4.34
Product Licensing, 4.14
Product-Related Exclusions, 5.27
Products and Completed Operations Liability Loss
    Exposure, 3.25–3.26
Products Liability, 3.26, 4.46, 4.46–4.47
Property, 5.9
Property and General Liability, 4.49
Property in Transit, 4.47
Public international law, **3.22**
Punitive Damages Exclusion Endorsements, 5.39
Punitive damages (exemplary damages), **3.8**
Pure and Speculative Risk, 1.3
Pure risk, **1.3**
Purpose and Duration of TRIA, 5.30
Purpose of a Risk Management Framework, 1.9

Q

Quadrants of Risk: Hazard, Operational, Financial, and
    Strategic, 1.7

R

Regulatory Compliance, 4.24
Reporting, 1.19
Requirements for Enforceability, 3.6
Residual risk, **1.27**
Retention, **5.21**
Revenue Growth and Financial Stability, 4.5
Reverse Flow Business, 4.30–4.31
Risk Assessment, 1.24, 3.31
Risk Avoidance, 3.10
Risk Classifications, 1.3–1.7
Risk Control, 5.5
Risk Control Measures for Cyber Risk, 5.15
Risk criteria, **1.11**
Risk Finance, 5.6
Risk Financing Measures for Cyber Risk, 5.19
Risk management framework, **1.9**
Risk Management Policy, 1.13
Risk Monitoring and Review, 1.25
Risk owner, **1.11**
Risk Transfer, 5.7
Risk Treatment, 1.25, 3.32
Roman-French Law, 3.18

S

Scan Environment, 1.34
Scandinavian Law, 3.19
Scope, 1.21
Selecting International Insurance Solutions, 4.43–4.54
Selling terms, **4.12**
Service-Related and Security-Related Exclusions, 5.27
Settlement of Claims and Disputes, 4.19
Short-Term Auto Rentals, 4.45, 4.45–4.46
Socialist-Communist Law, 3.21–3.22
Special damages, **3.8**
Specific performance, **3.9**
Specific Performance or Injunction, 3.9
Speculative risk, **1.3**
Stakeholder Communications, 2.18
Statutes and Regulations, 3.6
Strategic alliance, **4.8**
Strategic Reasons for Global Expansion, 4.4–4.5
Strategic Redeployment Planning, 2.10
Strategic Redeployment Planning Stages, 2.11
Strict liability, **3.5**
Strict Liability Torts, 3.5
Structuring an International Insurance Program, 4.54–4.59
Subjective and Objective Risk, 1.5
Subjective risk, **1.5**
Subsidiaries, 4.15
Subsidiary, **4.8**
Supply Chain Best Practices, 2.16
Supply Chain Risk Management, 2.13–2.16
Surplus lines law, **4.33**
Systemic risk, **1.6**

T

Tangible property, **5.9**
Technology Errors and Omissions Liability, 5.24
Territorial Endorsements to U.S. Market Policies, 4.36
Terrorism Coverage, 5.25
Terrorism Endorsements for Commercial Property and Liability Forms, 5.36
Terrorism Risk Insurance Act, 5.29–5.31
Terrorism Risk Insurance Program Reauthorization Act of 2015 (TRIPRA 2015), 5.33
Threats and Opportunities Inherent in Supply Chains, 2.14
Torts, **3.4**
Trade Sanction Laws, 4.20
Treat Risks, 1.35–1.36
Trends in Global Expansion, 4.3
TRIPRA 2015's Effect on Insurers, 5.35
Types of Climate Change Risks, 5.4
Types of Contracts, 3.6

U

Understanding Local Ways, 4.23
Understanding the Business, 2.6–2.7
Underwriting Reverse Flow Business, 4.33–4.34
Unenforceable contract, **3.6**
U.S.-Domiciled Subsidiary of the Home-Country Insurer, 4.32
Use of Language and Translations, 4.23

V

Valid contract, **3.6**
Void contract, **3.6**
Voidable contract, **3.6**

W

Workers Compensation and Employers Liability, 4.45, 4.49–4.50
Workers Compensation and Employers Liability Coverages, 4.37
Workers Compensation and Employers Liability Loss Exposure, 3.28
Workers Compensation Endorsements, 5.40